FINDING GOD *in the* SEASONS *of* DIVORCE

FINDING GOD *in the* SEASONS *of* DIVORCE

Vol I -
Autumn and Winter - Seasons of Loss and Sorrow

RICHARD D. CROOKS

WESTBOW
PRESS
A DIVISION OF THOMAS NELSON

Author photo by Cheryl Crooks
Cover photo by Richard Crooks

Scripture taken from the New King James Version. Copyright 1979, 1980, 1982 by Thomas Nelson, inc. Used by permission. All rights reserved.

Scripture quotations taken from the New American Standard Bible®, Copyright © 1960, 1962, 1963, 1968, 1971, 1972, 1973, 1975, 1977, 1995 by The Lockman Foundation. Used by permission." (www.Lockman.org)

Scripture quotations in this publication are taken from The Message. Copyright (c) by Eugene H. Peterson 1993, 1994, 1995, 1996, 2000, 2001, 2002. Used by permission of NavPress Publishing Group.

WestBow Press books may be ordered through booksellers or by contacting:

WestBow Press
A Division of Thomas Nelson
1663 Liberty Drive
Bloomington, IN 47403
www.westbowpress.com
1-(866) 928-1240

ISBN: 978-1-4497-6342-8 (sc)
ISBN: 978-1-4497-6386-2 (e)

Library of Congress Control Number: 2012916364

Printed in the United States of America

WestBow Press rev. date: 09/18/2012

And you will seek Me and find Me,
      when you search for Me with all your heart.
                  — Jeremiah 29:13 (NKJV)

I have always seen dedications like this, and thought they were just what people think they ought to do. At this point, I realize that is not the case, but that, indeed, there is very good reason to do the dedication I have included here....so just realize, I really do mean this! This book is dedicated to my wife, Nola, whose strength and love have brought so much healing and hope, and whose support has made these writings possible. I am truly a blessed man to know her and have her as my wife.

—Richard Crooks, 2012

CONTENTS

LETTER TO MY READERS

Dear Reader,

I am sorry you are reading this book, because this is not a book one reads just for fun. It is usually being read because loss, devastation, brokenness and struggles have come into your life. For that I am sorry; I know how hard it can be, and how much it can hurt. And I am sorry, because I believe marriage is intended by God as a wonderful thing, but obviously yours, like my first marriage, has become much less than that. I want you to know I am not here to judge you nor to tell you what to do. Instead, I have written this book as a tool to help you find your way through these tough times. More importantly, it is to help you connect with God in a time when God can seem far away.

I realize there are those who will believe I have handled this wrongly, that a book like this SHOULD tell you how to interpret the scriptures' teachings regarding marriage and divorce. Some may condemn this book because it does not do so, but I prefer you come to your own conclusions for a couple of reasons. First, the very fact that there are differing interpretations by various Christian teachers clearly implies that there is more than one way to understand these scriptures. Since you alone will be the one to give account for your life and choices, and since God's Spirit can lead and teach you just as effectively as He does me (or maybe more so), I offer this book as an aid to help you as you search out your own answers. Secondly, I am also aware that my life with God is an ongoing process, a relationship of continual learning and growing. With my limited understanding, It would be rather presumptuous of me to believe I should tell you what to think and believe about the situations of your own life. Romans 14:4 makes clear that it is not my place to judge you. It is to God you will have to give account, and God is able to make you stand strong before Him. So my hope is that this book will provide opportunities God can use for your faith walk with Christ through this time. God *will* get you through.

This book is about specific things in relation to divorce. It attempts to help you address two specific areas: 1) how does one get in touch with the God of the Bible during the process of a divorce to discover what God has to offer during this time? 2) if you are a Christian, how does one hold fast to his/her Christian faith and practice during a time of divorce so as to avoid the devastation that could cause loss of faith and direction in life? (Sadly, that happens more frequently than you might think.)

This book comes out of my own experiences of my wife filing for divorce, after 19 years of marriage and two children, and contains insights from that time of struggle and learning. I also share from things learned as a pastor, observing and assisting others going through this tumultuous experience, and reading I have done to help me be a more effective pastor to divorcing people. Some memories come out of journals I kept during my divorce. Other parts of the book are presented without name or incident as a composite of lots of situations I have seen or experienced. Though some pages may not apply to you at all, they may still contain something useful for your own life or to share as you encourage friends in divorce. Hopefully, there will be some scriptures and pages that will be precious for you as you walk through the struggles....at least, that is my prayer concerning these materials.

The book is set up as a daily devotional, but if your experience is anything like mine, sometimes you will want to read vociferously seeking hope and answers, and other times you don't feel like opening the book at all. You may end up using it a variety of ways. This first volume deals with the times of divorce I call "autumn and winter," when things are falling apart, hurts are intense and the uncertainties strong. I know I was really searching for something to help me through those times, and it is my prayer that this volume can be that for you. The second volume is for "spring and summer," the times when you start to get your equilibrium, and to find ways to move forward in the new structure of your life. The seasons of our calendar year are not relevant here, only the "seasons" you are experiencing in the divorce process. An index of topics in the back will enable you to jump around to find discussions about issues you experience when you want them. A scripture index allows you to search for devotions on specific scriptures, in case you happen to stumble upon a verse that speaks to you one day and want to see if there is a related devotion. However, I encourage you to try to read at least one each day, even on the days you don't really feel like reading, so as to give God an extra opportunity to speak to you and to help.

Well, that gives you the purposes behind these writings. The next section describes for you some of the underlying assumptions behind the writings, which can help you understand the perspective of the writings. In closing, I pray that, more than my purposes, God will reveal to you the purposes HE has for these pages coming into your possession. And that, somewhere in all these words, you will find some bits or pieces that will make your experience just a little bit easier and draw you just a little bit closer to God. Remember, the only words that matter from this book are the ones that God uses to personally touch your heart as only He can. May God do that many times as you and I share the struggles of divorce.

God bless you, and may His arms of love surround you in the days ahead.

Richard

P.S. By the way, I get really frustrated with the limits of English pronouns.... and tired of the whole he/she, him/her tedium when you really mean both and/or either. So in my writing, sometimes I will use a singular verb with the pronoun "they" or "their" to indicate that both genders are included. I know it's wrong, but don't like the other options either, so....please just overlook my little quirk if you are a stickler for grammar (or just think of the verb as being used with a collective noun instead!)

In the same vein, I follow the traditional use of "He" as the pronoun for God as a grammatical masculine (rather than a "gender indicating" masculine). I am fully aware that God is not just some guy, and that, truth is, God is far beyond male or female....in fact, Genesis indicates that both genders are made in his image.

Until we develop better pronouns for English, I guess I'll just be quirky.

ASSUMPTIONS UNDERLYING THE TEXT

The following assumptions have shaped this book and the way I perceive how to offer support and help. I share them to help you understand the context of the writing as you examine your own.

One assumption is that God is part of your life, or you at least *want* God to be part of your life. Closely tied to this assumption is the belief in the Bible as the inspired word of God, through which He can and does minister to the needs of our lives and hearts, if we approach the texts prayerfully with open hearts and minds. In scripture, God promises to reveal Himself to any who honestly seek to know Him. Whatever your connections with God, this devotional could help you discover God's help in fresh ways. You will most fully benefit from these pages if you know Christ personally as your avenue to God. An appendix in the back is a guide to help you as you seek to clarify your relationship with God. I encourage you to review it now, before you begin, and whenever else the need arises.

Maybe you are going through divorce and aren't what people would call a "church person." Perhaps you don't consider yourself a Christian, or aren't sure whether or not you are. This devotional book can help you, too, because the tragedy of divorce automatically brings with it an opportunity to examine yourself and your life to evaluate what you do and don't hold dear as you decide what kind of person you want to be. Those are the very things God can help you sort out, if you just give Him the opportunity. So, as you read this book, I encourage you not only to consider the words that are written in these pages, but to try to listen and discover if perhaps God is saying some other things to you as well.

Some readings may challenge you to take a long look in the mirror, to change a behavior, or to ask for forgiveness from someone. Information alone is not what this book is about. It is a practical resource to help support and encourage you in living your life as you find your way through the uncertain obstacles that are part of any divorce.

A second assumption is that you are not a person thrilled with the notion that you are getting divorced. This book is designed especially for those who are struggling with their divorce, whether you are the one who filed or not. It is my hope that this devotional will help you work through the struggles you face in the midst of this dramatically life changing experience. If, at this point, your divorce creates in you nothing but a sense of exuberant freedom, then odds are there may be lots of disconnects in this book for you…at least at this time. You might want to know that as you begin.

The third assumption is that you are willing to look at this material and yourself honestly, for your own benefit as your own choice, not because it is something imposed upon you by others. Where the scripture gives clear teachings, do your best to be obedient to those teachings, so as to experience God's blessings for you.

One final assumption is that there are some common experiences for people going through divorce, even though there is also a great deal of variation. People with children face difficult issues that those without children will not face. The person filing for divorce because they want out of an abusive situation will experience divorce differently from those who have an undesired divorce thrust upon them. Christians who believe that God is always opposed to any divorce will have struggles which a Christian who believes God allows divorce will face differently. The variations are endless….but I believe there are still some common threads, and it is those common threads that make these writings useful.

THE SEASONS OF DIVORCE: AUTUMN

I love autumn, with the beautiful leaves, the cooling of the weather, and even the raucous thunderstorms that are so much a part of autumn in the great plains region. There is a kind of sadness that takes place in autumn as so many trees become denuded of their foliage, and most of the plants on the ground turn brown. The blue skies turn grey, and the temperature doesn't stop at the midway point of cool and comfortable, but continues its trek downward into the bitter cold that signifies the arrival of winter. Birds and monarch butterflies begin their southward journey. Other animals seem to become more scarce, hibernating or spending more time in dens and caves. Everything around you warns that there is an inevitable progression toward the bitter winter days ahead. Just as the squirrel buries treasured food for the winter, we check doors, window caulk, attics, paint, and whatever else we need to do to prepare our residence for the impending cold and storms ahead.

In the cycle of a divorce, autumn is the time when things are falling apart all around you. As in many autumns, there may be times of warmth for a few days, but there is an awareness that winter winds are just around the corner, inevitably approaching closer day by day. It is hard to find much to look forward to or to maintain your sense of hope as your marriage moves into a cycle of endings. Days seem very dark. As one prepares for winter by cleaning out dying foliage and putting away summer tools for the season, one may attempt to make preparation for the cold days ahead as your divorce process advances…and yet, autumn does not predict with certainty when the winter storms will hit, or whether winter will bring ice storms or blowing snow. There is much you cannot predict about your divorce proceedings, either. Things may seem to be moving along nicely, but they can suddenly change and your preparations seem useless.

It is a hard time, an unpredictable time, a time that must be endured one day at a time. There can be much weeping at the loss of better times. There can be fears and emotional rollercoasters. Most of all, it can be a very, very lonely time. You can feel yourself pushed along inexorably to a winter season you do not want. But what you feel and want, may not have much impact on the march of time toward the final days of your marriage. There may be moments of fleeting beauty, much like the brilliant colors of autumn leaves, but they do not seem to last. These times are times when you must prepare as best you can, and then trust that God will get you through to better days....even when it seems those days might never come. Hopefully, these few pages will help encourage you during the losses and uncertainties you are experiencing.

Each week will begin with a special prayer for you for the week. Absorb it, receive the answer, reflect on it whenever you need some courage, and remember, odds are I am not the only person praying for you.

MY PRAYER FOR YOU THIS WEEK

This week, I pray that the tender mercies of God will be intimate and close at hand. May you feel His comfort as a soft handkerchief drying your tears and cooling your face. May you sense His arms enfolding you and pulling your head nestled into His shoulder with His gentle, soothing voice tenderly speaking your name. Amen.

Day 1   Malachi 2:13-16

If you are reading this devotional, then you are in the process of learning the meaning of this verse in a new way, sadly enough. Many Christian folks these days read this verse with a twisted interpretation. It is often read as if it says, "God hates divorced (or divorcing) people." But that isn't what it says. It says, "God hates divorce." (Actually, in the context, it is referring to divorces that were being pursued at that time where men were divorcing their wives in favor of a younger woman, thus abandoning the woman who has stood with them over time.) Odds are, before you finish the process of divorcing and the subsequent necessary healing, you will have a deeper understanding of why God hates divorce than you ever did before. Before it was easy to glibly talk about the broken families and how people should just stay together. But as you go through the processes ahead of you, you will never speak of this topic glibly again. It will be with a sadness in your tone, a tear in your eye and an ache in your heart as you remember the impact it has had on your life. My way of saying it is, "The Bible says that God hates divorce....and I know why." Or sometimes it comes out as, "Yeah, well, you think GOD hates divorce, let me tell you how I feel." Because even if it is a necessary divorce, or one that you experience with a sense of release, there still remains the aching of your heart that goes along with it, for lots of reasons.

There are things you will feel that you hate feeling. There are things you might end up thinking, that you will hate to admit you are the kind of person to have thought. There are choices you will have to make in which you hate every option available. And you very likely will hate that you have to go through some of the things you go through, or, even more, that you have to watch your children go through. And in the brokenness, in the loss, in the loneliness, in the fearfulness, in so many ways you will begin to have a deeper understanding of what the Bible means when it says that God hates divorce. He hates what you are going to be experiencing. And He hates the marring that has come into the world through the Fall, and has resulted in the kind of world where divorce is, at best, a necessary evil. And just as Jesus wept over Jerusalem when they would not gather to Him, so He weeps over the experiences you are having. His heart breaks with you. His desire is to heal your brokenness. His desire is to be there for you during this tough experience. Sure, His best choice would be for your marriage to be restored in such a way that each of you is a committed, humble partner, repenting of every wrong that you have been part of, and living with one another and with Him for the rest of your lives in holy marital bliss. But even if that is not how your situation turns out, He will walk with you through the days ahead. He will speak to you if you listen. He will comfort you if you draw near. He will give you courage when your courage fails, and He will get you through the days ahead. Not only that, but He will bring you out in a way He can use to make you more than you are and to prepare you for the ministry that awaits you beyond these dark days, if not in the midst of them. You have to trust Him through this, day by day, moment by moment, step by step, until the time that you see the sun shine again and feel the future holds promise and joy. It is my hope that as you spend time with the Lord and this devotional, it will assist you as you seek God's presence and guidance for this chapter of your life.

Day 2   Psalms 71:1-3; Proverbs 18:10

As a person experiencing or having recently experienced divorce, if there was any depth to your relationship and your love at all, you will be finding yourself in the midst of one of life's strongest storms. When a spouse dies, people gather around and try to encourage you, they express their sympathy and concern, they send cards, they have a special service to help bring a sense of closure and some strength to help you through. When you are in the midst of divorce, our society has few, if any, useful processes that will help and care for you. Some friends will try to encourage you, but may fail miserably. Others will try, and it will give you a lift, but it won't lift the heaviness that plagues your soul. Hopefully, there will be some who have been through divorce themselves, who help bring you the strength you need because they, to some degree, understand what you are going through. But many will not even try. They will feel awkward and not know what to say. They may feel threatened, afraid you might try to steal their spouse away. Or they may simply walk away from you, now that you have become a person whose life is marked by divorce....as if it is a contagious disease.

But as you start reading this devotional, I want to invite you to use this time in your life to deepen your relationship with God beyond anything you have experienced before. Make time to let Him be the friend who will not leave you aside. Seek His counsel that He may guide your steps and choices. Cling to Him that you may resist the temptations that will come which could lead you away from Him. In other words, make Him the strong tower into which you run and where you hide your heart. Let Him be the protection and encouragement you so desperately need. If you will choose even now to make Him the strong tower for this experience of your life, you will find that He reveals Himself and ministers to you in ways you would never have imagined possible. It boils down to making a covenant between you and God for this time….that you will use it to draw near to God, rather than allowing it to drive you away. God will honor His side of the covenant….always….that is the concept of His faithfulness. You have to be responsible for your side. You may not know God well, or maybe even not at all. There is an appendix in the back about knowing God that I would ask you to take time to read and consider. You may have known God well in your past, but find yourself extremely stretched right now, or will be soon. Choose deliberately and prayerfully before God that you will make Him your tower. Begin, even now, there in your heart, to envision yourself hidden inside the safety of His hands. Then, as you go through the months ahead, do regular checkups to see if that is where you are still hidden, or if you have started seeking refuge elsewhere. God will get you through this in a way that will bless you, especially when you come out on the other side.

Day 3   *Isaiah 41:10 and Philippians 4:13*

So how are you feeling this morning? Are you overwhelmed? Depressed? Fearful? All of those things are often part of divorce. In fact, you may even experience, as I did, rapid mood changes throughout the course of a day, sometimes triggered by things you run across that flood your mind with memories, sometimes triggered by songs on the radio that break your heart, and sometimes for no apparent reason at all. It can feel like you are tied to a yo-yo, spinning out of control as your spirits run up and down relentlessly. Perhaps this is one of those days when you feel like you just can't do it. Perhaps it is a time when you feel so beat down, that you just don't think you can go on, like it is too much, too hard, too frightening. It is for moments like those that God offers the promises like the one found in today's verse. At the moment you feel like you just can't, that is the time you need to hear that the strength of the Lord is greater than your own, and is available to help you conquer those things you cannot conquer on your own. You don't need God's strength, if you can do everything yourself. It is when you face challenges bigger than you think you can handle that God's strength becomes the key factor, to show you that with God, nothing is too hard.

For some people, and in some times of life, all it takes is a prayer in the morning...."*God, give me the strength to get through this hour, this day, this night.*" For others, it requires time and again in the course of the day seeking strength from God...."*God, help me be able to get dressed for work, help me be able to focus on and complete this task, God, help me even be able to make my kids dinner.*" One thing that happens in these times when you feel so weak is that you have the opportunity to learn how to draw on the strength of the Lord in ways and depths you may never have learned otherwise. God offers His strength. Promises His strength. Gives His strength. To all who seek Him when they need it. Is today a day you especially need it? All you have to do is turn to Him and ask, then go to the tasks with God as your partner.

Day 4   1 Timothy 4:11-16

In this time of divorce, you will have some choices to make about yourself. There are going to be lots of temptations and opportunities that will shape and reflect your character. It may be a decision about how you are going to report assets in your divorce proceedings. It may be whether you choose to act out of anger, or out of righteousness, or.... It may be an attraction to a member of the opposite sex long before you have settled your divorce, or allowed sufficient time to heal and regain your equilibrium. It may be the way you talk about your soon to be ex. But you will choose to respond to every situation either out of the best of who you and what God has taught you, or you will let less noble traits take over so that anger, revenge and spite become the dominant features of your life.

Paul's advice to Timothy was that he was to literally flee from those things that would drag him down and away from God, and instead set an example in righteousness, speech, faith and conduct. Have you realized that how you act in the divorce process is an example for those who are around you? Are you setting a good example, or a bad example? For your children, if you have any. For your attorney, if you have one. For the officers of the court. For your friends and acquaintances. I remember one time dropping my check by the court to pay child support, and asking some question about due dates. I was stunned when the court clerk said that if I paid it by that date each time, it would be the first time that ever happened! In this area, are least, my conduct was going to reflect the difference it makes to be a Christian.

Very possibly people you don't even realize are watching you, to see if your faith is real, to see if Christianity really has anything to offer in tough times, to see if you will give up on God, to see what difference it makes that you claim to be a Christian. I had an individual tell me that they were struck by the fact that in the terrible experience of divorce, I never blamed God or turned away from Him. Since that person was a Christian, too, I was a bit surprised that they thought I would do so, but I simply was doing my best to do what I thought God would want, and this person was watching from the sidelines. You have no way of knowing who is watching the way you handle this time in your life. In fact, this may be one of the most powerful opportunities for witness you ever have, because if Christ makes any difference in our lives, He certainly changes how we handle the struggles of life. And there are plenty of people who struggle with all sorts of things, who may come to you for guidance on how to receive help from God in the midst of struggles. The question for today is, "Will you let God have His way with you and be your source in this time, or will you walk your own way?" People are watching. And your character is on the line. Choose wisely.

Day 5   Reread Malachi 2:13-16

Today read the passage in several translations. You will discover that there is some uncertainty about the exact meaning of the text. And notice that the text begins with God laying a charge against those who have violated their marriage vows by forsaking their wives (the women were the ones put at risk by divorce and forsaken by husbands for frivolous causes in that culture). If you are in the midst of a divorce because of actions you have taken which violate the sacred vows you took before God, before you go any further in this book, you need to get that issue settled between you and God. Depending on your resulting situation, the marriage may or may not get restored, but you need to make sure that your relationship with God is restored through confession and forgiveness. Examine your heart prayerfully and carefully. Maybe you didn't commit adultery and violate your marriage vows that way, but did you cherish, did you honor? Was your work more important than your spouse, or did you let your children come between you and your spouse? Were you more faithful to money than to your partner? What about attitudes, forgivenesses, secret places of your heart? For this devotional to do any good at all, it is important that the first thing you do is get your heart clean and honest before the Lord. God is gracious to forgive, but He expects us to confess. And we cannot change what we refuse to face. So allow this passage to be a mirror as you examine your own heart.

There may be some reading this devotional who are the ones who were cheated against and betrayed. The hurts you feel may be devastating. The inadequacies you wrestle with may seem insurmountable. The anger may rise, and maybe even overwhelm. You need to read this passage in a different way. Allow it to speak to you about the fact that God does understand, and does take notice. It likely is not your place to go back to correct, confront and change the one who betrayed you. That is God's job. It is not your role to be their judge and avenger. That is God's job. And God has noticed what has happened. You have to trust Him with what has happened….and ask HBim to help you grow because of what you have experienced. After all, if anybody understands what betrayal feels like, it would be Jesus, wouldn't it? He suffered the ultimate betrayal Himself! And scripture is clear that God consistently has compassion on those who have been victimized through betrayal and abuse.

Day 6   Luke 22:39-46

I remember one of the awful times of my divorce, during a time when I was not sleeping well, and often would read scriptures in the middle of the night. On this particular time I ran across in my reading the scripture of Jesus in the Garden on the eve of his crucifixion. To that point, I had been praying that God would do something to prevent the divorce from occurring. I desperately wanted Him to intervene, and was willing to do whatever it would take. But that night, when I read the story of Jesus and His agony in the Garden, I experienced a huge turning point in my prayers and in my life with God. That night I felt I had a deeper understanding of what Jesus experienced as He prayed in the garden for God to take away the cup He was facing, though not as if Jesus was seeking to overrule in any way what the Father's will was for His life at that moment.

This translated for me in this way: when I became a Christian, I had given my life to Christ, therefore, it was no longer my life, and I no longer had the right to decide what would happen in my life….I had given my life to Christ, and it was His to use as He desired. Not that I think God's desire in our lives is divorce, but I did come to the conclusion that while I could ask God to intervene here, I had to leave the ultimate decision as to what would happen up to God. Only God knew the purposes He had for my life, and the events He would allow into my life to bring about those purposes.

I had to let go. I had to examine how seriously I meant that prayer in which I told God I would give Him my life. Was I willing to actually accept that God could alter all my plans, allow things I valued and loved to be torn away, even to let go of what I believed to be right so that God could do something different in my life. It reminded me of Kierkegaard's reflections on Abraham's offering of Isaac (see <u>Fear and Trembling</u>), as he pointed out that God was asking Abraham to give up the very thing God had once promised to give him, and to do it in a way that just did not seem right.

Is there something about what is happening in your life right now to which you are clinging? Something that God is challenging you to let go of and, instead, trust that if you let it go, God will still accomplish his will for you? Letting go is hard, especially if you feel that what is happening is simply not right, but sometimes the only way to see the ram God provides is to first give up the provision you have in your hand. (see Genesis 22) At this point in your life, perhaps it is time to pray this kind of prayer: *"God, I have given you my heart, given you my life. I relinquish all rights to my own life, and admit that my life is in your hands, to use however you will, to shape however you will. I let go of ownership over even my life in this divorce situation, and trust that you are doing something in me that will make me more like what you want me to be. Your will be done, God, not my own."* Maybe you could benefit from finding an old hymnal and praying the words to the hymn, "Have Thine Own Way." Remember, God's way is always the best way, whether it feels like it or not.

Day 7   Romans 8:28

This verse is one that can become an anchor to get you through, if you approach it properly. I want you to read this verse several times today and tomorrow, and reflect carefully on what it says to you about who you are and what God may desire to do with and for you in this time. Read carefully the last half of the verse, because we will focus upon it first, and if you can, do so in several different translations. This promise of God doing good for us is not a universal promise. It is only for those people who love Him, those who are called according to His purpose.

Before you let yourself get excited about what God might do that is good for you through this experience, first you need to reflect deeply on whether you are one of the people for whom this promise is given. In fact, this very experience will shake and sift you, will test who you are and reveal the depth of your commitment to Christ or the lack thereof. Some people face hard times such as this, and turn against God, blaming Him for the situation, angry at Him for not protecting them from it, or not guiding them in such a way that it would have been prevented. They blame God for all the pain that comes. And, theologically, we could have a very long and meaningful discussion as to how much happens to us because God allows Satan to attack, and how much is our own doing because God doesn't force us to do what is right, and how much is something God sends our way to teach and shape us. But that discussion is for another time. Right now, the focus needs to be simply, what is the current condition of your relationship with God? Have you committed your life to following Christ? Are you willing to continue to trust Him even now? Is this a time you will let God use to shape you, or are you going to blame Him and turn your back on Christ because He hasn't done what YOU think He should have done? Only you can make that choice. But I would suggest to you that the best way through this time of your life is to go through it with God at your side, seeking His guidance every step of the way. Because if you make that commitment, God will have a free hand to use you and to help you and to heal you. You may especially need to ask yourself about this if you know that you are in the situation you are in now BECAUSE you have ignored God and His commands in your past. Perhaps you stepped outside the bounds of marriage into adultery. Perhaps you ignored his nudge to not marry the person you did. None of that is the question that I am asking. What I am asking you to think and pray particularly

15

seriously about over the next day or two is what you will choose to do with the situation of your life right now and tomorrow and the next day. Regardless of what you have done in the past, God can help you if you will make Him the center of your life now. And if you feel like you have already done that and were doing that and yet still ended up in this nasty situation, then consider that God has not lost control of what He is doing, and you need to hang on so that He can bring it to completion.

MY PRAYER FOR YOU THIS WEEK

This week, my prayer is for your peace. In the midst of a whirlwind, through the confusing and uncertain moments of your life, may you know peace. May God's peace supersede the circumstances of your life. May God's peace give you the assurance that all will be well. May God's peace spread through you to those you love as together, you seek the will of God for this time. In the name of Jesus, the Prince of Peace, Amen.

Day 8   Romans 8:28

I hope that you have a renewed sense today that you belong to Christ, and that your love for Him is the driving force of your life. In that realization, I also hope you are marveling at the notion that God has called YOU, and called YOU for a purpose. And now, as we turn to the first half of the verse, I want you to realize and appreciate that He called you with a full knowledge that you would be going through the very things you are experiencing now in terms of your divorce. He already has in mind what good He can bring about because of what you are going through now. Don't misunderstand, I am not saying that God brought your divorce about. But I am saying He knew it was coming, and that He has already determined a way He can do something good through it.

There were times when, serving as a pastor, I would sit and listen to individuals struggling with divorce, and try to offer them encouragement and hope. Looking back now, I realize that some of the things I did were helpful, some were simply clueless. Not because I didn't care, but because I simply did not understand to the depth I do now, after having gone through the experience. After my own entrance into the world of "divorcees" I found that my connection with Christians struggling with divorce was transformed. I once wrote a letter to a man I didn't know, but whom I knew was struggling with a divorce himself. I just shared some thoughts from my own experiences and struggles, things I thought might be helpful to him. He told me later that he had hung it on his refrigerator to help him get through his divorce. I was struck by that when I realized that I could never have written that letter before my own divorce. One small good God had brought out of my tragedy. Perhaps this book will be used of God to accomplish good. Again, something I could not have done without the experience I so hated. I don't know what the good things are that God would want to bring into and through your life with your divorce….but I know there is something. Because God promises to do so. So many of the stories in the Bible are about the times when things were terrible, or about people who made mistakes and blunders, and in all of those stories, God manages to accomplish something good. It doesn't mean the bad things don't hurt, or aren't hard. It doesn't mean that God's desire is for the brokenness that comes into a home through divorce. It means that God can use even this experience to make you more like what He wants you to be, and to accomplish His good purposes in your life and the world. You have to choose, though, whether you are willing to let God do something good. Tomorrow we will look a little more in depth at how God works, but today, offer God your experience, asking Him to use it, to shape it, to guide you that He may accomplish something good through it.

Day 9   Romans 8:28 and Hebrews 12:1-3

We have looked at the Romans verse for two days, but I want you to understand it on its deepest level, and to do that well, we consider Hebrews 12 with it. When God says He can work something good for those who love them, no matter what, He means it always. No matter how awful things seem to be at the time. No matter how hopeless. No matter how wrong. And those of us who love Him need to keep that before us when things seem wrong. Jesus is the evidence that this is true.

When we go to churches, we see beautiful crosses, polished, lighted, shiny and smooth. Around our necks we see crosses of gold and silver, sometimes with diamonds or other gems. What a lovely thing a cross is. The church and its people are so proud of what the cross means, that it is embellished and celebrated throughout time and around the world. But that was not always the case. On the day Jesus was hanging on a cross, it was anything but beautiful. It was filthy, crude and ugly. It was vicious, cruel and hated. It was despised, and so were all who were placed on it. Spit upon, mocked, abhorred....that was the attitude people had toward crosses and those who would be placed on them. It was designed to be painful, awful, maybe even evil. And Jesus' journey to the cross was no exception. If anything, it was worse than many. He was beaten, mocked, thorns were driven into His scalp, and He was abandoned by even His most loyal followers. It was about as bad as life....or death.... can get. Every individual who loved Him and witnessed it at the time considered it absolutely awful. It felt like defeat and failure. They had all their hopes shattered as they watched Jesus' journey from the Garden of Gethsemane to the tomb in another garden. That, too, was a tragic time from a human perspective. But Hebrews reminds us that Jesus was not looking at it merely from a human perspective. He was seeing His struggle through the lens of the joy that was set before Him. What was the joy? The joy of resurrection. The joy of defeat of Satan. The joy of breaking sin and Satan's hold on humanity. The joy of making the way for literally millions of people to be welcomed into a holy heaven. The joy of being able to call YOU His brother or sister....of being able to say to you, "You are forgiven, and you are mine." The joy of hearing the Father say, "well done" as He returns to His eternal throne in heaven. In other words, Jesus knew that there would be good ahead of Him.

Did He know all those things I just listed? Theologians have debated the details of that for centuries, as they seek to understand the concept of fully human yet fully divine nature in the one Christ. But for us today, it isn't about whether or not He knew all the details. What matters is that He knew the character of God, and knew that the character of God is to work good for those who love Him when they follow Him in obedience. Maybe He knew exactly what all would happen (He clearly knew many details in advance), but even if He didn't, He trusted God to work the good....and, in trusting, He was right. God worked such a phenomenal good that the despised object of torture and execution became the celebrated symbol of the highest good and the greatest love. God did it for Jesus from the abyss of crucifixion....and He will use the same pattern for you from the abyss of divorce. God will work something good. If you love Him. If you do your best to be obedient. Follow the example of Jesus, and set your eyes beyond the pains and uncertainties of this moment....to the God who will work things for good. Because not only do *you* love Him....*He* also loves you.

Day 10   Isaiah 43:1-5

I will be with you. They shall not overwhelm you. You shall not be burned. Perhaps one of the greatest promises of the scriptures is the simple statement by Almighty God Himself: I will be with you. And when you combine that promise of the presence of God with the promise that He will make sure that anything that comes at you will not be great enough to defeat you creates one of the greatest promises of all. God is with you not only as a good friend to whom you can turn when you need to do so, but God also places Himself as a shield around you in the hard times of life.

I wonder if you can visualize that image for your own life and situation. There you are, fearful, uncertain, under attack and perhaps at the end of your rope. But step back a bit. Try to envision yourself with all those issues, not standing alone, but resting in the center of a fortress....right smack dab in the center of the care of God. Perhaps you could imagine the hardships coming at you like a tornado's winds, yet by the time they pass through the shield of God, they have become but a gentle blowing....the destructive energy absorbed before the winds ever reach you. Or maybe your view is that the winds are blowing hard against you, but like a person holding tight to a pillar or post to keep you steady so that the winds cannot move you. Or maybe you would compare yourself to a rock against which the waves crash, but the drops just scatter and the rock stands strong. Maybe a better image for you would be one of those fire safety boxes that protects precious papers from the intense heat all around. Whatever image works for you, let the reality of what this scripture promises sink into your spirit. While you are reading this, odds are, this isn't your toughest moment of the day....but if you develop this image now, then when the wind and waves start for the day, you can tap back into the deep recesses of your soul to remember exactly where you are....right in the center of the protection and care of God.

Let's make sure you notice one more fact found in this scripture. There is nothing in this scripture that would suggest you are exempted from the flames and floods of life. In fact, the preferred translation of this phrase is WHEN you pass through the fire and water, not IF. The assumption is that during your life on this earth, you will face hard times. And your divorce could certainly qualify as one of those times.... at least mine did. The promise isn't that you won't go through those hard times. The promise is that you never need go through them alone. And that God will meet for you the challenges that are beyond your capability. Hang in there. God will get you through this.

Day 11   Psalm 30:4-12

I remember a day early in my divorce when a good friend passed on to me a comment she had heard from another person going through divorce. What she passed on was that there is life after divorce. Her timing turned out to be ahead of schedule, in that I was not able yet to even think that life would ever be good again. But somehow I think it didn't hurt for me to hear it. It has often been said that a person can endure most anything if they know that it is only for a time. That is what has given hope to people captured as prisoners of war, and what has helped encourage people who have gone through chemotherapy, and it can be a good thing to know when you are going through a divorce. It is interesting to me that different states have such widely different time frames for a divorce....some are instant, some require a significant waiting period. But whatever time the state requires, remember this verse in the Psalms....the weeping you are experiencing is only for the night....there will come a morning when joy comes. The time frames vary, not just by law, but by experience. If you have children, the divorce results in entanglements and complications for many years, worst perhaps while they remain minors, but even after that. One friend told me that she didn't feel like it ever really ended until the day her ex died....that there was always an awareness she had. I had another friend who, many years out of her divorce, told me that she didn't think you really ever "got over it," but you didn't remain in the dark days, and you find new meanings in life.

Another good friend helped me understand that, during this time of divorce, my life was in a kind of limbo until the matters were settled at court so that I could start reordering my life, and that I needed to focus on dealing with the matters at hand to get through it as quickly as possible and as effectively as possible so that I could then begin to discover where my life might go next. Let me, in these early days, pass on to you an awareness that, indeed, there is life after divorce, and joy can come after the night has passed. There are so many things that I have found to be so good in this new chapter of my life that began only after the first marriage ended. Not that it has always been easy, or is anywhere near perfect, for there remain hard things that carry on. But, I have found there is a deep joy that has come to my life in this new chapter that I never really imagined could be in the midst of the night of the divorce. If you are struggling at this point in your life, remind yourself that there will one day come a time when you start a new chapter, and that chapter may be filled with more joy than you can even dream right now. The weeping only tarries for a night. You don't have to take my word for it. Instead, take this phrase from the Psalms as a promise of God for you.

Day 12   Ephesians 4:26

Have you gotten angry yet? It is absolutely amazing the intensity of the anger one can feel during the divorce process. Anger at your attorney for the exorbitant charges you may be having to pay. Anger at the court system that seems so impersonal and whose decisions sometimes seem anything but just. Anger at a soon-to-be-ex who just seems to be making everything more difficult than it needs to be. Maybe even anger at friends who all of a sudden don't want to spend time with you anymore. I have found it very interesting that so often, the partner who seeks the divorce becomes the one who is the most angry during and after the divorce.... perhaps because things don't go exactly like they thought they would when they filed. Sometimes it feels like you just get settled down from being angry over one issue, then another envelope comes in the mail, and the emotions start all over again.

One of the things so often overlooked is that this verse tells us to be angry....it doesn't declare anger to be a satanic evil thing. Instead, it acknowledges anger as part of the God created human experience. But the Bible regularly warns against misusing anger, reminding us in James that human anger falls short of the righteousness of God. Anger is bound to arise in the excruciatingly frustrating process called divorce. Anger at betrayal. Anger at rejection. Anger at abandonment. Anger at perceived injustice. Anger at shattered dreams. Anger at....well, you probably don't really need me to list it for you. Anger, anger, anger.

The key to handling the anger that comes along is found in this verse from Ephesians: don't allow dusk to become night's darkness while retaining your anger. That is, don't hold on to it. Cleanse off your emotional plate each day. Don't let it develop into a harbored grudge, or a gnawing bitterness. Anger is not something to be nurtured, cherished or fed. It is simply an emotional reaction to difficult times of frustration and hurt. Feel it, express it in appropriate ways if necessary, but then, let it go and move on. Kneel down before God, and let Him know what you are angry about. Let Him know how hard it is to let the anger go. Let Him know what hurts, what is frustrating, how angry it all makes you, and then walk away to a restful night with the anger abandoned with the falling sun.

Day 13   Romans 12:17-19

There may be days you seriously think about that friend of yours who has a friend who knows a guy who knows a professional hit man. There may be days when you would do anything to get back at your ex for things that have been said or done. You may have been betrayed by the adultery by your ex. You may be shocked at recently discovered mismanagement of money. You may feel cheated by your ex as they pull the rug out from under you in area after area of your life. You may just hurt so badly that you want your ex to hurt, too. But guess what!?! It isn't your job to get your own revenge. It isn't even your right. Both you and your ex will have to answer to God for every choice and every word and every action of your own during this time, and during the marriage. God is the only one with the perspective to justly evaluate everything in your life and the life of your ex. And God will do that and recompense accordingly. Much as you think your ex should be punished, what you think is not what matters, ultimately. Only God's opinion really matters, so you must simply live each day with an awareness that you, too, are under God's scrutiny, and trust that the Lord of all the earth shall do right. Perhaps it would be helpful to take a few minutes today to honestly discuss with God all the feelings you have that arise out of anger, bitterness, spite or revenge, and ask Him to help you make your choices out of obedience and righteousness, rather than those feelings that so many times take over during people's divorces. If you do that, and then follow through on that, then afterward you can look back with a sense of peace about your actions, rather than shame, embarrassment or guilt. And having a clean conscience at the end of the divorce process is worth more than anything you are going to get pursuing those negative feelings. Keep your place, don't try to take God's. Vengeance belongs to Him, and to Him alone. Do your best to live in a way that God will commend, rather than condemn.

Day 14   Isaiah 1:1-3

Many people who go through divorce will find this verse a very troubling one, because it hits too close to home, too close to our nearest and dearest. Children going through their parents' divorce are placed in a very precarious position. If both parents put their children's best interest first, then they can work together to make the experience less difficult for the kids. However, more often than not, the parents are divorcing because they have different points of view on many of life's issues, and that can easily include how the children are to be raised. I have seen all sorts of things, from all sorts of angles. I have had adult children of divorce tell me that it wasn't until they were adults with children themselves that they really began to have an understanding of what happened to their family. I have heard of parents offering all the child support to their children as a bribe to get the kids to move in with them so they don't have to pay child support any longer. I have seen kids treading so carefully, trying to negotiate their way through the swamp of their parents' emotions. I have known of children literally shaking in their boots as they hear a parent rage at them, releasing all the anger of the divorce upon the child. I have heard of children being used as spies to find out what is going on at mommy or daddy's house, and the child foolishly plays along because they are pleasing their parent. I have seen children use the two household system to their advantage to get their way, threatening to move in with the other parent if they don't get what they want....and if the parents are not working together, the parent is often virtually powerless to deal effectively with the child. And I have also seen times when the children's minds are so poisoned with slander that they refuse to see or speak to one of their parents, sometimes even for decades. Children can literally turn against a parent.

How are you doing with your children? It is very hard. I remember the great freedom I felt in that I no longer had to compromise with my ex if I wanted to do something nice for my kids....I could just do it, since I was the only adult in the household. At one moment, the kids may think you are wonderful. At the next, you may be the worst person on earth. You may hear things come out of their mouths that break your heart...I know I have. What can you do? The answer is: you can pray. If there is a way to work out your problems with your ex to make a real and honest fresh start on the marriage, that is certainly the best route for the children. But all too often couples reunite with no change in the unhealthy patterns that had led them to divorce. If your situation is such that reconciliation is not apparently the best or even a possible option, then you need to remember your children. They are not the adults with the problems. They did not create the divorce. They desperately need to know they are loved in this time, regardless of where they live or how they feel about the other parent. And there are things in their broken little hearts about which you can do nothing.... that is why prayer is so essential. God can do for them what you cannot. In every decision you make, remember the children. I was so thankful for a good attorney who regularly helped me consider how my decisions might affect my children. I won't say I did things perfectly— I made mistakes, as will you, but I always tried to make choices with the children's best interest at heart. God bless you, as you seek to minister to your children in a difficult time, not only in your life, but also in theirs.

```
┌─────────────────────────────────────────────────────┐
│                                                       │
│      MY PRAYER FOR YOU THIS WEEK                      │
│                                                       │
│   This week, my prayer for you is God's guidance, in matters small │
│   and large, in decisions you face and choices you make. When       │
│   you cannot see the path to take, may God order your steps for      │
│   you. When your future is dark and gloomy, may his light go         │
│   before you. May his assurance be yours as you walk step by step,   │
│   day by day, hour by hour. In the name of Jesus, the Wonderful      │
│   Counselor, Amen.                                                   │
│                                                       │
└─────────────────────────────────────────────────────┘
```

Day 15   1 Kings 19:1-13

One of my favorite things about this story is the fact that Elijah was depressed. Here was this man who was a great hero of the Bible, a man through whom God spoke prophecies, and who did mighty acts in the name of God, one of the great examples of faith. But after his showdown with the prophets of Baal in Mt. Carmel, in which he came out the victor, he reaches rock bottom when threatened by Jezebel. He feels like the only one left and is on the verge of despair. So he just wants to get away by himself and hide out somewhere and complain to God while feeling sorry for himself. I had days I felt like that. Have you? Days it all seems too much, days you just want to hide and have a good cry. God, why is it all so bad? God, I feel so alone, so abandoned.

Then Elijah is sent by an angel to a faraway place, a special holy place. So he goes there. Why? Who knows? Maybe looking for answers. Maybe because he hopes God will take him home there. Maybe he just is tired, lonely, frustrated and just wants to get away from the mess. So he goes. And there, on that mountain, he experiences a whirlwind, an earthquake, a fire, but not God. What about your life? Have you felt like you're in a whirlwind? Have the foundations of your life been shaken like in an earthquake? Is there a fire consuming your world? And God feels so far away, so silent?

Something then happens for Elijah. All gets quiet, and in the silence, he hears God speaking to him. Quietly. Gently. Tenderly. A voice speaking to Elijah. Personally. Uniquely. The words Elijah needs to hear. If you are having a hard time hearing God speak because you feel like your life is in a whirlwind, or is being shaken like in an earthquake, or like your world is being consumed by a fire, carve out for yourself a holy place. Make a place, a time, where you can be alone with God. And then, listen. Perhaps read your Bible, and God will lead you to that special scripture you need today. Or maybe in the silence you will quietly hear his voice within. But you have to listen. You have to quit looking for God in all the turmoil, and find a quiet place where you can meet with God once in a while….just to let Him speak. He may say something profound, He may say something simple, but whatever message He brings for you is just that….a message for YOU. Personal Powerful. Genuine. For you. Go to your place right now. Or if you simply cannot now, commit yourself to a time you will go sometime today.

Day 16   Psalm 46:1-11

Isn't that an incredible phrase? "Be still and know that I am God." Many a day, being still felt virtually impossible. My gut was in turmoil, my stomach churned, my knees were weak, my mind racing, and my heart so agitated I could barely think straight, let alone be still. Yesterday you were challenged to spend some time with God to just listen. Today, I want you to see one more level….just being still in the presence of God. Stop and allow yourself to quiet within. It may take some time. It may take some effort. It may take forcing your thoughts to focus, and your heart to stop racing, and your lungs to breathe just a little bit slower. You may have to turn off the television, the cell phone, the mp3 player. But whatever it takes, be still, not just for the sake of being still, but that you may know that He is indeed God. In uncertain days like often occur during divorce proceedings, it is good to know, to really, really know for sure, that He is, indeed, God. To know that God is still there. To know that God is present with you. To know that God cares. To know that God has not lost control. To know that God understands all the mix of feelings within you. Not just with a mental assent, but to truly know. To truly, deeply, fully know that HE **_IS_** God. Not only that He is God, but that He is the kind of God you need at this time of your life. And that He is God above all other things that are part of your life. And that, being God, He is worthy of your worship, your obedience and your trust....even now. Maybe especially now.

Part of this being still and knowing that He is God means you also must recognize that it is **_HE_** who is God, not anyone or anything else. You are not the god who has total control of your life....perhaps trying to live like you are got you into this mess in the first place. Don't turn to your attorney as god to solve all your problems. The attorney can help, but does not have infallible advice, and will charge you for every bit of help you get anyway. You are forced to see that the security of your family cannot be your god....for it has become very unstable. Maybe you are having to face the fact that you have let almighty dollar become your god, and now find that even your well laid plans for retirement are at risk. No, be still....only **_HE_** is God, and He **_IS_** God, and He is **_GOD_**. And if you get those three things into your spirit so deep that you know that you know that you know them....then you will be all right, no matter what else happens.

Day 17   Matthew 18:21-22

This is the first time we will talk about forgiveness. Emotionally, you may be thinking about skipping today's reading, because you really don't like the topic. I don't blame you. Today, I am not going to suggest that you forgive your ex for everything. I know some people who say they forgive, but say it so glibly and so sharply that you know it isn't true. No, I just want you to begin thinking about the fact that God will want to help you be able to forgive. Not mouth words of forgiveness, but really forgive. And that is not easy. In fact, you will probably be able to literally face the concept of forgiving 70 times 7, maybe even 70 times 7 a day. You are going to have lots of opportunity to practice being a forgiving person. And it isn't easy. In fact, it may be the greatest challenge you ever face. But it has been said that a person is most like Christ when he or she forgives. Today, I want you to take time to pray and ask God to help you learn how to forgive well, because you cut yourself off from the experience of God's forgiveness when you choose to live in unforgiveness. Read Matthew 6. If you don't forgive, neither will God forgive you!?!? Wow! Is that really what it says? Have you ever stopped to consider whether or not you really believe that, whether you *live* like you believe that? Sometimes we look for an out by pointing out that in the 70 times 7 passage, Jesus refers to your brother turning and asking forgiveness….and your ex may not be doing anything like that. That doesn't give you an out. Jesus did not wait until we asked Him to forgive us to die on the cross on our behalf. His forgiveness was in place and ready for us to receive, because He had already determined that forgiveness was going to be His attitude. Begin now to consider prayerfully what attitude you are going to have. Later on we will return to this topic, but for now, ask God to help prepare your heart. I once heard Billy Graham say something like this: "If you're not willing, are you willing to be made willing?"….of course, he was referring to giving your heart to Christ, but I'm sure he wouldn't mind if you applied that same principle to forgiving those who have wronged you.

Day 18   Genesis 32:22-33:9

Do you know this story? The last time Jacob saw Esau was when he was getting ready to trick his father into giving him the special blessing that was actually reserved for Esau. This was after he managed to get Esau to sign over his future inheritance in exchange for a bowl of food when he was hungry. Those events had occurred years previously, and Jacob had run away quickly so that Esau wouldn't find him to pay him back for his deceptions. So, knowing those things, when you read this story, you can imagine the anxiety Jacob is feeling as he heads back home and hears his brother is coming to meet him with a large crowd. Jacob probably knew what he deserved, and what HE would have done if the situation was reversed, and had no idea what kind of person his brother Esau had grown into, so he was scared. Have you ever felt that kind of anxiety?

I had an interesting conversation with a friend the other day who was sharing with me a recent experience of meeting with his soon-to-be-ex to sign some papers and work out some details in preparation for the court settlement. As we discussed the event, including the apparent maneuvering and bargaining that had taken place, I found myself going back in my mind to those days when I was going through his experience. I think this Jacob story is a pretty good parallel. The night before he was going to meet his brother, his sleep was troubled, and he wrestled through the night with an angel, begging for the blessing of God. I recall having many sleepless nights, usually the night before or the night after I was to meet with my divorcing wife to hammer out details. I hated those meetings. I doubt that she cared much for them, either. Each of us guarded, uncertain, untrusting….wondering what words and actions really meant, and what information was NOT shared with each proposal. The makers of nighttime pain medicine with sleep aids built in made some pretty good money from me during those nights. I learned fairly early in this that I could not do much to change my emotional unease during those meetings, but I could schedule carefully before and after to reduce the impact. For example, I would make sure I had a good night's sleep before and after, even if it meant taking a sleep aid of some sort. I also tried to think through some things so that I could leave the meeting knowing I had done my best, instead of being vindictive and mean…that was my parallel to Jacob's advance gifts….although that doesn't mean she interpreted any of them as gifts or even fair. (My attorney once suggested that if both parties feel like they didn't get their fair share in everything, then the settlement probably was pretty equitable.) And then, I tried to schedule something afterward to relieve the stress. Sometimes I'd go to a movie, sometimes take the dog for a walk and playtime in the park, sometimes spend time with a friend, or even occasionally just reading something humorous. If you are still having to have those meetings, realize, they don't last forever. And just because you feel anxious about having to do something, does not mean you cannot do it. Then make sure you add in a little bit of self-care….whether that is counseling and some temporary medications, or extra rest, or that fun activity to take your mind off of things. Some things in life truly are Esaus….something you just have to face without knowing what the outcome will be. But you can rise above them a bit if you look out for your own spiritual and emotional well being in the midst of it.

Day 19   2 Corinthians 8:1-15

How are your finances right now? For many people going through divorce, the finances of your life undergo great upheaval and uncertainty. You may feel like you don't have a penny to spare. And when you go to church, the time comes when they pass an offering plate, and all you can think about is how to pay the bills, pay the attorneys, get by on one income and what is going to happen to your nest egg. One of the things that you may have to deal with is the question of tithing, that is, giving 10% back to God though his church. Maybe you never did tithe before. In that case, you would need to know that the Bible contains promises for those who honor God with their finances. Perhaps another time we will look at that. But at this time, you feel surrounded with uncertainty, and are simply not sure what you can afford to do, or what you should do. What should you do? What should you put in?

In fact, this is one of the areas in which your divorce will test you. How much do you trust God? Do you really believe He knows about your needs and will provide for them? Does He have first place in your financial world, or does television or leased cars or whatever other bills you may have coming? This also gives you an opportunity not only to reveal who you are at the core, but to determine who you WANT to be at the core. You no longer have to negotiate with your spouse as to what you will give to God….it is entirely your choice. You can decide to develop a new core value in relation to your money and your giving. Maybe you don't feel like you can give what you would like, or aren't sure you are ready to try tithing yet, but you can choose whether or not you are going to be a giving person. While I believe tithing is important, and that the more you give to God and trust Him, the more He will honor that choice, I also believe God does not want it to turn into legalism for you. Instead, He wants a cheerful giver, and one whose giving reflects trust. Notice the passage today, it says God is not interested in your giving based on what you don't have, but on what you do have. It isn't about what you would do with a million dollars if you won the lottery, it's about what you will do with whatever you have in your pocket today. Don't give in to the temptation to quit giving to the church. Keep steady the habit of being a giver….even if it is just a few dollars, don't let your divorce rob you of the blessings of giving to God. The discipline of giving, trusting God's provision, and stepping out in faith are important disciplines that are going to be tested during this time. Choose to pass the test well. I know a woman who told me about her time of divorce, when money was extremely tight. She had $20 in her purse to get her and her children through the coming week. She believed she still needed to give to God, so she put the twenty in the offering not knowing how she would get by without it. On her way out of church, she was handed $100 by somebody in the church. And then, people in that church supported her as she went back to school to train for a new career. I know personally all the people involved in that story, and know it to be true. I wonder how the story would have been different if she hadn't put in the $20. I wonder how your story will be. That of course depends on what you choose to do with this opportunity. Choose wisely.

Day 20   Luke 21:1-2

Let's take one more day to consider finances. Odds are there is a lot of stress for you if you are in the midst of a divorce, and maybe more stress if you just finished that process. What does God expect of you in terms of finances? What God expects is for you to learn how to trust Him. I love the story of this lady who put in just the two copper coins.... two pennies, essentially. Jesus holds her up as the example, even though there were lots of others who were putting in extravagant and costly gifts. You see, we as people may be impressed when somebody donates a million dollars to a cause. But that doesn't mean God is impressed. God is impressed when whatever you put in demonstrates that you are willing to put yourself on the line, and that you are willing to believe He will meet your need. This lady, Jesus said, put in everything she had to live on, while others put in out of their surplus. Much like the lady I mentioned yesterday who put in what she had for the week. Don't compare what you do with what other people do. That is irrelevant. God doesn't compare you to others. He compares you to you, and looks on your heart.

I so love the story of the time David wanted to make an offering to God, and a man offered to give him his oxen as a sacrifice. (see 1 Chronicles 21:23-25) David refused to accept them as a gift because he was unwilling to give to God something that cost him nothing. That is the key....what does it cost you to give to God? What are you giving up? What are you doing without? What are you risking? You may remember the parable Jesus told about the three men the master gave varying amounts of monetary units called talents. (see Matthew 25:14-31) One had five and doubled it, and was commended. Another had two and doubled and was commended. The third had one and hid it away to preserve it. While the point of the story is that God expects us to use what He entrusts to us and rewards us accordingly, it is worth noting in our context today that the master does not rebuke the one who only had two for only using two when the other man had five. Nor does the one who hid his get in trouble for only having one. No, he gets into trouble for not using the one he has. So it is with you. God looks to see what you are doing with what you do have.

Maybe you don't have any cash, and literally feel like all you can put in is a penny. Then put in the penny....God counts that. Or maybe what you do have to give is time....time to help the soup kitchen or delivering meals or watching a nursery during Bible study or folding papers and stuffing envelopes to help the church office. Whatever it is you can do, that is what God is looking at to see what you do with what you have. And God always honors faithfulness. View this time as an opportunity to demonstrate whether or not you will continue to be faithful to God, including the area of your finances, during a time of testing. Your faithfulness can be a witness and encouragement to others who are struggling, and your giving means that you have included God as a financial partner in your life. He promises over and again He will meet your needs and make sure you are cared for when you faithfully include Him in your life. Sit down, look at what you have and what you have coming in, pray and ask God to show you what He would want you to give, and then commit to doing that to the best of your understanding. If it needs to change, God can show you that as well. I just want to encourage you not to miss this opportunity for God to work in your life to deepen your faith and to experience his provision and care.

Day 21   Proverbs 3:5-6

How quickly we quote this verse when things are going well, and how often we don't have time to mess with it when we are scurrying about trying to figure out how to handle our various decisions when the pressure is on. But the verse applies when the pressure is on just as much as when it is not. I remember feeling so off balance, like I just couldn't think straight, and yet had so many decisions to make so quickly. That, of course, is part of why we hire attorneys....they are experts in the laws that apply, and are supposed to be able to give us dispassionate, although expensive, advice. And God may well use them to help guide you through the maze you are in. And for me, friends who had been through divorce themselves were also a good source of advice. But do not make the mistake of substituting those advisors for God. And don't make the mistake of just using your own figuring as the way God guides you. Certainly He expects you to use your own brain and think things through, but sometimes God calls us to do things that no attorney would advise, things that make no sense even to our own brains. To know that what you are choosing fits into the plans God has, requires that you faithfully keep some time set aside to pray about decisions and keep yourself in the scriptures where guidance is readily available. God promises time and again that He will guide you, and we will see some of those scriptures through the course of the year. But you first have to decide that, in this time, what you want is to do whatever God asks, and therefore you actively seek to know what He wants. He may or may not send you specific guidance on each and every little detail. You can shampoo with whatever brand you prefer. You can keep the china and let him have the toolchest. But it is important to make sure that you cultivate those opportunities for God to guide. Sometimes God may want you to make a particular choice about something that seems minute at the time, but which fits into a plan He has down the road you cannot yet see. Sometimes He takes the choices we make and weaves them into the fabric of what He is creating in your life. Don't merely trust your own insight. Don't lean on your own figuring things out. Don't sell short what God will do for you during this time. God's guidance is the greatest thing you will ever know.... because then you make your choices with confidence, or at least with a small degree of faith, knowing that God has a purpose in all that is going on, even if you can't see it.

MY PRAYER FOR YOU THIS WEEK

This week, my prayer is for your faith, that it will not be shaken. Through the testings that come your way, through the attacks that may seem to undermine everything you believe and hope, may your faith in Christ sustain and carry you. May your faith grow stronger through the testing, and may you come through it purified and holy, to the glory of God our Father. Amen.

Day 22   1 Kings 19:13-18

Before you read any further today, I want to ask you to get up and walk over into a corner of the room, as close to the corner as you can, facing the corner, and read the rest of the devotional there. Without turning your head, I want you to notice what you can see. Do you see any pictures on the wall behind you....without turning around mind you? Do you see any of the doors or windows in the other parts of the room? No. All you see is the corner, and maybe just a little bit at the edges around through your peripheral vision. Make a mental list of all the things you can see without turning at all. Now, I want you to estimate what percentage of the room and its contents that list represents. In most cases, it might be less than 10%. Now that you have done all that, you may be asking yourself, "so, what is the point?" Well, the point relates to something I use a lot in my pastoral counseling with people who are struggling for various reasons. Let me explain it to you.

In the corner of the room, you miss seeing so much of the room. And, in fact, you also miss seeing all the rest of the rooms in the house. That may well be an analogy of what you are experiencing emotionally and mentally at this time. The divorce process looms large in your observations. Everything you experience day by day is tainted by it. All your decisions are affected by it. And, there may even be significant periods of time that you literally obsess about it. It may be all you can see, or you may simply be dwelling on it significantly more than is helpful. If you are like I was, it may be very hard to do otherwise. However, think about the room. There is so much more to that room than what you can see in the corner, and there is so much more in your life than this divorce you are experiencing. If you but turn around, you would see pictures, windows, doors, furniture, rooms beyond. If you can, once in a while, do the same in relation to the divorce, you will see hobbies, friendships, family relations, work successes, physical activities, Christian involvements....the list is virtually endless.

God did the same kind of turning for Elijah. He was so struggling that he felt like nothing but a failure, abandoned and all alone. But God turned him around out of his corner. There are some people yet for him to anoint. There are 7,000 others who are still loyal to the Lord as Elijah was. But he just couldn't see them. All he could see was the corner he was living in. Maybe that is all you can see, too. I encourage you today to get a journal, and start making a list of what would be behind you if divorce is the only corner you see....all the areas of your life that are meaningful to you that exist for you and in you regardless of the divorce. It is simply a part of what one must do regain your perspective.

Day 23   1 Samuel 20:1-23

One of the things I remember so much from my divorce time was the precariousness of my situation. Financially, things were in terrible upheaval and I did not know how it would turn out, or how I was going to make it. I felt so devastated. But God did something special in my life. Actually, He had already done that something special, I just hadn't realized yet how special it was. God surrounded me with good friends. Friends who were willing to share their experiences with me from their own divorces when I asked for advice regarding my situation. Friends who were willing to open their homes to me temporarily until I could find a place of my own. Friends who would take time out of their busy day to listen, encourage and pray. And in those moments God showed me something. Though I was feeling so broke as I watched money go to attorneys and get divided between my ex and myself....I suddenly realized that I actually was very wealthy. I had one of the greatest treasures a person can have in this life: good friends. Friends with whom I could shed tears. Friends who would share moments of joy with me. Friends to stand with me in the midst of the storms. Friends to turn to when I needed help and advice. And those friends are the treasures of a lifetime. David and Jonathan had that kind of experience, in all the hard times they shared together.

I know I can never repay all those friends did for me, or the time they so graciously and generously gave to me in my time of need, but I do know that God noticed their care, and God will repay what I cannot. For me, those were the friends I had developed over a lifetime. Have you found those friends in your life? If not, then perhaps now is the time to reach out and find some. At your church....or a church you may need to start attending if you don't have one. At your divorce support group. Maybe you could help start a home Bible study. One of my favorite movies is "It's a Wonderful Life," and the message that comes through that movie as well is that you can never be poor if you have friends. It may well be that you will discover in this time of your life, just how great a treasure your friendships are.

Day 24   Matthew 19:3-12

When my second wife and I got married, because we met through the assistance of our dogs, my step-daughter made candy bar wrappers for the wedding dinner that had pictures of the dogs on it with the slogan printed in the middle: "what dog has brought together..." Well, you get the idea. The trouble is, if we are indeed Christian, no matter how we get together as a couple, we believe it is God who brings us together. And it is before God that we exchange our vows. And we know that the scripture says, "what God has brought together, let not man put asunder." And the vows are sacred. "Till death do you part." When I took my wedding vows that first time, I meant them. And when things got hard in that marriage, I would remind myself—I promised. I took the vow. When the divorce came, it felt like there was a betrayal of those very vows. So what do you do when you see those sacred vows shattered before your eyes? Well, perhaps the first thing you do is your very best to keep those vows. Is there any possibility of reconciliation? Would you go back and make it work if there were a chance not just to be back together, but to go back and make the marriage work, really work. To make it the kind of marriage that doesn't careen toward divorce, but one where love truly abounds. That is different from just going back for the sake of going back...especially if the marriage was abusive, or if adultery was a factor. But whatever the cause, when the sacred vows are broken, what do you do?

Well, the Bible does speak of an unforgiveable sin....but divorce isn't it. In fact, if you read today's passage carefully, you will discover that divorce, though not God's original intention, was given because of the brokenness of this world due to the hard heartedness of we humans. And even if you were the one who chose to end the marriage, you need to know that God still has a place for you. Confess to God your part in the dissolution of the marriage....even if you feel yourself mainly to be the victim. Tell Him how you feel about it, ask His forgiveness, be open to follow His leading wherever it goes, and let go. That is the hardest part, to let go. In some ways, you never do. Especially if you believe that vows you make are sacred. But when the vows have been rejected and shattered, not just by the divorce, but by the relationship styles that are so different from what was vowed, then you have to sort out where you go from now, and part of that, once things are final and irreversible, is that you have to begin the process of letting go. That is a critical part of any grieving process.

Day 25   Jonah 2:1-7

Doesn't this passage of Jonah take on a different feeling as you read it in this time? I imagine Jonah, feeling himself dragging downward, pulled along with hope disappearing quickly, while he felt the overwhelming aloneness there in the depths of the sea. Though the situation he was in, and the choices that led up to it may have been entirely different from your own, yet the emotional heartcry of Jonah expresses well the lonely feelings that may overwhelm you now. I remember what it felt like many a day walking into an empty house, footsteps echoing, no voice to call out hello. And, if you have children, whether they live primarily with you or with your ex, the empty spots at the table when they are away seem so empty during this time. Later on, you may experience their time with your ex as giving you a break, sort of a built in baby sitter, but in the early days, the emptiness is what you feel, as you sit alone eating a meal prepared for one. If, that is, you even bother to make a meal. Maybe just popcorn. Maybe a frozen dinner. When you feel the seaweed of loneliness dragging you down, it is hard to see the brighter days ahead. But that doesn't mean they aren't there….it only means you cannot see them. It might feel easier to just give up. And Satan and despair would love to see you quit, dragged down to the depths of despair. But remember, just as the night does not mean the sun has stopped shining, only that it is not shining upon the place you are dwelling, so when life's shadows come our way, it does not mean that the light of God's face has stopped shining. It only means that time in the shadows keeps us from seeing the brightness of his light, and we must wait until we round the bend, till the light climbs over the horizon to feel the warmth of God's glow upon us again. God's warmth remains constant, even when we cannot feel it.

Let these times build within you his compassion for others as you experience something of what others also feel in their times of distress. The next time you see a fellow servant suffering, or downcast and despairing, remember these times and do for them what you wish someone would do for you just now...become for them the light of God in the shadows of life. Put your arm around them. Kneel down in prayer with them. Send that card with words of hope. Take them to an evening out away from the pressing walls of home. Paul said it best when he wrote in Romans 12: *"Rejoice with those who rejoice, and weep with those who weep."* (NASB) And, for that to actually happen, it may require you to allow someone else to weep a bit with you, as well.

Day 26   Matthew 5:44-45

So, have you been praying for your ex? Or maybe I ought to ask, what have you been praying for your ex? I am sure there are days you want to pray like the two disciples who wanted to call down fire upon people who had rejected them. Surely you can relate to those feelings at times. But Jesus says that is not the spirit we believers are to be following. Instead, we are to bless those who hate us, and pray for those who use us badly. Wow. That is hard to do, isn't it? Maybe not so hard to mouth the words, but to really mean it? Perhaps you have been praying that God will help him change his mind about what is happening. Or maybe you have been praying that God will change her so that what is happening will be different. Maybe you want God to make him hurt like you have been hurt. Maybe you just don't even want to bother to talk to God about that person....like you are so angry you simply can't pray for them, or if you did pray for them, you know it wouldn't be a good thing you'd be asking. Or, maybe you are a bit more noble minded, and you really do want to pray well for your ex, and want to pray in a way that God can do something in his or her life. That is not such a bad place to be. The difficulties come when we decide exactly what God should be doing in that life....giving God advice if you will. No matter which of these categories fits you, the scripture remains that we need to be on our knees before God on behalf of people who treat us poorly....including your ex. So what do you do?

I might suggest a few that were what I learned to pray. What is wrong with praying, "God, do what you know is best in the life of my ex-spouse to accomplish what you desire to accomplish during this time"? Or how about this one: "God, you know my ex's heart, and you know what needs to change. Bring about the circumstances and opportunities to work your will into his/her heart." Perhaps a more general view would be, "God, work in such a way as to reveal to him/her what Your will is for his/her life, and make him/her into the man/woman you desire them to be." Or, "God help him/her in this trying time to not make foolish and hurtful choices." Or maybe even, "God, send the people into the life of my ex who will be able to represent you to them in this difficult time." You get the idea.

Sometimes, God speaks to people and they respond quickly because their hearts are tender. Other people come to God the hard way, through the path of selfishness and rebellion. And others live their lives without ever bending their knee to Christ. God alone knows the path your ex will pursue. At this time, it is very likely your ex will not hear God's voice through anything you say or do, so unless you feel a strong, clear leading from God, it is probably a time for you to commit your ex to the hands of God, and concentrate on keeping your own heart tender so that God can work in you as well. Which may mean you may have to be open with God about your own feelings as you consider praying for your ex.

Day 27   Hosea 7:8-12

Does that image make sense to you at all? Haven't you seen people acting the way Hosea describes, flitting from here to there and back again, no stability, no roots, no logic. Perhaps that describes how your life is right now. You may be feeling so off balance. You may be running from a support group, to a close friend, to your pastor, to a counselor, to another friend, to your doctor, to the antidepressants, to….well, you get the idea. Not to say that some of those things aren't good things, in fact great sources of help. But, all too often we let those things become the primary source of our help, and then turn to God as an incidental part of our lives. It is exactly that sort of thing that God condemns through Hosea. Israel was facing a national crisis. Their continued existence as a country was precarious at best, as one empire after another grew around them, and threatened them because the land of Israel was in the way of their international conquests. Like so many other countries in our world today, the leadership of the country was assessing the volatile situation around them, and trying to ally themselves with whoever they thought would be the country to come out on top. The problem wasn't so much that it was inappropriate to seek to make international alliances on the world scene. They had done that before. It was part of being a world leader. But the problem was they were seeking these alliances as their source of strength, as their source of hope, as their source of protection and deliverance. In other words, they were allowing somebody else to be what God has promised He would be….and He never allows somebody or something else to take His place in the hearts of His people.

So, are you getting the help and encouragement you are seeking BECAUSE those sources are the ones God has provided and has led you toward? Or are they the things you are seeking as your source INSTEAD of God. God is still a jealous God, He shares His space in your heart with nothing else. Perhaps you need to consider what you are making as the source that keeps your going. Is God that primary source? Do you turn to God FIRST with the decisions facing you? When you need to unburden your heart to someone, is God the first someone you share with, or do you treat God as your last resort? Do you turn to God only when nothing else works, and nobody else is around? This time in your life is a time that will bring to the surface what your real priorities are. Don't be a silly dove. Stay connected to God, and you will be able to withstand the storms that are blowing. If you make time for God to be first, then He may lead you to a friend for support, or a counselor to help you through, or to a doctor whose prescriptions can help you through the day. But keep your priorities straight. God must be first.

Day 28   Matthew 27:1-5

Once the trial and crucifixion process began, Judas seemed to suddenly realize the full implication of his betrayal. (Have you ever done something, and not really thought through the implications? I know I have.) Realizing what he had set in motion, in despair, Judas committed suicide. Such tragic despair and regret. It is very possible that at some point in your divorce process, your emotions may get so cloudy, your situation so difficult and your mind so confused that you may well begin considering ending your life. Or, as we hear all too often on the news, you may even consider a combination murder/suicide. It is incredible to say, especially if you are a Christian, but the tide of your emotions can become so over-whelming that the boundaries you usually live with can become weak and you may be tempted to end your life or even the life of others in despair. You begin to think there is no future, that you have lost everything, that nothing matters any longer. As I looked at my life, I felt like so many of the things I valued most.... my family, my marriage, my wedding vows, time with my children, my homelife, things like that....so many of them were shattered out of my life in an instant by a piece of paper from the court....a paper indicating a divorce had been filed. I remember saying, as I was sorting out all the odds and ends we had accumulated, that it was all just stuff....what mattered most to me was gone, the rest was just stuff. Can you relate to that feeling of shatteredness and loss? Are you finding your heart blessing that you handle things differently, or it may be that things may hit you this way another day, and this may help prepare you.

I have mentioned before that one of my friends wanted to offer me some encouragement, and so one day told me something she heard from a divorced friend of hers, which she thought was worth passing on. The phrase was, "There IS life after divorce." At the time, it was hard to understand or appreciate the depth of the reality of that statement. In fact, it can actually seem unbelievable....so many things seem so shattered, so hopeless, that it is hard to imagine that anything could ever be good again. Sometimes, people get stuck at that point.... and in their despair, they choose to bail out, thinking that choosing to end their lives will also end their pain. I have had a number of people contemplating suicide who have asked me what happens to them if they die by their own hand. My main response is to consider what it would feel like to stand before the Almighty God and have the first thing you hear from God be, "Wait a minute, what are you doing here already? This is too early."

Well, I don't want to actually get into the speculations and theology around the topic of suicide. What I do want us to get into, is the fact that the person who decides to shortcut their lives never sees what would have happened if they had hung on. Kind of the reverse of that old Christmas movie, 'It's a Wonderful Life." In that movie, George Bailey is given the opportunity to see what the world would have been like without his influence over the past years of his life. You and I don't know what the world will be like because of our influence over the future years of our lives....the future that one abandons when giving up through suicide. Judas never got to see the end of the story. Just a few days later Jesus rose from the dead. Nobody knows what might have happened had Judas lived until Jesus' resurrection. I know the pain can be intense. I know things can seem hopeless. But that is not the end of the story unless you make it the end. If you are struggling with despair, I just want to encourage you to hang on....these hard times will pass, and the things beyond these hard times may well be better than you can imagine now. Give God that chance....simply by not giving up. There IS life after divorce....and that life can be very good.

MY PRAYER FOR YOU THIS WEEK

This week, my prayer is for your children, if you have any. May God protect them, and keep tender their wounded hearts. May they experience Your healing and protection. May they know and experience the love each parent has for them, even if they express that love in radically different ways. Help the readers of these words to experience an anointing from You as they seek to be a quality parent for their offspring in crisis. Hold before the readers a mirror reflecting every word and every deed, that they will be able to see how their behavior impacts their children. God forgive the readers for their shortcomings as parents, and help each one to always strive to be the kind of parent You would have them be.... regardless of how the children respond. Help the children to forgive this reader for errors they make, and to someday understand how hard this parent has tried to do those things that are pleasing to You. In the name of the Everlasting Father, from whom all families are named, Amen.

Day 29   Jeremiah 42:1-43:7

There is a fascinating story in the book of Jeremiah. After their country had been invaded, and all the resulting turmoil had taken its toll, there were some leaders who were struggling to know what to do, and wanted to know if there was guidance from God available to them. They asked Jeremiah to seek the Lord and guide them. Jeremiah promised he would go seek God's guidance, and in their exuberance, the people insisted they would do whatever God told them. Jeremiah came back with the message they didn't want to hear....he told them they needed to stay and endure. What they wanted to hear was that it was okay to escape their troubles by running to Egypt. But they were told God wanted them to stay. At that point, they were faced with a choice....do we stay in obedience to our best understanding of what God wants, or do we take what *we* consider to be the safest path and head out to Egypt for protection? If only they had remembered and believed the warning in Proverbs 3:5-6 not to trust their own understanding, but to trust God instead, they would have done what Jeremiah said. They let their fears get the best of them, decided to take their destiny into their own hands and headed off to Egypt....where disaster befell them. You see, sometimes people say they want to know God's will, but what they really want is for God to will what they want themselves. We don't get to decide what God's will should be....God decides His own will. We merely are given the opportunity to be obedient or not to those pieces of God's will revealed to us. Disaster always waits in the path of those who choose to live their lives in opposition to God's guidance....maybe soon or maybe later, maybe external, but maybe internal, maybe earthly and maybe eternally, but ignoring the guidance of God is perilous.

So, do you *really* want to know what God wants from you at this time so that you can do it? Or have you already decided what you want and are only asking God's guidance as a formality before you do what you have already decided to do? In our situation, that question may arise in a variety of ways. Like whether or not you will do your best to abide by your wedding vows, or look for an "easy" way out called divorce. Or whether or not you will see somebody else while still married. Or how vicious you will be in your court battles against a spouse who refuses to reconcile. Or whether you will drown your sorrows in alcohol or drugs. Or....well, you know better than I where the question arises in your life. Are you really open to God's will for anything? Even if God asks you to do something you don't really want to do?

There is a wonderful story in the ancient Jewish legends in which God is seeking a nation with whom He could entrust the scriptures of Moses. God approaches one nation after another, each of which asks what is commanded in the scriptures, and then finding something there that is disagreeable to their heritage, they refuse to accept the scriptures. But when God approaches the nation of Israel to ask if they would accept the Torah, their response is that they will receive it and obey it.... even before they find out what is in it. Of course, the history recorded

43

in the scripture reveals all the times they did NOT obey it after it was given to them....but what an attitude! Whatever God wants, I will do! I will not put conditions on my acceptance of the Lordship of Christ in my life! Think of Paul, and all the hardship he experienced; he was committed to God, and was not about to change that commitment just because the things God asked him to do were not what he wanted. In this time, how about you? Are you committed to do whatever God asks of you....no matter what? Or are you only willing to do what God wants as long as it coincides with what you want? Think carefully before you answer. And give your answer to God, not to me. God will guide you. The question is, will you allow yourself to be guided?

Day 30   Psalm 15:1-5

During the process and aftermath of a divorce, your own sense of personal ethics is pushed to the extreme. You have to decide time and again who you are, what you stand for and how you will behave. What being a Christian means to you will be exposed in many different ways, from your actions toward your spouse, to your style of negotiating, to your methods of handling the stress, to future dating morality. In fact, it may be one of the most severe tests of your morality you have ever faced.

I have known of individuals who claim to be Christian, but when they deal with the divorce process and their ex, all Christian morality vanishes, and the hypocrisy of who they truly are is evident. Examples? I have told you some already, but let's consider them and others today, too. I know of some divorcing couples where one spouse found creative ways to hide money and income so as to avoid having to divide things fairly with their spouse. Maybe it was done in self protection, maybe it was done in revenge, but regardless of the why, it was done dishonestly. I have known of some who are unwilling to submit to the authority of the court, ignoring court orders hoping to force their ex to impoverish themselves with attorney fees trying to recoup whatever was ordered. I even know a situation in which a spouse was awarded alimony (or maintenance) for a certain period of time or until remarriage, who kept her remarriage a secret from her ex as long as possible so that she could continue to receive monthly checks to which she was not entitled.

She thought it was funny. I think it is reprehensible.... especially for someone who claims to be a follower of Christ.

This verse in Psalms is an incredible challenge for people going through the trials you may be facing just now. Swearing your allegiance to Christ means doing what is right, to the best of your ability, even if it costs or hurts you. It may cost you money. It may cost you time with your kids. It may hurt so deep in your soul you didn't even know you could hurt there. I know, I have experienced these kind of things myself. I will not claim that I did everything "right". But I will claim that I have done my best to do what I believe is right and what would be honorable from Christ's point of view. I know of many choices where it was very tempting to do something other than what I did. I know of many ways my heart has been broken, and the choices I made had results that were more painful than I could have imagined. But I have tried. After all, that is all God asks, isn't it? Remember the other Psalm (103:14) where it says that God is mindful of our frailty, that we are but dust?

It is your turn now. As you go through what you are experiencing, what will be exposed of YOUR character? What will be the basis out of which you make your choices? When all is said and done, one thing you have that nobody can take away from you is your own character. Even if things get twisted around so as to damage your reputation, you can still have a clear conscience toward God, knowing you have been as true as you know how to the high calling called "Christian".

Day 31   Matthew 23:23-28

Have you been caught up in the maelstrom of attorney papers flying back and forth, enough legalese to turn your stomach, and then those financial statements from your attorney that just seem so unbelievable?!? Things that seem like they could be done so easily are, instead, complicated and obfuscated by legal intricacies that seem absurd, but you know if it isn't noted, then the law is structured in such a way that there will be all sorts of unintended consequences. And who structured that law in such a convoluted way? Lawyers! There is a reason so many lawyer jokes exists. (Like the one about the lawyer who billed his client because his client's name popped into his head during a dream at night.) Assuming you have an attorney, there will be days you think of them as the best friend you have in your times of struggle, and other days you hate walking into the office because of the endless details that seem to continually arise for discussion, each detail at more money per hour than most people make in a day….or even a week.

For a couple of days, we are going to consider your relationship with the attorney, and some insights into how that teaches us about God. Today, let's talk about the frustration. As the incredible number of attorney jokes and slurs would indicate, you are not alone when you are frustrated with your attorney, your spouse's attorney, or the whole court system. I have personally wondered how some attorneys sleep at night, especially those who make their fortune through the charges they assess clients who cannot afford the exorbitant rates, but also cannot afford to go to court without an attorney. (Although I have known some who did, trusting that God would take care of them….that was just what they felt they needed to do.) This can especially be true of individuals going through a divorce….many have to take bankruptcy afterwards. Even Jesus railed against the practices of some of the attorney types of His day for straining gnats and swallowing camels. These individuals would make the simplest things so difficult, so condemning….I can't imagine but that some of the people back then just cried out, "Do you have to make it so complicated? I just want to serve God….surely it doesn't have to be so frustrating!"

What I want to note in this particular passage for today is this: attorneys have a job to do. Sometimes I am sure they feel very satisfied knowing they helped someone who desperately needed their expertise. I have made sure my attorney knows how much I appreciated the help I needed. I am also sure there are some who couldn't care less about their clients, as long as the bills are paid. These attorneys seem to go out of their way to find one more billable minute, one more issue that could be added to increase paperwork, motions and costs. And some are probably sadistic in the way they go after their opponent in ways that are sleazy and unnecessary. Maybe yours is like this latter type. You should be careful if the attorney is that way…it is too easy to get sucked into that kind of ethic, to make your choices from down in the gutter. You could choose to remember that your attorney works for you, not vice versa, and you do have the right to set limits….although doing so may mean your attorney will refer you to somebody else. Or you could choose to deal with the issue yourself and seek another attorney. Finally, you can simply endure your way through, doing your best to keep yourself and your attorney in line with what is morally acceptable in your relationship with God. But remember, it is not your place to judge your attorney. You don't have to keep the same attorney, but those who abuse the authority and trust placed in them will have to answer for themselves in the highest court of all, the throneroom of God. That can be an especially encouraging insight when you get frustrated or angry at the behavior of the opposing attorney....and I can practically guarantee that you will. Focus on the issues of your own that you need to deal with, and let God take care of the other people in His own time and way.

Day 32   1 John 2:1-2

Once again, let us reflect upon what we can learn from attorneys and your relationships with them. This time, let us reflect on the great service they provide for us. I remember more than once in my divorce proceedings, I would think that everything was lost, or be overwhelmed by some of the challenges I would face, and then my attorney would say to me something like, "but the law covers that, you have a right to have...." I would suddenly have hope, realizing that there were protections I was not aware of but, thankfully, my attorney did know about. That was her job, her role as my attorney. When papers would come from the court, or from my ex's attorney, my attorney would counter with something that was more considerate of my needs. More often than not, she would present me with the various options I had, make her recommendation, and then offer her services to prepare the papers or motions or whatever to accomplish on my behalf what was decided. I know that different states have vastly differing procedures in these matters, but in my state, when it came time for the final settlement, my attorney presented me with three options. I could go to court by myself, or I could have her go with me, or she could go instead of me. Given the emotional trauma I had been feeling and going through, I was grateful for the opportunity to not have to stand before the judge (who was also a personal friend) in the strange environment of court to go through what I knew would be a tremendously emotional experience. She went in my stead and took care of everything that needed to be done. During that time and since, I have always been grateful for the quality work she did on my behalf, and the wisdom and knowledge she made available to me. Of course, on the other hand, I also received the bill, and one is never grateful for that!

If you have ever had the sinking feeling of having to walk into a courtroom to stand before a judge for something, whether in your divorce or otherwise, then you may also know how much it helped to know that the attorney at your side was going to be watching out for you. Today's verse makes clear that we have our attorney, our advocate, who is standing before the ultimate judge, God Himself, and interceding for us, looking our for our best interests. He has made sure we have access to the promises God has provided, ones we wouldn't even have known were available if He wasn't our advocate. Just as my attorney guided me through the unfamiliar processes of the court, so Jesus is our guide through this foreign territory of sojourning upon earth. Just as my attorney had the priority of looking out for my best interests when there were those who would try to undermine them, so Jesus stands against Satan, the thief, liar and murderer who is out to destroy us and sell us short. And best of all, there will be no bill from God coming our way, because it was already stamped "paid in full" at the cross of our advocate, Jesus. (By the way, if you want to read some fun comments about attorneys, you might look at Ben Franklin's <u>Poor Richard's Almanack</u>.)

Day 33   Genesis 7:17-20 and 1 Peter 3:18-22

I have lived several places in my life near rivers that reach flood stage and overflow their banks when there are extended periods of heavy rainfall. Often, I have seen fields and parks changed into temporary lakes, and have also seen waters flood into a riverside town's main streets. On the news, there are often stories about places where waters flooding out of their banks wreak all sorts of havoc. In the Midwest a few years back, the television frequently portrayed people rapidly filling and stacking sandbags in preparation for floodwaters that were going to come, but they weren't sure when, or how high, or if the sandbags would work. There is always a higher ground area to head to, or a distance one can travel to get away from the waters, but I cannot begin to imagine what it must have been like for Noah and his family. Waters rising rapidly everywhere. Danger at every turn. Damage and death must have surrounded them as the ark began to float and they were carried away to destinations unknown. Floods are just kind of like that, waters out sweep in, things are carried off, lots of uncertainty, everything way out of control. With all those things taking place, they must have been very grateful for the ark, the one safe haven in the midst of all the devastation. And they must have been so humbled and grateful that God had prepared them so many months in advance so they could be protected from the danger. God even closed the door of the ark once they were inside, an assurance that they were in his protective care.

Do you ever feel like flood waters are swirling around you? Do you ever think that too much of your life is being swept away? Are things spinning out of control, and all your frantic efforts to protect yourself, all the sandbags you have stacked into your life, now seem precarious and insufficient? God prepared for your flood in advance. If you look carefully, you will find things He has done, things He has taught you, preparations He has made to help you through this time. But all the preparations of Noah would have been to no avail had they never run into the ark. The same is true for you....place yourself within the ark of God. Let Him close the protecting door around you. 1 Peter makes clear that your commitment to Christ and the seal of water baptism are the Christian parallels of God's deliverance for Noah. And that is the place you have to begin....you first have to place yourself within the salvation of God by coming to Christ seeking forgiveness and salvation. But afterwards, in the midst of the floodwaters you may be experiencing, God's provision of an ark may have many forms. Maybe it is your local church to whom you turn for encouragement and support. Maybe it is hiding away in your private prayer space with God to gain the strength and wisdom you need. Maybe it is finding those promises in the Bible that are relevant to your current situation, and then hanging on to them by faith for dear life. Maybe it is looking back to find those things that God has woven into your life to prepare you for the floods you are experiencing, and then trusting that God will use them to help you through. It could be a special job skill, it could be inner emotional strength, it could be the ability to make wise choices.... Whatever your ark is for you just now, God knew exactly what you would need to get through this particular flood, and his hand rests upon the door to hold you in. Hang on, and trust that God knows what He is doing....even if the flood waters continue to rise.

Day 34   Luke 16:10-11

Honesty is the best policy. Remember that old saying? Sometimes, honesty can cost you money. Like when you report money on your income taxes that somebody else might choose not to report. Or when you sell your car and explain to the buyer what all is wrong with the vehicle. Sometimes it could cost you a job. Like if your employer is skimping on some things, and wants you to cut corners or be less than candid with a customer. You have to choose whether you are going to compromise your honesty and keep your job, or refuse to do what is asked and risk losing your employment. There are lots of opportunities in our culture to be dishonest.

I have seen many people who are not willing to be honest. Not with their friends. Not with their spouse. Not with themselves. Not even with God. Not really. They keep their little secrets. They cut corners, and skirt the edges. And they are people I have learned are not trustworthy. They are also people who cannot look you in the eye, or when they do, you know it isn't real, it is just a façade. Because when someone cuts corners in their honesty, they also cut corners in their character. Instead of being a person of conviction, they become a person of compromise.

I knew of a woman who, during her divorce process, was systematically pulling money out and giving it to another family member for her to be able to access afterwards, believing that her husband didn't keep the books and would have no idea the money was missing. But God saw each dollar she hid. I knew a couple of men who, to avoid settling with their spouses and to protect themselves from having to pay much child support, hid substantial sums in their businesses, that they would access for themselves later on after the divorce. But they didn't really protect themselves, they protected only their finances. Instead of protecting themselves, they endangered themselves, opening the door that made money more important than character. We make choices, and those choices determine not only who we are, but also who we become. You will be making choices today, and those choices affect your character. I doubt that anybody ever regretted making choices that established their reputation as an honest and trustworthy individual. God is never dishonest with us. If we are going to be followers of Christ, can we be any less than honest?

Day 35   Isaiah 46:8-13

Who is it you turn to in times of trouble? Who is your most trusted advisor? Whose shoulder do you cry upon? When you think of a faithful friend, whose name comes to mind? When you need someone you can truly trust in a desperate time, who would that be? When you think of a person whose life has been an example for you, whose name comes to mind? What about the person you would want to have at your side if you were under attack and needed defensive help? Who would be the one you would turn to in a time you need good moral support? When you think of the kindest, most upright person you have ever known, one you consider to be truly good, who would that be? What about the greatest artist you admire? Or the most creative thinker you have ever seen? Lots of people fill lots of different roles in our lives. If you are like most of the people I know, then at the end of those questions you would have a wide variety of names listed. Today, as you think of those people, I want you to consider that any one of those people fits their category only to a point. That is, someone whose life is an example would still have characteristics you would *not* want to emulate as well as those ones you admire. The same is true with all the other issues. Individuals exemplify one trait or another, but none of them are perfect, nor does any one person possess all the characteristics you treasure to a full degree. Each of us has our frailties and failings, our shortcomings and our faults. But each of those good characteristics we admire and appreciate in others, and seek to develop within ourselves, are just a hint, a trace of the true character of God Himself.

Today's scripture says that there is no one like God. Your friend in trouble may or may not be able to help you solve the situation. Even the best of advisors sometimes gives us bad advice. Sometimes when you need a shoulder to cry on, your best friend is unavailable because of other obligations. We have all been let down by even the most faithful of people. You can see where this is going, can't you? There is no one like God. God is absolutely unique in all the universe. And your relationship with Him is different from all others, both in kind and in degree. He will always be there. He will never make a mistake. He never fails. He will always love you, without reservation or reticence. He is more loyal than your best friend. He is absolutely trustworthy, and His guidance infallible. He is a mighty defender of the defenseless, and a powerful warrior in battle. There is no one who is so completely, so perfectly wise, good, loving, righteous, just, creative, so....well, the list is actually as infinite as God Himself. There is simply no one like God. Our mistake in life is that all too often, we try to replace God with lesser beings, or lesser things. We worship money or fame or security. We turn to others in times of need before we turn to God. We trust so many other people or other things, and yet question the guidance we are given by God. We want to feel safe and loved, but settle for door alarms and quick thrills instead of holding out for the perfect security and love that comes only from a relationship with Him. We count on others, or our own solutions, when we should be counting on God. God alone can meet the needs of our hearts, the longing of our souls, and expand the limits of our minds. There is no one else like Him, and we must never let another take the place in our lives that He longs to fill.

MY PRAYER FOR YOU THIS WEEK

This week, my prayer is for the tender touch of God when your world seems to have fallen apart, when the hurts and burdens have become more than you think you can bear. May you sense the nearness of God as He catches each tear you shed and carefully stores it away, until the day that tears will no more be shed. May you experience the arms of God wrapped around you to keep you safe and warm, his hands beneath you helping you to stand, his shoulder against you to lean upon when you weep. May you never doubt the profound and eternal love that God has for you, today, tomorrow, and with every new day. Amen.

Day 36   Job 23:8-10

Job was one of the few people in the scriptures described with the adjectives blameless and upright (or something similar depending on your translation). He must have been quite a man of faith to receive that kind of commendation out of the mouth of God. I have always been amazed at this statement of Job's during the midst of his grief and suffering. This is only one of some pretty profound statements, and we consider the others elsewhere. He was a man who lost most everything he had acquired in life: possessions, family, friends, health, pretty nearly everything. Even his character and good name were being called into question. Not only that, but even his own wife wished he would just die and get it over with. He had hit rock bottom in life, and was clinging to God as his only hope. This passage strikes me as so powerful, because in the midst of this incredibly tough season of life, Job was convinced there was purpose: the severe testing that had come upon him would only serve to refine his faith and character, and he would come out like gold—pure, shining, beautiful and valuable. What a hope!

What is your expectation when tough times are in your life? Do you hope just to get through them? Do you feel like a piece of paper too close to the fireplace, as if you are at risk of being totally consumed by the flames of trial? <u>Or</u> do you hold on to the sense that God is working even in this time, that He has purpose, and that purpose will ultimately be good. Sometimes I think we don't hope for enough out of our faith. Like we only hope that we get through the testing, or that we will come out only slightly charred. Are you hoping for more than that? Are you aware that God can use it for more if you are faithful and obedient?

Some of us are going through fire hoping to come out like a clay brick….not broken and just a bit stronger, but still mud. Some hope to come out a little cleaner, like a cast iron skillet burned through a fire to remove the gunk that has formed. But Job's vision was for more than that, to be not only strong and pure, but to be beautiful, valuable, glorious. I want you to try to envision yourself as a great champion of God, a person whose character is flawless, a person of deep, spiritual beauty. And I invite you to look at the hard things in your life and begin to see them as fires of testing and purification, rather than flames of agony and destruction. Job knew he would get through it, because he knew God was with him. God is with you, too. Let that certainty sink deep, and begin to praise God for what He is producing in you.

Day 37   Job 2:1-10

Job and his wife suffered almost the same tragedies. The herds they lost were their livelihood. Their children were their future. Their harvest was their sustenance. All gone in an instant. But then Job also lost his health, while his wife seems to have lost her faith. Her response to him was that he should just curse God and die. Actually, in the

Hebrew, the word used is not, "to curse," but an intense form of the word for blessing used in a form to indicate that blessing is not what is meant. It was such a reprehensible thing that no self respecting Jew would dare to write "curse God." For her to say such a thing was clearly beyond the pale. Job's response, on the other hand, was to respond with acceptance of whatever life might bring under the hand of God. He knew it makes no sense to accept only good as part of life under God's reign, when the world also has so many hard and evil things. So he responds with his famous statement that he arrived naked, would leave naked, and the name of the Lord is to be blessed. You gotta admire a fellow who can still offer praise to God when life has dealt such a traumatic blow as he suffered. Times of severe struggle are also severe tests of faith in this life. Some people rise to the occasion out of the depths of their being. Some people crash into the rocks. And some make it through when given appropriate support and encouragement. What kind of person are you?

One of the things that is a core struggle in the book of Job is whether or not God has to explain his actions to humankind. Lots of people throughout history have asked the question of why. Why did God allow Abel to be killed by Cain? Why did God allow evil into the world at all? Why did Joseph have to get sold into bondage in Egypt? Why did the Jews have to be oppressed there as slaves? Why did God allow Peter and Stephen and Paul to be beaten or stoned? Why did God allow Hitler to come to power? Why did He allow the millions to be killed in the holocaust? I bet you can name a few whys of your own, if you tried.

Job begins pretty well, he acknowledges that he brought nothing into the world, and would leave without anything, something the apostle Paul echoes in his letter to Timothy. But as time wears on, Job begins to struggle to understand why things are so bad, and why they don't get better. In fact, he spouts off with great bravado how he would make God answer and explain if only God would show up for a debate. But when God does show up, Job backs off from his claims, and even says he will keep his hand over his mouth in silence. God makes clear to Job, and to us in chapters 38-41, that his knowledge, power and wisdom are far beyond human understanding. Once Job gets the point that just because *HE* doesn't understand what God is doing, does not mean *GOD* doesn't understand. In fact, part of the point is that Job wouldn't be able to understand it all even if God *did* explain it to him.

Most of all, it seems to me, the point of it all is to remind Job (and us) of who is God and who is human.

Somehow, when things become hard in life, we develop an attitude that God owes us an explanation. We never think He needs to explain Himself when good things happen, only when hard or bad things occur. But the truth is, God is the Creator, we are the creation, God owes us nothing, least of all that He should have to defend Himself and His actions to us! After all, we aren't the judges, God is the judge, we are the judged. God is not accountable to us. If we receive good things in life, it is by the grace and mercy of God. If we receive hard things in life that we feel we don't deserve, then we must trust that God has His reasons, and whether we realize it or not, it may be because of the same grace and mercy! The example, of course, is Christ Himself, the One we claim to follow. He certainly experienced some awful things during His days upon earth, if we are following Him, why should we assume that we won't? The Lord gives, the Lord takes away, blessed be the name of the Lord. Because, after all, H*e is the Lord!*

Day 38   Job 13:13-16

This is one of the more powerful passages declaring Job's faith in God. He has lost everything near and dear to him. His wife wishes he were dead. His friends gather round and blame him. He sits on a dung heap with ashes on his head. To all appearances God has abandoned him. When he cries out to God, he hears nothing. When he prays for help, he receives nothing. Alone. In pain. His past a vague memory. His future bleak. And his present a constant state of misery. Ever felt like that? Then he proclaims that he is going to trust God, *even if* God were to kill him. How can he say that?

In essence, he is saying two things, it seems to me. First, he is saying that his relationship with God means more to him than life itself. Secondly, he is saying that he believes that whatever God does is done with purpose, and that purpose must be what is best for Job, because only God knows what is best. Now, maybe I am overreading the text, maybe Job's intent was much simpler than this, but I doubt it. Because you find the same kind of faith demonstrated in the book of Daniel, where Hananiah, Mishael and Azariah are about to be cast into a fiery furnace. They announce to the king that God is perfectly able to save them, but that even if He chooses not to save them, they still won't worship anybody else. To me, this statement and the statement of Job are confessions of faith that carry a special kind of weight. It is what I would call faith under duress, or faith in the extremities of life. Much like Corrie ten Boom and her family. It is one thing to believe in God when everything is going your way and you are living on easy street. It is another when things are hard. And it is one step more to acknowledge that you are going to trust God even if things go from bad to worse, even to the point of death.

How can Job say something like that? I believe it is because he had walked with God, that he had studied and sought God in the intimacy of relationship, so he understood what kind of being God is. He knew by study, experience, and faith the character of God. The one thing that stood out to him above all other things is the fact that God is absolutely trustworthy. In every situation. With every need. And in every event that would come into his life from the hand of God, God can be trusted. Whether it makes sense or not. Whether it is what Job would have chosen or not. Job knew that above all else, God could be trusted at all times, with all things, for all time.

Do you believe that? Are you willing to trust God as He moves you beyond where you are now? Are you willing to stand in faith in the current circumstances of your life? If God allows things to get worse and worse,....even to the point of death....are you willing to declare, "I will trust you, God, no matter what may come?" Not that Job liked the situation of his life, nor must you like all of your situations. But Job, and you, can trust that God truly does know best, and trust that He truly does love you, and trust that He truly will work out the perfect plan for your life, because He is God, and He is YOUR God, and He will never do less than perfection in your life.

Day 39   Job 19: 26-27

Once again, we have the opportunity to stand amazed at the faith of Job. Today's passage is one of the very few in the Hebrew Scriptures (or Old Testament) that indicates a hope of resurrection and eternal life. The understanding of heaven was gradually revealed to humanity over centuries, culminating finally in the revelation given to John, recorded in the last book of the New Testament. At best, it seems that most of the Jewish believers of old thought that this life was all there is, or that whatever one experienced after death was shadowy or undesirable. That attitude was revealed in such questions as posed by the Psalmist when he asks if the dead can praise God (Psalm 88:10-12). But every once in a while, somebody gains a glimpse into eternity and discovers God has plans beyond this earth. Job was one of those people. It is interesting that we know so little of his life. Most of what we know is encapsulated in the time of his tribulation, and a few comments of his life afterward. How he came to know God personally is a mystery. How he learned about the character and trustworthiness of God is not recorded. We see bits and pieces of how he had lived from some of the statements made in the book. For example, we know he was generous with the poor and needy (Job 31:16). We know that he was concerned about his children's relationship with God....he did sacrifice on their behalf (Job 1:5). So much, though, is clouded in shadows and suppositions. Somehow, in his faith experiences with God, he developed the assurance that his relationship with God extended not only through this life, but on into the world to come called eternity. He was sure of his God. He was sure that God would see him through life and beyond the grave.

It is with that perspective Job struggles through his afflictions. That assurance gave him the strength to endure, but not merely to endure, rather to endure with hope. Not a hope that is groundless and nothing more than wishful thinking. Job endured with a hope that is based in the character and promises of God. He says that he knows. What claims can you make in your life? What is it YOU know? Many years ago, during an interview with a board of deacons, I was asked whether or not I knew I was saved. My response apparently caught the board off guard, because all I said was, "yes." One of them asked me to elaborate. But I was simply sure, it had already been settled. There are other things of which I am sure. Rather than my sharing those things, though, it is better for you to consider what things you know and believe with assurance.

Job knew that beyond the grave, he would see God in the flesh, for he had come to know God in such a way that God was able to reveal to him at the deepest level assurances that were critical in helping Job through this tough time of life. At your deepest level, what are you sure of about God and your relationship with Him? What will get you through the tough times where nothing makes sense? What is the one thing you can hold on to, no matter what? What things has God revealed to you through your learnings and your experiences, that have shaped who you are and how you respond to life's challenges? Can you articulate those things to your friends as Job did to his friends in his time of distress? His words became a testimony that has blessed countless generations. Your words could be a blessing and encouragement, too.

Day 40   Job 19:23-27

There is one more area I'd like to examine before we abandon our little excursion into the book of Job. We have talked about some of the things Job believed, and the things he confessed, and the reasons for them. We did not yet comment on the aspect of God that is mentioned in today's passage: my Redeemer lives! At the heart of all Jewish and Christian theology, and at the core of our experiences with God is the central truth that our Redeemer lives. In the days in which Job's story is set, not everything that was worshiped could make the same claim. There were statues and groves for worship. There were images and constellations. There were gold and silver, wood and gems, sun and moon. But there was no breath, no activity, no moving lips, no beating heart, no creative activity, nothing except people offering their gifts, uttering prayers that ascended to nowhere, and gyrations with lewdness all in the name of a religion of belief in something that doesn't even exist!

But Israel had a God who lives, a God whose name is the essence of the very meaning of being itself. And in the fullness of time, that God took on flesh, walked our earth as a man who taught and healed until the day He was killed on the cross. But He did not stay in the tomb, for Job was right those many years before....our Redeemer lives! It is a living God we serve, a living Christ who redeemed us, and the living Spirit who fills us and guides us.

The faith which we have inherited is not a faith of ceremonies and rituals. It is not a faith of incantations and spells. It is not a faith of deeds done to earn something. How sad when we allow it to be clouded by such things, and forget what it really IS all about. Ours is a faith based in a relationship, a living and vital relationship with a living and life giving God. That relationship is as real as any marriage or parent child relationship we experience in this world. In fact, it is more real, because it is based on an absolute knowledge by the lover of the one loved; that is to say, God's love for us is not based on appearances or fleeting passion, but by One who knows all things and yet out of His own nature, chooses to love beings desperately in need of love and forgiveness. An inanimate object can love no one, and has no awareness of being loved. A god who is no god can neither forgive nor save, it has no power to do either.

Job knew, more than he knew anything else in life, that his God was not just his God, but also his Redeemer, and that his Redeemer lives and he would one day see Him face to face. His life, his faith, his destiny were all bound up in that single, and ultimate reality. Is that the way your life is? Is your relationship one that is alive with the God who lives, the Redeemer who rose from the grave because death could not overwhelm life? Do you know that for sure, at the core of your being? Is that the hope that drives you forward? Is that the faith that sees you through? No matter what the world says, or how much the scoffers mock, our Redeemer lives and makes those who love Him live forever, eternally in the presence of the one and only living God.

Day 41   Acts 11:1-18 and Luke 10:17-20

Peter had an unusual experience that changed the course of church history. God made very clear to Peter through the vision and his experience with Cornelius that the salvation through Christ is not just for the Jews, but for non-Jews as well, that it is a gospel for the world. After Peter's startling encounter with God and Cornelius, he reported back to the other disciples what had happened and what it meant. Paul also reported back, both in Antioch and in Jerusalem. In much the same way, the disciples returned to Jesus in Luke 10 to share with Him what had happened in their lives, at which time they received further instructions from Jesus.

One of the important relationships in a church setting is the relationship between you and someone who is over you in the role of spiritual guide or mentor. This could be your pastor, your small group leader, or a good friend whose role is your spiritual partner. If you don't have someone like that, ask your pastor to help you find someone who can fill that role. This relationship is important to maintain during the process and aftermath of divorce. Sometimes people who go through the emotions of divorce, isolate themselves from other people for a variety of reasons. It is important, though, for your spiritual health and future, that you keep in contact with a spiritual mentor. Partly to keep yourself from becoming isolated from the church in the midst of your struggles, and partly to provide an opportunity for God to guide you through godly counsel. This does not mean you have to share everything that is going on, nor that you shouldn't be careful not to overly consume that person's time. But it does mean that you keep the connection alive and vital. God has brought these individuals into your life for a reason. They have been used of God for you prior to this experience, and perhaps were even placed in your life by God specifically so that they could help you through this rearrangement of your life. It may be that one or more of them may turn away from you, rather than stand with you. If so, then perhaps it is because God is seeking to use someone else in your life now. The important thing is, keep an honest and ongoing connection with a Christian advisor who can help you keep on track with God during a tumultuous time in your life. You may easily say that you don't need to do that, that you will be fine. But I will warn you, I have seen individuals who were pillars in their churches, yet in the fallout of divorce, they have gotten out of touch with their leaders and fallen by the wayside over time. Don't kid yourself, it **could** happen to you. You have to choose to make sure the connections are kept strong so that it doesn't. And know that as I wrote this particular devotion, I am praying right now for each person who will read it, that God will protect you and keep you from falling. But you need to be doing your part as well.

Day 42   *2 Timothy 3:14-17 and 2 Peter 1:19-21*

In this day and age, there are plenty of folks who question the value and trustworthiness of the Bible. Odds are, that is probably not you, since you bothered to read in a devotional book to begin with, however, I'd still like to say a few words on this topic as we begin. The Bible makes some pretty strong claims for itself in relation to its uniqueness as the holy word from God, and the difference between itself and all other books....even other "holy" writings. Maybe you are a bit skeptical that this collection of writings from thousands of years ago can have anything helpful for you in your modern situation. That is fine. There is nothing wrong with that kind of skepticism. I have known many people who would voice that very sentiment. But I always try to raise a question with them that I want to raise with you now. Does your skepticism arise from what you have heard, or have you ever actually taken the time yourself, as an adult, to read from the scriptures to see whether they have anything to say to you? Often I find that people are skeptical of the Bible because that is what they think "scientific and modern" people are, but they have no first hand experience of the scripture's power to speak to them because they have never given it a chance.

My desire in these devotions is not that I will speak to you, but that God will use these words of mine to help you find scriptures that are relevant and useful for your life. Some of the words may encourage you. Some may strongly challenge you. In fact, some may even chastise you. Some will offer guidance, some hope, some offer security or peace, and others help you sort out your values and your purpose in life. But not if you don't give them a chance. Oh, I could put together an argument explaining the way these writings have been preserved, or how various prophecies have come true in remarkable ways, or all those things people explain when they are trying to offer a defense for the validity of the Bible. But I am not interested in doing that in this context. This is not designed to be a class on biblical history or an introduction to the Bible. Instead, I desire to simply let the scriptures speak for themselves to you as I share with you how they have spoken to me. So, in some ways, I am inviting you into my personal spiritual life, as you seek to understand your own. There is a great likelihood that some of the things you will read from me will seem totally irrelevant for you. There is also a likelihood that you will read the scripture, read my devotional, and find that the scripture means something totally different to you than it did to me when I wrote.

My friend, that is fine, I encourage you not to let that become a stumbling block in your journey. Let God speak to you however works best between the two of you, with this book as merely a tool that might help you hear his voice in your prayers, in your life, and, most of all, in the scripture. One of my favorite scriptures is from Isaiah 55:10-11, where God speaks about his word indicating that not a word of his will be empty, but will accomplish something of his purposes. I want to strongly encourage you to never just read the writings I present, but always read the scripture given, and maybe even extra scriptures around that one, or those listed in the cross reference footnotes of your

Bible. God's promise is not to honor MY words, but His. I am simply hoping that as I share how God has spoken to my heart through these scriptures, you will sense God's Spirit speaking to your heart what is useful for your life at this time. With that said, I want you to look at your Bible, and realize that right there, in your hand, on your lap or coffee table, is a treasure that you are about to delve into for this new situation in life. My prayer is that it will become even more precious to you than it has ever been, and that you will find, as so many have, that it is more precious than gold.

MY PRAYER FOR YOU THIS WEEK

This week, I come before the throne of God to offer thanks for you. Because this is being read, God, it means, that my friend here has travelled a long road since the day they first heard the word, "divorce" from the lips of his or her spouse, or even his or her own lips. I thank you, God for the ways You have sent encouragement and hope, and the ways You have kept the reader when things seemed too hard. I pray that You will help the individual now holding this book as You guide her/him in restructuring life. I pray that with each passing day, more and more of the cloud's silver lining and greater glimmers of hope will become visible as Your expanding light envelopes and warms the heart of this child of Yours. Amen.

Day 43   1 Samuel 17:31-54

When you really read this story carefully, it is actually kind of gruesome, don't you think? And yet, the PG version has been standard fare in children's Sunday School books and in the celebrations of Jewish culture for so long that David and Goliath have moved into the common vernacular as the epitome of the underdog versus the big guy. How many times have you heard sermons or lessons on the example he sets for us to follow as we face the various giants in our lives? Plenty, I am sure. Well, I'd like to offer this story in another way. Actually, there are many stories in the Bible I could have used, but this one is so popular, I wanted to start with it.

Many teachers like to refer to David's reference to having battled lions and bears in the wild as evidence of how God used his daily routine out in the pasture as the training ground to prepare him for this confrontation with Goliath. Other times, I have heard folks who liked to focus on the way he clings to God as he draws the contrast between Goliath coming with weapons of war versus David himself, who was coming in the name of God. Indeed, that also is a great lesson in faith, reminding us that we, too, need to trust the unseen God as our source and strength rather than any earthly powers. Good as those things are, though, they serve my purpose today as merely the foundations for what happened in David's life.

As I examine the stories of David, it seems to me that this meeting with Goliath, this standing before the Philistine giant is also one of the, *if not the*, defining moments of his life. It is all well and good to believe in God while you are out pasturing sheep. It is great to have learned the skills to trick, trap and kill wild beasts. But both of those are a far cry from standing before a mighty warrior, seasoned and trained for battle, with nothing but a sling and a few pebbles in your hand. To be able to realize that God is still present, and to act like God is still powerful….that is a lot of faith when you realize he laid both his life and his nation's honor on the line when he took up the challenge. This was a defining moment for David: would he be able at this moment to act on the lessons he learned about God as he grew up and as he wandered those pastures? This is such a now or never, sink or swim, the rubber meets the road sort of moment….will what he has always claimed to be his faith stand the test of this time of extremity? In many ways, how he handled this moment would shape his life and character in so many ways for the days ahead.

When I think of defining moments in the Bible, I think of many people. Like Adam and Eve at the tree. Or Joseph with Potiphar's wife. Or Joshua and Caleb spying out the Promised Land. Or Elisha as he approached the Jordan River, or stood by the king surrounded by enemy troops. Daniel when he heard the decree of Nebuchadnezzar, or Esther after the treachery of Haman. The list is practically endless. The question is, do the moments come to us as clearly defining moments, or do the moments simply come and could it be that how we choose to view and respond to them is what transforms them into defining moments in our lives? Like this Goliath story. David could have let the moment pass and nobody would have been the wiser. After all, he was just a kid, nobody expected him to be on the battlefield anyway. Had he walked back home, nobody would have thought the less of him, he would have already accomplished the mission his father had entrusted to him. I don't know that David saw it as a defining moment himself, but the convictions he had long held caused him to see things in such a way that what most people saw as discouraging and filled with despair was, to him, an opportunity God could use.

With all the challenges you have been facing, and all the temptations that have come along the way, nobody will think the less of you if you handle them poorly. After all, everybody knows that divorce is a tough experience, and none of us is perfect, right? But I wonder if you have considered that perhaps this period of your life is something God can use as a defining moment for you. One of those moments for you to rise to the occasion and face the challenges in such a way that all the lessons you have learned from God bear fruit in the decisions and actions you make now. I believe that the time of divorce, as I experienced it and walked with others as they wrestled with it, is a time of the kind of testing that will, indeed, give you many opportunities to demonstrate what you stand for, and what difference your faith makes. And the defining that takes place in your life **now** can impact your life and your future for many years to come. Look around, and ahead….will what you see become an opportunity for faith and victory? Or discouragement and despair?

Day 44   Luke 18:1-8

Have you ever felt like the judge in today's story? I can remember times when my kids just kept on and on with some request or another, hoping to wear me down so that I, like that judge, would give in to their request. Maybe you have had friends who just tire you to death as they go on and on. I know many of us feel that way when someone just wants to complain and complain about their illnesses, the political world, the problems they have in life, whatever. One of the things I have learned through my divorce is that I am a person who needs to talk out the struggles I have. Part of the way I learned this is that my current wife is just the opposite, and sometimes when she and I have visited about things, she has pointed out this difference between us. That is, she processes struggles inwardly through personal reflection while I process them verbally with friends.

During my time of divorce, I felt more like the widow in the story than the judge, because of the fact that I had two or three friends with whom I was processing my struggle, and who were probably getting worn out with my ongoing struggles. As a pastor, I had individuals who were going through divorce who would sometimes come to sit and talk for what seemed like an interminably long time. When my divorce hit, I understood why those people had needed my time and my listening ear, because I needed the same thing during my divorce. I want to suggest that you take time to understand yourself and how you process struggles. And then, if that is a need of yours, realize what a gift those listening ears are in your life. Let them know what they mean to you. Let God know how much you appreciate them. And try to find a good balance so that you don't wear out your friendships....maybe even asking your friends to help you set limits, if necessary.

Most of all, today I want you to realize on a deep level just exactly how much God is willing to listen to whatever you want to tell Him from your life. In the parable, God is compared to the judge. The judge only grudgingly grants a request because he is worn out with the begging. But the parable is what is called in terms of style, the "how much the more so" format, the argument from lesser to greater, in which a minimal example proves the point of the greater example. The judge is the minimal person. If that unfeeling judge was willing to finally grant her request, then God, who is so much more caring and kind, is more than willing to help those who cry out to Him with persistence. The scriptures are filled with invitations from God to you, for you to come and tell Him your requests, your struggles, your needs, your desires, your hurts....whatever is on your heart and mind. Your friends listen because they love you, and they are your friends....but they have limits. The best listening ear you can experience in life is the listening ear of God, who is ready to give ear to every cry of your heart, any time, any where, about any thing. Nurture the ability to share your heart with God.

Day 45   Mark 8:34-37

It is sometimes amazing what things people fight over during a divorce. A piece of furniture, a knick-knack, or big things like the house, the car, the kids. It is also amazing how aggressively people will pursue even the smallest things. Thousands of dollars wasted on attorneys seeking frivolous things. Sometimes, the things sought aren't so frivolous. But the assets and energy expended pursuing these things can easily become far out of balance. Maybe you are in the midst of such a battle, or are licking the wounds after an intense court proceeding, or trying to get your life back in order now that the divorce has been finalized. My attorney was such a great guide for me....willing to pursue what needed pursuing, but willing to temper the process where she felt it wasn't worth a hassle. One of the issues that concerned me she said she felt pretty sure I could pursue and win, but to do so would require a lot of proceedings and costs. Her comment was that some things could be pursued and won, but that, after the battle would be over, she wondered whether anybody really ever comes out the winner. I think she was a very wise lady. It sounded to me a lot like Jesus' comment that somebody can gain the whole world, but it is worthless if they forfeit their soul doing so. It was extremely difficult to walk away from some of the issues I desperately wanted to pursue. And, over the years, I have wondered whether I should have chased harder after some of them or not, because some of the consequences of not pursuing have been very hurtful for me over the years. The financial cost would have been tremendous, and the emotional wear and tear excruciating....but even worse, I might have ended up selling my soul to chase them. Though some things have been hard to deal with, I don't think they have been as hard to deal with as might have been the case if I had compromised who I was or who I served to go after what I wanted in unhealthy ways.

Day 46   Mark 15:1-5; 1 Peter 2:20-23

This is really an interesting event in the life of Jesus. Here are all these people making all these radical claims about Jesus, giving false evidence and twisting His words around to make it sound like He said something He didn't, all in the midst of a legal proceeding attempting to get Him sentenced. What did He say in His defense? Nothing. He stood silently. Pilate marveled that Jesus didn't at least present His side of the story. And His silence becomes an example for us when we are bitterly accused falsely.

Perhaps one of the most difficult things in a divorce is how to handle false accusations. Especially when you know those false statements are not merely being given to a court, but also to your children or to friends. The danger with your children, of course, is that if your ex has already told them one version of an incident, if you tell them your version it can come across as running down their mom or dad, or at least implying that your ex is lying. The consequence of that is putting the children into the position where they are having to decide between parents, and that is a lousy place for a child to be. On the other hand, I know a family where the child never heard "the other side of the story," and, as a consequence she never spoke to her father again….at least for 50 years and counting….I suppose she could still come back and make it right, but I'm not very optimistic. The upshot is that the dilemma is a hard one. Jesus did set us an example, and surely in this time there is wisdom in keeping silent on some things, perhaps especially when it comes to your friends….true friends know you well enough to know what is most likely true and what is untruth. But there is also the issue of guiding children in the way of truth. Sometimes they may need to understand when they have been misinformed, because keeping silent may also be misleading them.

It is a difficult position to have to be in….it would be better if both spouses were just very careful about what they said in front of their children or to the public in general. Now, twelve years out of my divorce, I would love to say that the choices I made in this area always resulted in good. But the truth is, there are times I tried to say things and found that it made matters worse, rather than better, and there were other times I chose to keep silent that seem to have fostered an ongoing lack of perspective. Most of my friends seem to have formed their own opinion, and have an understanding of both sides of the issues. But the opinions of friends is not the hard one….though it hurts to lose a good friend, I can always make new friends if necessary. But when it comes to the children, it is much more critical….they remain our children for life. And the difficulties of the issue are not ones that are completed the day the gavel strikes in the courtroom. The issues continue for many years and, depending on how considerate each spouse is to the other, can keep going much longer than need be.

So today, I'll tell you what. I'll pray for God to protect your children and grant them understanding, and encourage you to ask a prayer partner to do the same. And I'll pray for you to be wise and have godly counsel as you handle the falsehoods that arise....but I'll also ask you to pray the same for me....because, even now, you and I share many common challenges and issues because we are divorced. And then, after you pray and make your choices, you simply must trust that God will take care of the rest, and will let you know if you need to do something differently. Bottom line is that you simply have to do the best you can to do what is honorable and trust God to take care of the rest.

Day 47   Revelation 6:9-11

We live in a world that all too often seems very uncertain. Things change in an instant, sometimes very unexpectedly, sometimes very delightfully, sometimes very frustratingly. We can look around the world at so many problems, so many injustices, so many inexplicable evils, such as famines, cancers, the inequity of poverty and wealth to name a few. To watch these things, it is easy to think that things are just spinning madly out of control, and wonder why God doesn't put an end to it all and send Jesus back to finish things up. Even in heaven, there are apparently those who wonder why God doesn't do that. But in heaven, there is one thing they see that we don't see: God on the throne. The martyrs in today's passage are depicted looking down upon the evils of earth, and crying out for God's justice to come and put an end to everything, and ask how long. But God simply tells them to wait, it isn't time yet, things are not done. He doesn't panic and say, "Oh dear, you are right, things are terrible, what will we do?" He doesn't say, "Yes, I better get in there right now, before anything else happens." In fact, there seems to be no surprise, no sense that things have gotten out of hand, no sense of anything but complete calm, certainty and deliberateness by the One on the throne. The same is true with your cries to God. He is still on the throne. Nothing takes Him by surprise. Nothing makes Him panic. He is in complete and utter control with perfect calm and perfect timing. Sometimes we just don't see things that clearly from down here. Today, whatever happens, whatever you are struggling with, whatever answers you don't know, rest assured, God is on the throne and He is in perfect control.

Day 48   *Ecclesiastes 12:13-14 and Romans 14:12*

Do you ever resent how things progressed in the divorce? Do you sometimes feel like it just isn't fair? That your ex is just getting away with all sorts of things, and everything you try to do "right" just blows up in your face or is misinterpreted and thrown back at you? Maybe it seems your ex is getting everything he or she wants, and the judge just seems to hand it to him/her, while everything else seems to be stacked against you. Or maybe you even feel like your ex just keeps prospering while doing things that are clearly wrong (at least to you). Maybe there are days you just want to throw up your hands to God and say, "God, what is going on? Why are you letting these things happen?"

Well, those feelings certainly may come. And if you read your Bible closely, God is not obligated to explain anything to you or me. And, the truth is, even if He tried, it would probably be bigger than we could understand. You may be right in thinking that some of the deeds of your ex deserve judgment and punishment by God. However, you have to choose to lay aside your concerns about the justice of God in relation to choices and actions of your ex, and focus instead upon your own standing before God. Romans 14:12 reminds us that each of us shall have to give account of our own choices before God. Your ex will have to explain their choices and actions. You will have to do the same before God. During this entire process, never forget that. Every motive. Every word. Every choice. Every action. They all will come under the scrutiny of God. Trust, as Abraham said, that the Judge of all the earth will do right in relation to your ex. And live so that you will be pleased with how He responds when you are called to give account before your Maker.

Day 49   *Genesis 49:1-27*

What a time that must have been. Jacob, now called Israel, gathering his grown sons around him, for a final time of blessing. It wouldn't be long before he was going to be gone. Time was short. The future precarious, and death was looming large. Israel chose to make his first priority be time with his children so he could bless them.

Down through the years, I have known people despairing in the midst of divorce, people who just wanted to give up, to quit, even to end their own lives. Of course, they are not thinking rationally at the time, the extreme emotions and depression have overwhelmed them, and they have lost their hope. While the stories are never the same, the emotions of divorce are relatively common. While I cannot prove it, I suspect that the intensity of those emotions is determined by certain factors: 1) how long term the marriage; 2) whether the person involved was the one who filed or was filed upon; 3) whether or not the person was still in love with their spouse or the two had drifted far apart. A combination of those factors can be devastating. One spouse may be on their own for the first time in years, maybe the first time ever. Sometimes one spouse has not been working outside the home, and finds him or herself facing a very uncertain future. Bills demand payment. Court papers demand action. The pressures can become so great as to make someone simply give up and start believing ending it all is the only answer. Or, the stresses can become so great that they consume all the attention and energy the person has within them. Some of us have illnesses that have already been diagnosed as terminal, and some have even been abandoned by their spouse in the midst of the illness, leaving us in incredibly difficult situations.

By this time you may be wondering how today's scripture relates to the thoughts I have just shared. The answer is this: don't let the emotions and pressures cause you to neglect the most important things in your lives. You have people who depend on you, people who care about you. Children, grandchildren, nieces, nephews, siblings, maybe children you teach in Sunday School, friends....just like in the life of Jacob, life is precarious. None of us know how long we have left here on earth. ***But people do need you***....don't get so caught up in your own pain you overlook the kids, the relatives, the friends. Jacob knew that it was important for him to be a blessing and to give a blessing to his children. It is important that you be the blessing to others you also were intended to be. It is very true that you will have to focus on a lot of personal issues to get through this time of divorce. But it is imperative that you not focus exclusively on yourself and your issues. There are still folks around you, maybe children, or grandchildren, maybe just long term friends, who long to know that you care. They still need hugs. They still long to hear words of appreciation, encouragement and affirmation. Don't withhold the blessings that are yours to give. The fact that you are going through a divorce does not mean that there aren't people who still need you, people who love you, people who depend on you. Only one person has said that you don't matter to them anymore, one person and maybe their family. But everybody else is still there, looking to you for the help you give, the caring you provide, the hope you offer. Take the example of Israel to heart, and intentionally find ways and times to bless those around you.

MY PRAYER FOR YOU THIS WEEK

This week, I pray that you will experience on a deeper level what the forgiveness of God means in your life. May you understand the awesomeness of God's grace, and the great lengths He has gone to on the cross to cleanse you, redeem you, and make you His own. And in that experience, I pray that not only will you gain a deeper insight into the grace and forgiveness God offers to you, but that you also will find within you the urge to pass that grace on to others. Amen.

Day 50   Mark 1:35 and 1 Corinthians 7:32-34

One of the hardest things about divorce can be the overwhelming sense of emptiness in your home when nobody is around but yourself. It can feel like the walls are closing in around you. I remember one of those times when I was alone, and tripped on a stair in the house. I caught myself, but I found myself wondering, if I had fallen and seriously injured myself, how long it could be before someone might find me and get me to the hospital. You think things like that when the solitude is strong. The silence can sometimes be deafening. But there is also a useful place for solitude in our lives.

In the Mark passage, we find Jesus heading out away from people so that He can be alone with God. In this time of your single status, you actually have the opportunity to spend unhampered time alone with God in ways that were not available when you were married, and will not be if you marry again. In my case, some of those times were middle of the night Bible reading and prayer, or early morning walks and devotional times. During that time, there was nobody telling me to turn off the light because it bothered their sleep. There was nobody waiting for me to get back to help with some task or another. There was nobody turning on a distracting television or radio that made it hard for me to concentrate. It was my time to carve out special space with God however I chose to do so. You have the same opportunity. Oh, I know, if you are a single parent with young children around, time and energy is at a premium and you may feel it is very hard to find any time for God. But the time is there. Maybe when you finally lay your head on the pillow at night, when it is just you and the Lord. Maybe it is during the weekend when the kids are at the other parent's home. Maybe it is early on the weekend morning while everyone else is still in bed. And, yes, it may mean you have to let something else go.

Paul's way of saying it is that when you are married, one of the concerns you have is how to do things that would please your spouse. Even the decisions about what you do with your money has to take into consideration your spouse. But when you are single, the only person you have to please is God. Your attention is not divided in the same way as it would be if you were married, although if you have children, obviously there are concerns and responsibilities there. In the midst of the busy hubbub of this chapter of your life, make some time to cultivate a healthy habit of quality solitude with God. You may not have these opportunities forever.

Day 51   Psalm 136:1-9

For today, I offer a contemporary reflection of this ancient Psalm. Hopefully, it will speak to you. First, (and at the end) are a few verses of the Psalm, then let's see where it leads as I add in my own reflections. (By the way, NASB uses the word lovingkindness, you can use mercy, steadfast love, covenant loyalty....whichever translation speaks most to you today.)

"Give thanks to the Lord, for He is good, for His lovingkindness is everlasting.

Give thanks to the God of gods, for His lovingkindness is everlasting.

Give thanks to the Lord of lords, for His lovingkindness is everlasting."
(Psalm 136:1-3, NASB)

To Him who knows the end from the beginning, for His lovingkindness is everlasting.

Who will carry you through this time of struggle, for His lovingkindness is everlasting.

And will love your children as His own, for His lovingkindness is everlasting.

For He is a God who turns tragedy to triumph, for His lovingkindness is everlasting.

And He can make the desert places of your life blossom like the orchid, for His lovingkindness is everlasting.

He walks beside you in the dark nights of your life, for His lovingkindness is everlasting.

And will not abandon you when the storms impend, for His lovingkindness is everlasting.

God is the Great Physician to heal the wounds in your soul, for His lovingkindness is everlasting.

And He will one day wipe every tear from your eye, for His lovingkindness is everlasting.

When you stumble, He will pick you up, for His lovingkindness is everlasting.

And will set your foot upon a rock, for His lovingkindness is everlasting.

He gives strength in the time of weakness, for His lovingkindness is everlasting.

And loves you when others have rejected you, for His lovingkindness is everlasting.

He made you unique, with a special plan for your life, for His lovingkindness is everlasting.

And promises to always guide your steps, for His lovingkindness is everlasting.

God restores you when you are empty, for His lovingkindness is everlasting.

And gives you hope when all seems hopeless, for His lovingkindness is everlasting.

For God is able to do all things, even when it seems nothing can be done, for His lovingkindness is everlasting.

And, as He raised Jesus from the dead, so He will raise you up to
stand before Him again, for His lovingkindness is everlasting.

Since He did not spare His own Son, but gave Him up for you, for
His lovingkindness is everlasting.

Know that He will give you everything that is needful for your life,
for His lovingkindness is everlasting.

Your God is a God whose promise is to lead you to glory, for His
lovingkindness is everlasting.

So today, bow your knee and humbly give Him thanks, for His
lovingkindness is everlasting.

*"Give thanks to the Lord, for He is good, for His lovingkindness is
everlasting.*

*Give thanks to the God of gods, for His lovingkindness is
everlasting.*

Give thanks to the Lord of lords, for His lovingkindness is everlasting."
(Psalm 136:1–3, NASB)

Perhaps you'd like to add a few lines of your own.

Day 52   *Genesis 15:12-21 and Exodus 10:21-22*

There are times in our lives that can be described as none other than
darkness. Divorce is one of those times. In it there are times when you
simply cannot see your way. There are times when you feel you have
become completely lost. There are times when you cry out with Job that
no matter which way you turn you cannot find God. There are times
when it is like you have fallen into a deep, deep hole, and the darkness in
that hole is clutching at you to draw you down, down, down. And that
darkness is, like the Exodus story mentioned above, so strong a darkness
that it is a darkness that can be felt. I cannot explain it to those who
have not experienced it. And for you who have or are experiencing it,
it needs no explanation anyway, you know exactly what I mean.

While it may or may not be the best interpretation of this very odd
story from Abraham's life, I believe the imagery found in the story can
be very poignant for those of us who experience divorce. Abraham
stands before a God he cannot see, having split the sacrifices in half,
part on one side, part on the other. Isn't that what you are experiencing

with your marriage....a brokenness, a splitting apart, a deep divide? And just as the sacrifices were killed, don't you feel the death that has sucked the life out of your marriage and devastated the vows you made so long ago? And while you are looking at it, don't you find it hard to see God and his purpose anywhere in it? And if you could step outside yourself and look down upon yourself, don't you feel that what you would see is a heart that has been shattered and broken, a person torn between vows and violation, a person half in the past, half in the future, and mostly in the limbo between? I invite you to take all that brokenness and turn it into a sacrifice that you lay down before God just as Abraham did that night. You may have to protect what you offer; there will be birds of temptation, doubt, despair, despondency, well-intentioned advice, hostility, so many birds that will come to devour what you are trying to offer to God. You have to shoo them away, and maintain the sacred portion of your life.

But then comes the rest of Abraham's story. The light appears, a torch passing between the pieces. A glowing little lamp, passing back and forth. It isn't the brilliance that Moses experienced, when even his face was shining as he walked away from God's presence. Nor is it the overwhelming presence of God at the dedication of the temple that prevented the priests from standing up to do their ministry. It is a quiet, solemn time with God. Not all clear, not all the answers, not even a lovely place to be....but God is there....a quiet glow passing back and forth among the parts of your life, sanctifying the pieces you have laid before Him.

Day 53   Matthew 18:1-6

Children always suffer in divorce....even adult children struggle. People like to say that children are resilient, but that is more rationalization than reality. Sure, the kids survive. But if you read the statistics, they have many more problems than those from intact families of origin. Children from intact marriages often find their own marriages someday are more secure, with trust less of an issue. If you do not have children, then read this and realize what God is sparing you from in this trying time of life. For those of us with kids, the hardest thing to experience as you go through divorce is to see the impact it has on your kids. The impact is one that does not end with an announcement that mommy and daddy are going separate ways. It does not end just because the child is 17. It does not end when the divorce is final, even if each of you end up in a new marriage that is healthy and stable….the divorce has its shaping impact on the lives of your children, as well as the relationship between you and your children. However, sometimes that impact is more intense than others.

All too often angry parents, trying hard to retaliate against the one who has betrayed and hurt them, try to turn their children into weapons against the ex-spouse, or try to use them as spies. Or they manipulate the children, telling them extremely one sided stories, coloring the other parent as the demon from which the family is now delivered. The trouble is, regardless of how bad a marriage was, or how bad a parent the mother or father is, for the child, it is still "my mom" or "my dad"….as well it should be. But the poison planted into the hearts of children by angry parents sometimes takes on, sadly, a twisted result, with children who had been raised by both parents together now finding themselves forced into a bizarre loyalty to one parent or the other at the cost of the relationship with the other parent. Parents have even told kids during a divorce that they have to choose which parent they are going to believe, to trust, to be loyal to, and that they must exclude the other parent. Granted, some parents need boundaries set for them, and "supervised visitation" (an obnoxious phrase….you will find plenty of them) has a place in this messy thing called divorce. However….the issues of mom and dad need to not be played out through the agents of the children.

Today, I want to urge you to do your best to be very careful. Do your best to not be one who adds unnecessary emotional burdens upon your children. Seek to be a caring parent who actually looks out for their best interest. Put their welfare ahead of your own. And keep the strong emotions you feel toward your divorcing spouse as your own….allow the children to have their own emotions and their own relationship with your ex.

Day 54   1 Corinthians 12:11, 27-31

This devotional book will hopefully have something along the way that helps you. Odds are, there will also be things to which you do not relate at all. That is because you are a unique individual, and God will deal with you as the unique individual you are. Some individuals find they handle the stresses of divorce best by keeping themselves busy and keeping their minds occupied lest they overly dwell on their struggle and end up so depressed they can do nothing. Others do best by having time to reflect, to weep, to plan, or maybe to journal. One of the things that happens as you work through your experience is that you can develop a different kind of self-understanding.

The most incredible thing about this passage is the insistence that God deals with us as individuals. It is okay that you respond differently than others. God knows exactly what it is YOU need in this time, and what He wants to accomplish through this time. It may or may not match what anybody else does. In a world where we are often nothing more than a number, one of the masses, God offers us something different....a PERSONAL relationship on the deepest level. The more you seek that relationship, the more you will find the answers you need. The more you seek His touch, the more you will find He meets you at every turn. He may send along a song that brings peace to your soul. He may send you a friend with whom you can share your heart. It may even be something as simple as a beautiful sunrise that gives you hope. Whatever it is you need, God is ready to provide. Give Him plenty of opportunities to do just that for you. Take time to offer yourself to God in that way as you begin this journey through the raging waters of divorce.

Day 55   Mark 14:43-52 and Luke 23:44-49

Let's think again about the sense of shock that comes with divorce. Sometimes it feels like you are walking around in a nightmare, thinking surely you will wake up soon and everything will be back to normal. Or you almost feel like you are standing outside yourself watching somebody else go through this awful experience, and think....I just can't believe this is really happening to me. Somehow, that is what I think the disciples must have felt starting with the arrest in the Garden of Gethsemane all the way to the death on Golgotha. How can this be? Surely it is just a bad dream. Surely this can't really be happening. And then when they began to realize it really was happening, not only were they in shock, they were also in fear of their lives....if Jesus was first, surely the soldiers would come after them next....so they huddled behind locked doors. I know there were days in the midst of my crashing world when I just wanted to find a hole and hide in it....just curl up by myself in a chair and sit. Not even sit and think. Just sit.

I can't imagine the disciples weren't wandering around asking themselves, or maybe each other, "why?" Why did they do this to Jesus? Why did God let it happen? How can God be a good God and allow something like this? What will we do now? And they received no answer from God. I wonder if it was because they were so busy worrying and being scared and confused that none of them thought to ask God what it was about. God could have reminded them of things Jesus had taught them about his upcoming death and resurrection. But that reminder never came. And it seems to me it never came for one of two reasons. Either they were so caught up in themselves and their own little worlds that they really weren't open to listening to God speaking, or, it just wasn't any of their business yet....God would reveal to them the reasons why when the time for revelation came, and not before.

Maybe that is the same way it is for us when we go through divorce. Maybe we run the risk of becoming so agitated or so caught up with all the garbage demanding our attention that we hardly stop long enough to hear God. Or maybe the whys are just things we don't need to know until God is ready to reveal it to us. Maybe He will reveal it to us during the divorce process, maybe a few years later, maybe not until He explains it to us face to face. We can do nothing about the timing God chooses....God alone knows the perfect timing and the perfect amount of information we truly need. But we can do something about our attitudes and our receptivity to God's voice. Make sure you are providing appropriate opportunities for God to speak. Attend church. Get involved in a Bible study. Read your Bible daily. Read good Christian books. Listen to some good Christian music. Share some time with some Christian friends or support groups. And make time for prayer. Because if God would speak to you about some kind of resurrection, like He did the disciples, you don't want to miss it because you were out of commission behind locked doors.

Day 56   1 Peter 2:18-23

When you stop and think about it, Christ must have had amazing self control to be able to endure the kangaroo courts, the beatings, the thorns, the mocking, the pain of the nails, the thirst....all those terrible experiences of the crucifixion....and the whole while refuse to lash out with angry words or spiteful replies. The scripture says He was as a sheep silent before its shearers. Jesus could have said so much. He could have called out for the angels. But He was silent. He did not let the hatred infect His heart and cause Him to "lose his cool" if you will. How is your "cool" holding up these days? How tempting it is sometimes to spit out words of venom, or to run down your ex as you try to explain to your kids or friends "your side of the story." Jesus chose not to do that....He kept His silence. And the scripture says He did that as an example for me. And for you. It is easy, sometimes, for things to get under your skin. In fact, your ex probably knows all the right buttons to push. And in this adversarial time when you both are having to look out for yourselves and your own future, those buttons may get pushed left and right. But Jesus showed us by example that even though you may be abused, mistreated, maligned, slandered and despised....you don't have to respond in kind. You can choose to be something more. One of my friends one time said it in a very colorful and descriptive way: the trouble with getting into a spitting match with a skunk is that you both come out smelling like skunks. Determine now to do your best to spread the fragrance of Christ (2 Cor. 2:14), not the stench of a skunk!

MY PRAYER FOR YOU THIS WEEK

This week, I pray that your foundation will stand firm as the tempests of life and divorce blast through your life. May the example of Jesus, who stood firm through life's extremities and prevailed give you hope and assurance that God will see you through as well. And I pray that those things that have come into your life that are distractions and unnecessary will be washed away, so that you will be able to withstand the final testing with a life built on the foundation of Christ and obedience to his Word. Amen.

Day 57   Matthew 18:10-14

Let's go back to revisit children in our topic of divorce. If you don't have kids, and would like to skip over this, you may do so, although you might still find something useful for your heart and life. You may also have friends who are going through divorce....hopefully you have some friends in a Christian divorce support group of some kind, and this might help you as you seek to encourage them. Going through a divorce always has impact on children. Period. In some cases, there may be lots of good mixed into that impact, like when a child is rescued through divorce from an abusive parent. But there is always impact that isn't so good. You can find that information in other resources. No longer being a husband or a wife *does not* relieve you of continuing to be a father or mother. And it is a heart wrenching experience to be a parent during a divorce. You see the struggle they experience and the shattered, sadness in their eyes. You sense the tension they feel. You hear their sobs and words of uncertainty. And then they learn how to navigate the turbulent waters as they enter the survival mode. What can you do?

There are lots of things you can do. I would highly recommend making sure the kids have opportunity to talk with a good counselor... preferably a Christian one....if they want to do so. And you can make things easier by leaving them out of your dispute with your ex.... difficult as that may be when you see things happening that so violate your values....realizing that you will make some mistakes along the way. I did. But you can try your best. In this devotional I want to highlight two simple things. First, the highest responsibility for any parent, even a divorcing parent, is to stand before God to intercede for them in prayer. Earnest, passionate prayer. Of all the times in your life when you have prayed for your kids, for their safety, for the ability to accomplish something, for the future spouses, for their well being and anything else you have prayed for, right now they need your prayers more than any other time in your life. And while you pray for them, realize that you are not alone in interceding for them....their angels always behold the heavenly Father's face. Now, I don't know exactly what that means, but it is clear there is a special place in the heart of God for your children.

Secondly, you have to trust. Trust your children to God....and that is extremely hard. As you practice that trust, I wonder if you have ever realized that God loves them MORE THAN YOU DO!!!! A *LOT* more than you do. However much you love your child....and if you are like me, that is pretty hard to begin to quantify....but however much you love that child, realize that God loves them something like a kazillion times more. And He loves them with a more perfect love than you do. Now, read this paragraph again, it is important to know this about God.

There are things you are not going to be able to do for your kids....whether you get divorced or not. You may not be able to explain everything to them. You may not be able to protect them from poisonous thoughts that are being planted in their minds. So many things are suddenly outside of your grasp. You need to TRUST GOD to do the things that YOU cannot. As my wife sometimes says, "Realize, you don't know what God is doing in their lives right now." And that is true. God may be speaking to them through one of their friends. God may be preparing them for a future ministry to kids of divorce. God may be sending across their path a teacher or other caring adult to help them gain the perspective and caring they need. You can only do what you can do....and, of course, you are responsible to do that. Your kids need you to not only work on your issues that you are struggling with just now, but also to do your best to help them through this tough time. Most of all, you need to be asking God to protect them, care for them, guide them and help them in all the ways that you cannot. Ask that with the awareness that He loves them more than you, so you can trust Him to do what is best. The plan He has for them may be outside your understanding, but it is not outside God's. There is much to be done, if your children are to come through this time well. Get busy. Get on your knees.

Day 58   John 11:17-37

Some people compare divorce with the experience of the death of a loved one with the subsequent grief. The death of the marriage. The death of the relationship. And there is truth in it, because when you walk around your house, your spouse is no longer there. When you go to bed, he or she is absent. When your birthday comes around, you probably won't be getting a card from your ex. And, when you read the studies on grief, such as Elisabeth Kubler-Ross's important contribution to the studies, there are many of the same emotional issues—denial, shock, bargaining, anger, and acceptance. The feelings may not come in that order, or may bounce back and forth between emotions, but many of those emotions will be there. And there is usually not much control over them....they are just part of the healing process called grief. If you have experienced the grief of losing a loved one, then remembering things that helped you through that may also be helpful now. But there are differences.

For example, in most cases of death, the one lost did not die to intentionally get away from you. Feelings of outright and blatant rejection are rarely part of grief. And, generally speaking, when someone dies, they don't do so in a spiteful way. People in divorce often do. When there is a death of a loved one, songs on the radio and memorabilia or old pictures you run across tend to bring back pleasant memories, not stir painful feelings of rejection. And, as people often point out, when a loved one dies, the corpse isn't still walking around or interfering in your life. In divorce, that lost loved one may turn up at the same grocery store or church. In divorce, that loved one may complicate your Christmas plans or mess with your finances. So while there are parallels to death's grief, there are also significant differences. Worst of all, the grief may drag on and resurface time and again with the ongoing complications of divorce.

Let's reflect just a bit on what this grief implies. Someone you don't know will die today, and you may hear about it on the news, but it probably won't have a major impact on you....because that person is not someone you know and love dearly. The grief only comes because you have loved. And people grieve differently based on the depth of that love. A friend passing away will have a different impact than your brother, your Lazarus, dying. One of your aging parent's death is experienced differently than if your young teen is killed in a car wreck. The depth of grief is directly related to the depth of love and the circumstances under which the death occurred. The same is true in divorce. If you are really struggling, realize that is an indicator of how much you loved your spouse. If you are not struggling so badly, perhaps it is because you realized a long time ago that your marriage was not what it should be, perhaps it had even died. But the sadness is real. Allow time for yourself to grieve, to shed tears, and to remember the precious things from your love relationship. As with grief at death, the passing of time does help as you move on to the next chapter of your life.

Day 59   Psalm 73:1-17

Probably one of the most unsettling facts of life here on earth is that people do evil things and get away with them….in fact, are sometimes even rewarded for their evil efforts, while there are some people who do genuinely good things and end up in worse shape than if they hadn't done the good. Have you ever noticed that? Do you feel it in this divorce process of yours? I have seen many times when one of the spouses in a divorce proceeding do things that border on evil, and get away with it in court. Some of them hide money in a friends account so they don't have to report it. Others destroy property they know the other spouse would want. Others use their children in spiteful ways. And others avoid their financial responsibilities through inaccurate financial disclosures, bankruptcy proceedings, or simply skipping out on their child support. And the sad thing about that is some of those people even claim that they are Christians! Meanwhile, the person victimized by these immoral acts cannot understand how a person doing these things can get away with it, or why the court doesn't do something about it, or how a person can do things like that and still face themselves in the mirror, or why the children can't see what their mother/father is doing is wrong. And you may even be asking yourself why God doesn't do something about it. It can feel like beating your head against a wall in frustration, wouldn't you agree? You know it isn't right. You also know that if you decide to pursue it in court, it will cost thousands of dollars that you really can't afford to waste in that way. So what do you do?

Well, the Psalmist felt that same kind of frustration at people who were getting away with all this garbage, too. And he struggled with why God would allow these things to happen. The Psalmist recommends a longer view on things. When we only look at the here and now, we can resent what people get away with when we are trying to do our best to live like God would desire. Maybe you even feel that way right now concerning your ex. But the long view goes like this: nobody really gets away with anything. Maybe they think nobody notices their actions, maybe the court doesn't take jurisdiction, maybe they sit smugly thinking they have pulled off their deception. But God sees it all, and will hold each to account for their actions. Maybe it will happen here. Maybe it will happen at the throne of God. But rest assured, it will happen. God does notice your efforts at obedience, and that will also be rewarded at the appropriate time. And remember one more thing:

just because what you see on the outside suggests that they got away with it and don't seem troubled, the truth is you don't really know the torments, guilt and shame they may be experiencing deep within. You need to focus on your own choices, and leave to God the discernment of justice, trusting that in the long run, your obedience to God will prove to have been the wise decision.

Day 60   Colossians 3:1-4

Have you ever tried to pay attention to some bookwork or something you were reading while somebody else had the television at full volume in the next room? It can drive you nuts, can't it? Or maybe you were trying to have a quiet conversation at your favorite restaurant, but can hardly follow it because at the next table are some people who have had perhaps too much to drink, or are just too gregarious as if everybody else in the restaurant is delighted to hear their conversation? It is simply hard to focus on a task when someone is screaming at you. Well, that is very possibly a lot like trying to find God in the midst of your divorce process. All the things whirling around you literally scream for you attention, and many of them require your attention. But those things can also function as a distraction to keep you from hearing God's voice. So what do you do? The key is in today's passage.

We are told to set our mind on things above, not on things on earth. This indicates we have a choice. We can spend our time thinking about and worrying about everything going on here around us, or we can focus on the grandeur of heaven and the glory of God and the Almighty King who sits on the throne to rule all creation. We can realize that our true home is there, and that these things that seem so huge and so hard here, are in fact merely a fleeting moment in eternity. Jesus said the same kind of thing about storing up our treasure up there, instead of here. The notion is, if you really pay attention to everything that is going on in your life here and around you here, you can quickly get discouraged and overwhelmed. Oh, how this world screams to capture, in fact, demands your attention. Part of what is happening in this verse in Colossians is that we are being challenged to take control of our own minds. Don't let the world, your ex, your divorce process, your job….anything here, do not let them dictate how you will use your mind. After all, its YOUR mind! And your mind is part of your life that you have given to Christ! So, why let somebody or something else control it? "How?" you ask. The answer is simple. I invite you to take charge of your mind by giving it once again to God for renewal (Romans 12:1-2). And then, apply that mind by taking time right now to begin a thought list based on Philippians 4:8. Read it carefully, noticing all the categories. Find a piece of paper on which you can list those categories, and start noting individual items in each category. When the world screams at you, when your emotions jump onto a wild rollercoaster, instead, remind yourself of your list. These are the things that are from above. And you, as his child, have your real life there, too.

Day 61   Matthew 26:52-56

When Jesus was arrested in the Garden, He was taken away alone. When He stood before Herod and Pilate, He stood there alone. When He was scourged, or the crown of thorns was placed on His head, He experienced these things alone. There are some things that you have to do alone. You may have friends, but they will not get divorced for you, or with you. They might attend the proceeding, offer their encouragement, provide a shoulder to cry on....but the divorce is happening to you, and you alone (and, of course, for your spouse). Yes, your kids will be affected. Other things may be affected. But you stand alone before the courts.... perhaps with an attorney as your advocate, but not as your substitute. There are simply some things you have to do alone. Alone, that is, from a human point of view. But God never makes you go through anything alone. Remember his promise: "I will NEVER desert you" (Hebrews 13:5, NASB), or "I am with you always, even to the end of the age" (Matthew 28:20, NASB).

The things you face are not things somebody can do for you....you have to make the decisions, you have to go through the experience. But God will get you through it. I believe that God places limits on what may come your way, based on 1 Corinthians 10:13 and Zechariah 2:4-5, and so you can face the things before you knowing that you will get through it and come out on top. It is an incredible thing to know that even when facing life's challenges that *only you* can face, you still do not face them alone. To know that God is watching closely to make sure that you will come through a stronger, wiser and better person is a great assurance to help you through the tough times you are experiencing these days.

Day 62   *Hebrews 13:10-16*

It is easy to offer praise and thanks to God when everything is going well. It is quite another thing to be expected to do the same in times that seem not so good. Yet, especially with the emphases on the Holy Spirit in recent decades, there is a focus on the biblical call to be a people of praise and thanksgiving regardless of one's circumstances. The verse in Ephesians clearly does not say we are to thank God FOR everything, but that IN everything we are to give thanks. Praise is to be offered at all times. In fact, some have suggested that it is only when you are in difficult circumstances are you able to offer praise as a sacrifice as suggested in Hebrews….in other situations, it costs you nothing, but when things are hard, it may take every ounce of your strength to be able to sing or speak praise to God. Generally speaking, thanksgiving has to do with things God has given or done on your behalf. Praise has to do with who God is, and that character of God is the source out of which the deeds and gifts flow. What you may give thanks for can vary in different situations. But what you praise God for, the character of who God is, never changes, and so praise is always appropriate.

To praise God when you don't feel like it may feel hypocritical, but in fact it is an expression of faith. Faith that God has not changed who He is. Faith that God is still keeping His promises. Faith that, in spite of circumstances and feelings, God still loves you and reigns in your life and the world for good….for YOUR good. Praise sometimes requires having to stretch yourself to see beyond what you see around you, to acknowledge that the wisdom, justice, righteousness and goodness of God are all far beyond your knowledge and experience, beyond what you can figure out on your own. And that is a good thing. Do you really want God to be limited to what *you* can understand? Do you want a God who bases His actions on your own variable and fickle emotions? Do you really want a God who is limited in such a way that He is at the mercy of earthly circumstances, and cannot possibly take seemingly wrong situations and use them for good? If the answer to those questions is, 'no' then you will want to praise God. Because those things are specifically what God is not limited by! God is incredibly great and awesomely good and indescribably wise....God is worthy of your praise. Now, and always. When you recognize the character of God in your praise, you confess your trust in Him, and ultimately, invite Him into your situation, rather than resist the very thing He may be going to use on your behalf. Praise God!

Day 63   Philippians 4:6-7

Have no anxiety about anything?!?!? If you are like I was, that seems like the most incredible idea that anybody could ever suggest....especially in the midst of all the upheaval and uncertainties and choices of the process called divorce! No anxiety? And it is said in such a way that it implies you actually have the option of living without anxiety. Maybe even that you are *commanded* to live without anxiety. That is absolutely incredible. Sounds kind of like a fairy tale castle, doesn't it? Sort of a pie in the sky dream that doesn't have anything to do with real life. But that isn't so. Especially when you realize that when Paul penned this particular book, he was sitting in a prison in Rome, probably under one of the most vicious emperors that ever lived, Nero, and facing charges that would ultimately result in his execution. It is under those conditions that Paul can write to fellow believers who face lots of trials and questions the instruction not to have any anxiety about anything. So, it even applies to you in this time of your life's upheaval and restructuring. But, thankfully, this instruction doesn't come to us without instructions for making it possible. He doesn't just tell us not to have anxiety, he offers what we are supposed to do instead. The verse presents us with two options for our lives, and then an instruction not to pursue one of the options: 1) have anxiety, or 2) let your requests me known to God.

Have you fretted over anything recently? One of the great things that impressed me was when a person I know was struggling with a terribly tough situation in her divorce, and simply said, "God has always taken care of me before, I figure He will take care of me now." That is living without anxiety. I know it had to be hard for her....her husband left her in a really lousy situation in his mean spirited way. She faced challenges and greater causes for despair than I have ever known. But she lived these verses in her life. When anxiety arose....and I know it did....she didn't let it take root. Instead, she quickly passed it on to God. That is the kind of prayer and petitioning that Paul is talking about!

Paul says the way to do this is not to pretend there is no anxiety. Nor that there is nothing in your life about which to be anxious. Instead, it is that you choose not to allow those things to dominate you. The anxieties surface in your mind....maybe with a panic, maybe slowly over time, maybe something that eats on you, maybe something that is suddenly sprung on you....the concern appears and creates anxiety. It is at that point you make a choice. Either you spend your time wrestling with the issue, seeking to figure out a solution, and let it weigh you down, or you decide to pass it on to God by articulating the anxiety to Him. You simply tell Him what you are afraid of, what you cannot handle, how your feelings have gotten off track, and ask Him to handle whatever needs to be done, and to let you know if there is anything you need to do about it. Do you remember being a kid, and playing a game called "hot potato"? The potato would come to your hands, or land in your lap, but the last thing you wanted to do with that potato is to hang on to it. Instead, your goal was to get hold of it and get it out of your possession as quickly as possible by dumping it over to somebody else. See the parallel? Anxiety coming your way? Use it to play hot potato with God. The only difference is, God doesn't pass it back....it only comes back if you grab it out of His hands. If you do take it back, remind yourself that you are supposed to be playing hot potato, and get it back where it belongs....out of your hands.

MY PRAYER FOR YOU THIS WEEK

This week, I pray that you will find significant moments of joy to lift your spirits and lighten your heart. May the serendipitous blossoms, sunbeams and smiles saturate your being with the presence of God. As you go through your days, may God open your eyes and ears to the wonder and beauty around you, to the songs of the birds and the laughter of children, that you may find things to enjoy from the hand of God. Amen.

Day 64   Philippians 4:6-7

So how did the hot potato game go since you last picked this up? If you are like me, it requires a lot of reminders that you are supposed to pass it on. But I wonder if you have finished your experience of the verse. The second half of the verse talks about the consequence of the first half....if you take those anxieties to God, the result is a sense of peace. And that is the part of the experience I am wondering if you have received yet. Have you given over the anxieties enough that you are sensing that peace? Perhaps I should take a few lines to discuss that peace. It is more than just a feeling. Way too often, I hear Christians claiming God's guidance or whatever else because they "just felt a peace about it." Feelings are very fickle. You can experience a feeling of peace because you just finished a good meal. Or because you woke up from a great night's rest. Or you paid off that bill. Or even when you just took some time to relax, or take a stroll. I don't believe the Lord means that we will merely live with a feeling of peace. Instead, I think He is talking about a peace that is a result of assurance in the midst of upheaval. The kind of peace that gives you the energy to solve the problems before you. In John 14:1, Jesus tells his disciples not to let their heart be troubled, and then later on in the chapter He talks about the peace He gives, not like the world gives. So when we look at this scripture and ask if we are experiencing peace, it does not make sense to think it is the feeling of peace that comes in other situations in this world. Rather, it means peace that is different from the common experience of peace, which, of course, is why it is beyond comprehension. The peace that comes from taking your anxieties to God is the peace perhaps best described as an assurance that you will be okay, that nothing is out of God's control, in spite of how things would seem. It is a calm trust of God's guiding and providing hand when there is more reason to be upset than to be peaceful. It is a peace that comes from God to us within, not from without. It is a peace that does not change just because things around us change. It is more than a mood....you are probably very aware of how much your mood can change back and forth, sometimes for no apparent reason at all. It is a peace that comes because you know that the cares and concerns and fears have all been placed into the hands of God, so they are not yours to fret over, because you know He is in charge.

Again, I ask, have you experienced the peace of the second part of the passage? It is an incredible thing to think that God's peace is what will keep your heart and mind where they belong....in Christ. It is almost as if our hearts and minds only have so much storage space. When they are full of anxieties, there is no room left for the peace of Christ. But the more you can empty that space out by transferring the hot potato of anxiety over to God, the more you can be filled with the peace that is beyond reason. In the time of divorce, it is a peace that God will take care of you. It is a peace that you will be given the strength you need. It is a peace that comes from the assurance of your personal relationship with God, and the practice of trusting Him with all the things that trouble you, because you know that God is trustworthy and there is nothing He cannot handle.

Day 65   Philippians 4:8

We have talked before about what things you choose to focus upon, but today we want to look at it in the context of the previous two devotionals. We too often make the mistake of stopping at verse seven because we like the idea of that peace. But we must not stop there. When you choose to give God your anxieties, then a vacuum is created within you that God fills with His peace. Paul knows that vacuum is there, and you are going to be faced with the question of what you will fill the vacuum with....so he provides the godly alternative for you. If you aren't going to think about your anxieties, because you gave them away to God and they aren't yours to fret over anymore, what will you think about? Paul says think about things that are noble, excellent, worthy of praise and so on. Can you do that? Take each category listed, and come up with something that fits each category.

Is there something worthy of praise in your life? For example, God is worthy of praise for his goodness, for his faithfulness, for his love, for his willingness to sacrifice His Son for you. What about all the things in your life that *have* gone right, the opportunities you *have* had, for the health you *do* have, aren't those things worth praising God about? Paul offers here the antidote to so much of life's troubles for so many of us. The antidote is learning to focus on good things, not the troubling things. It is kind of the glass half empty or half full thing. In life, we truly do focus all too often on the negative things that literally scream for our attention, but the discipline of godliness means we learn to focus on the other things in life....the kinds of things Paul suggests here in today's verse. This reading is short, because the exercise is long. If you want this devotional to do you any good today, then take the instructions Paul gives here and put them into practice. Take some time to reflect on things in each of the categories listed in our verse. And then, rejoice that you even have things like that to reflect upon, because you could be in much worse shape. That is the assignment for you as you learn to let go of the anxiety.

Day 66   Acts 20:32-35

I remember a friend coming up to me one day in college way back when, and quoting this verse from Romans. He asked me if I believed that scripture, and, of course, I had to say yes. Then he surprised me by saying that he had something he wanted to give me, and that I had better receive it or I would be cheating him out of a blessing. He placed a hundred dollar bill in my hand and walked away. That was the day I learned how important it is to learn the grace of receiving as a Christian, not just the discipline of giving.

One of the lessons to learn in this time of rebuilding your life after divorce is to learn how to receive from those around you who want to give, so that in their giving they may experience the blessings God has for them. There may be a day you just need a hug—and to meet that need, you must allow somebody to wrap their arms around you. You may even have to ask someone to give you that hug. Perhaps there is a neighbor who might want to mow your lawn. Or you may come home one day to find a bag of groceries on your porch. There may be someone wanting to help you financially, but they may not know the need. You can lay the need before God, but you may also need to lay it before your pastor or a trusted family member or friend.

I know a woman who, after her divorce, went back to school to finish a college degree, even though she had children to care for in her home. Talk about taking on a challenge!! Someone in her church heard what she was doing, and so every month put a significant amount of money into the church's care fund to be given to her as long as she was in school. They were **all** blessed in that event. In these times, you have an opportunity to learn how to be a gracious receiver. Give God the glory, recognizing that it is He who placed these people in your life to meet your needs. Give thanks to God for these people, and share with the people how God has used them to bless you. Then, most of all, realize there will come a day when you are back on track, and then it may become *your* turn to be the agent of blessing for someone like you, so you can receive the blessing of giving, too.

Day 67   Matthew 10:17-23

This story of the rich young ruler is one of the most fascinating in scripture. Here is a man, purportedly desiring to be righteous before God, longing to know God on a deeper level, who comes to Jesus seeking the answers to those desires. Jesus recognizes the kind of person this man is....a good man, a kind man, a man who follows all the rules, but also a man who is owned by his money. The great profound truth is found in the words recorded in only one of the Gospel accounts of this episode, where the text says that Jesus loved him, indicating that it was because of his love for the man that Jesus challenged him at the deepest level. Jesus so loved this man that He wouldn't allow him to spend the rest of his life deceiving himself....He confronted Him with the fact that, at the deepest level, the young man loved wealth more than God. It is revealed in the fact that he was forced to choose, and when forced to choose he chose wealth and walked away. Interestingly enough, Jesus did not chase the man down begging him to reconsider. He did not warn the man he was making the wrong choice and try to coerce him to come back. He does not want followers who follow Him because they have been somehow forced to do so. He wants those who follow willingly. He also doesn't change the terms....He doesn't say, "well, how about if you give away half of your wealth," or, "take a week to think about it." Again, He doesn't want followers who only love Him half-heartedly. He wants disciples who are totally committed to Him.

And now it is your turn. Crisis moments in life, such as a divorce, deal with us at our very core. They often expose what is really in our hearts, who we really are. The sudden turning point in life lends itself very strongly to times of self-examination, and a review of choices and actions of the past. It is important to remember that just as it takes two to make a good marriage, it also takes two to make a divorce. The divorce was not entirely caused by the behavior of your spouse, nor entirely by yours. It is probably an exercise in futility to try to figure out exactly how much fault lies with whom and so on. However, there are things that you can learn. What are the issues about yourself that you are being forced to face right now? Are there some things about who you are, or about choices you have made, that reveal something from your core that you may have not been willing to see before? Could it be that God is allowing you to see something that you hold more dear than your relationship with God? Is there something you are clinging to as tightly as that man clutched his wealth, that God is challenging you to release? The choice is now yours. Will you walk away from the One who loves you so much that He doesn't want you deceiving yourself for the rest of your life? From the One who will not force you to choose Him over everything else, but certainly desires that you choose Him over those things? The challenge that is before you now is to choose, knowing that this may be the one chance in your life to really make a difference in your relationship with God forever. Tough as it may be to face what you are having to face, it is because God loves you that He brings these things to your attention. Choose wisely. He loves you so much.

Day 68   1 Kings 19:1-5

People handle their grief in lots of ways. Some, sadly enough, cannot handle it, and so try to drown it in drugs, drink, or sex. I remember an alcoholic friend of mine saying to me one time that believing you can drink to forget your problems is believing a lie....because when you sober up the problems are still there along with the new ones you created by getting plastered. Some people handle their grief by leaning on the strength and love of others, drawing near to their dear friends and family to help them cope with their loss. But others handle their grief the way Elijah did....they have to get away by themselves. Maybe they do that to sort things out. Maybe they do it to experience the feelings until it is time to step into new feelings. I knew a lady who handled the grief of her divorce that way, she didn't want people around, she didn't want to talk it out with anybody, she just needed some time to cry by herself. And that is what she did. Then one day she was done crying and went on to her life as a single woman. What she didn't do is what Elijah seems to have been tempted to do, and that was to allow the time alone to drive her deeper into despair, even into the despair that wants to die. If you are a person who needs that alone time....and

I think all of us do need some of that....then I want to encourage you to be alone wisely. Set some boundaries for yourself that will keep you from letting your sorrow turn into despair. Counselors who deal with suicide often say that if you get so sorrowful that you actually start considering suicide as an option, or even start planning ways you could end your life, then you need to intervene with yourself right then and go seek help. They are right. Sorrow moving into despair can become a vortex that will suck you down to destruction. You will need to observe the difference between sorrow and despair, and draw the line so you don't confuse the two.

Elijah was on the verge of despair....it is a normal reaction to extreme sorrow and loss. But notice what happened in Elijah's time of lonely sorrow. He did not just stay in sorrow. He tried to reach out to God. Maybe not in the best of ways...."I'm the only one, poor me, kill me now, God"....not the best of examples, perhaps. Except that it is an example of the fact that you don't always have to have it together to be a person of faith. You don't always have to have all the answers to be a true believer. You don't always have to be Mr. or Mrs. Sunshine-Smile-on-your Face to be one of God's chosen. What you have to be is real, really experiencing all life has to offer, feeling the feelings life brings our way, that, in fact, we were created to be able to feel. But, like Elijah, you need to feel those things while also reaching out toward God. And in the alone time, you need to allow God to nourish you as He did Elijah by that brook. Oh, you may not have ravens drop by with groceries, but God will find ways to nourish you. I do know of people to whom God DID minister by sending somebody by with some groceries in the midst of their divorce. But God will nourish you the way you need it, not the way Elijah needed. He may indeed send you to some Mt. Horeb of your own to meet with God face to face. One thing I do know, however, is the thing Elijah had to learn on that mountain: there does come a time when you need to go back. You need to get back among people. Go back because there may be some Elisha out there you need to take under your wing. Go back because there may be some Hazael, Jehu or Elisha for whom you need to point out God's anointing. Go back because the Great Commission has never been revoked....you remain a witness with a job to do, and you cannot be witnessing to the power of Christ in your life if there is nobody present to hear or see that witness. Being alone for awhile is not necessarily a bad thing. In fact, it may be crucial for you. But that period of time soon will pass, and you will move on to the next chapter in your life. Being alone too long isn't so good....whether you get married again or not. The point is whether you love people the way God does....by seeking out the lost, by caring for the body of Christ, by giving yourself for others. Are there people you have isolated yourself from? When are you going to come out of the desert and reconnect with those who need YOU?

Day 69   Galatians 6:9-10

Life with the divorce process is very tiring. Even when the court stuff is all over (or at least, mostly over), you have so much to rebuild after having been devastated and drained by the whole process. Kids still need to be fed and clothed. You may need to figure out where you are going to live from now on, how bills are going to be paid. The job may feel like drudgery, and you may even be considering picking up the pieces and moving somewhere you can start all over again. Attending worship at church may feel awkward. You may have had so many times when you have tried your best to do what you think is right, only to have it backfire and disappoint you. You may have had times when you got your hopes up thinking things were finally going okay at court, only to have it fall apart at the last minute.

This verse in Galatians may be just what you need to remember. Don't grow weary, don't grow weary in well doing. It isn't just about being weary, but about being weary in well doing. Just because when you do your best to do the right thing, it doesn't always turn out the way you want, you can't let that make you quit....you still need to do the things pleasing to God. Don't let things wear you down, make you give up. Keep trying. Keep doing your best. Keep offering every task of your hands up to God. Hang on, and then keep hanging on. Do try to do the right thing, whether it is appreciated or not, and then continue to be committed to doing your best to do what is right. In due season, at the right time, God who notices everything, will one day make it all worth your while. Just don't let it all get to you, don't grow weary, keep on doing your best to do the things that are pleasing to God.

Day 70   Matthew 5:43-48

Bitterness is one thing we can struggle with, however all too often things escalate within us, not just to bitterness, but to the stronger emotion of hate. With the shattering of love and a broken heart, all too often the intensity of feelings can lead to hatred. Especially when the offenses keep mounting over and over as issues arise. I have even seen a car bearing a personalized license plate that said something like: IH8MYX! Not only did that person hate, but paid good money to be able to proclaim their hatred to the entire world! Some people think that hate is the opposite of love. But some friends of mine pointed out the fact that hatred absorbs just as much, if not more, emotional energy and involvement as love does. Instead of hatred, progress comes when you move, emotionally, to more of an indifference. To a time when you really aren't that concerned about what goes on in your ex's home, when the choices they make become irrelevant to your emotional state, when instead of wishing them ill in life you wish them to be able to just move on.

Many will tell you it is okay to hate your ex, especially if you have experienced a lot of betrayal and abuse in the process. And some of us who have been through divorce suffered a lot through the experience. But for that to justify hatred? Jesus says we are to even love our enemies, so how does bad treatment excuse ignoring the command of Jesus to love our enemies? I think it is hard to come to a proper understanding of how to apply this command to your relationship with your ex, because it is such a mixed bag, as you have been entangled with him or her in the past in a love relationship that was an entirely different category from the love of neighbor and love of enemy. So what do these teachings mean for your life now?

It certainly must include not actively seeking their ill, but it probably does not include the extreme of overcompensating with codependent type "love" either (that is, you don't have to pretend you have all these positive feelings toward them when you don't). Additionally, it may have more to do with your actions, than with your emotions….at least, in the beginning. It may mean doing something kind when you feel like kindness is the last thing you want to do. It may mean looking out for their best interest, even though you believe it won't be appreciated or reciprocated. It can manifest itself in lots of different ways. But at the least, it means choosing not to allow hate to take root. And, unless your divorce is very unusual, hate will try to take root many times.

We hear so often in the news where an estranged spouse kills their ex and children, and then themselves. While that is not what everyone does, obviously, that is certainly a good example of how twisted you can become if you allow hatred to take root even in the midst of the agony of divorce. Fight it with all your energy....and sometimes it will take all your energy, because it is a nasty opponent. But fight it you must, lest it consume you. Practice love, even when it seems like the last thing you want to do. Not necessarily the kind of love that seeks to win a lover's heart, but the kind of love that is willing to give up one's self interest for the sake of demonstrating the kind of love God has for us all. It is quite a challenge, but it is the challenge God gives us.

MY PRAYER FOR YOU THIS WEEK

This week, I pray for your family....your parents, your siblings, your children, your grandchildren.... whatever your family may consist of, I pray that God will help them in this time. Maybe they need to know you are going to be okay, maybe they need to know they are going to be okay. I pray that God will make His presence real in each of their lives, that He will reveal Himself in fresh and practical ways for the needs of their lives. Amen.

Day 71   Matthew 18:21-22

Many people teaching from this scripture like to point out that the point Jesus is making is through the method known as hyperbole.... He pushes the example to the extreme to teach His disciples that they need to always be ready to forgive, not to come up with a magical number of how many times they have to forgive. However, in the process of divorce, 70 times 7 does not seem like such a far-fetched figure. You may very well get to see in real life whether or not you can take this teaching of Jesus seriously, not in theory, but in practice! You may literally have 490 offenses to forgive. You may have more! And the hard part, at least for me, is that just about the time you manage to really let go of some offense and forgive, another one occurs that is even more difficult to forgive. Sometimes it seems like it will never end. Sometimes it seems like nothing could possibly be more hurtful, until the next thing happens. Some things you may be able to work through and forgive in a matter of minutes, some in a matter of days, some may take a long time to truly forgive. The point isn't how long it takes, the point is that your decision, your commitment is that you *will* forgive….no matter how long it takes, no matter how difficult. Why? Because you want to be like Christ. And because you want to know God better. Even in the Lord's Prayer, we ask God to forgive us in the same way we forgive others, and if we refuse to forgive, we have put up barriers that are simply not healthy for our relationship with God. So many times in the scripture, the admonishment is to forgive just as God has forgiven you.

One of the greatest examples in scripture is found in the story of Stephen. Arrested, convicted, in the process of being unjustly executed, with his dying words, not only does Stephen indicate that he has forgiven his killers, he asks God not to hold their actions against them. Kind of reminds you of what Jesus said there on the cross, doesn't it? You will have plenty of opportunities to measure your discipleship, your commitment to God, by dealing with this very issue. Can you not only forgive your ex for each of the times that you are wronged by him or her, can you go the next step and ask God not to count the wrongs they do to you against them? Not can you say it, but can you ask it and mean it? Tough to do. Seventy times seven. That's a lot. Now some would point out that in Jesus' illustration, the step is included of the person repenting, and your ex may not be repenting to you. In fact, he or she may never admit to any wrongdoing in it. But that is not the point. You have no control over what your ex does or does not do. And you also have no responsibility for that, God does not ask you to do their part. God asks you to do your part….you forgive so that you are right with God. I would suggest that by the time you are completely healed from your divorce experience, you will either be an expert at forgiveness, or you will be an expert at bearing grudges of unforgiveness….because you will have had plenty of practice. Seventy times seven. That's a lot. Get started.

Day 72   Genesis 47:7-10

Have you ever felt like Jacob/Israel? As if the days of your life have just been too hard? It's kind of funny that he said this when he did. The hard days were the days that had already past. Past the days when he had been cheated by Laban over his wives and herds. He had a daughter who had been raped, and then, his sons slaughtered a town because of it, placing the family in a precarious situation of possible revenge by the neighbors. He had lost his son, Joseph, and lived for many years not even knowing that he was still alive. He had survived famines, primarily by sending his sons to Egypt to buy food. And then, on one of those trips, another son was kept in Egypt and he felt like he had lost the only other son of his favorite wife. Yup, that sounds like some pretty hard times. But at this point, he has just been rescued from all his hardship. He has been brought down to Egypt at the insistence of the son he thought he had lost. That son is wealthy and willing to provide for all of the family as long as the famine lasts....and beyond! The family is all together again, and a life of ease is ahead. But the weight had been pretty heavy on him throughout his life, and now it is pretty hard for him to change his perspective and focus on the good things that are happening, and the joy that is ahead.

Hard times take their toll, no doubt. But it is imperative that you not let them control who you are, or let them alone dominate your outlook. Sure, you have to be realistic, and deal with the responsibilities and hard things that come. And yet, looking back, all of us experience some moments of joy in the midst of even the hardest of lives. Why focus only upon the hard times? I have always been amazed by the folks who lived through the Great Depression here in the United States, and yet when they talk about their lives, they don't focus on the dust storms, they don't focus on the years they had little to eat or wear, they don't focus on all the hard things. Rather, they recognize that those hard things have shaped them into "can-do" sorts of people, the kind of people who are willing and able to take on whatever challenges come their way. Our world is going to miss those folks as slowly age catches up with them. Jacob/Israel was probably a lot like that. He had faced hard things, and survived. At this time of his life, as he enters his "retirement years in the sun belt" of Egypt, he also prepares to pass off the baton to the next generation. Just a few passages later, we find him on his death bed, not complaining about all the hard times, but pronouncing blessings on those who will follow. What are you going to do with the hard times that have come into your life?

Day 73   2 Kings 6:24-25, 7:1-15

This is one of the great stories of the Bible. God accomplishes a mighty deliverance. The whole nation was in a crisis, on the verge of destruction, and many were deep in despair, about to give up. It is kind of an odd thing, but we often feel when things are bad, that we are the only ones with hard stuff going on, or that nobody else has ever had it quite as bad. But the truth is, hardship has always been a part of the human experience. So much of the story of scripture is about the hardships people experienced and how God delivered them out of it or sustained them through it.

So today's story is just that....after the people were despairing and crying out to God for help, God worked things so that the attackers simply panicked and fled in the middle of the night. The beggars who discovered it were ecstatic. Riches untold. Feast instead of famine.... literally. They were saved, having been miraculously delivered when they were at death's door. So they began to take advantage of the moment by storing up some treasure and preparing for the future. Then they realized they were wrong to keep God's deliverance a secret by keeping the news to themselves.

In the midst of the hard things you are experiencing, you will find times when God does something for you that helps you through or gets you out. Are you keeping those deliverances to yourself, as if they are some kind of secret? It is wrong to do so. God is working on your behalf, but He also wants to use you to make a difference in the lives of others. The first step is simply choosing to get outside of yourself a bit. I know personally how difficult that can be in the midst of divorce. Your self-esteem may be weak. Your interest in other people and other things may have waned. And your own personal struggles may seem overwhelming. But you simply cannot let yourself end up like those two beggars, only paying attention to themselves. There is somebody you know, or whom you will have opportunity to meet, who needs God's deliverance just as much as you. They need to know that God is working. They need to know that there is reason to hope. They need to know that God can get them through it. And God's little deliverances for you are some of the things He wants to use to reach them.

Today, call someone you know is struggling, and find a way to be an encouragement to them. Maybe you are involved in a divorce support group, and know a person there really struggling who could be encouraged by your story (not for the purpose of romance, but for the purpose of sharing God's blessings). Maybe you could go to spend a few hours at the soup kitchen, food pantry, or inner city ministry center. There are lonely people in every nursing home, hurting people in every hospital, and anxious people in every surgery waiting room. The card store has cards that are intended to brighten somebody's day; who could you send one to, or write a personal note of appreciation and prayer? Don't let God's dawn come to this world and find that you have been hoarding all that God has done, when there are people around you who need deliverance as much as you do.

Day 74   1 Peter 3:14-15

We talked yesterday about the need to pass on the deliverance God brings. It could be that somebody else is experiencing the same struggles you are....concerned about their future, uncertain about their finances, grieving the loss of their spouse and home, or maybe just feeling battered by love gone sour. Whatever ways God has given you strength in these things are ways that would not only encourage you, but could encourage those others if you would pass them along. After all, the truth is, that is all this little book is anyway. I've been there, done that, God helped me through that traumatic time and I am simply trying to pass along some of the things that I learned from God so that maybe somebody else will have an easier time than I did....or at least not feel so alone. The things that happen in your life that are helpful and encouraging to you may be the very thing that somebody else needs to know for them to believe that God cares about them, or that God hasn't given up on them, or maybe even that God could make a difference in their lives if they gave Him the chance. And that could happen all because you choose to pass on information about the difference God is making in your life

But you may feel like you really don't have anything to share, like things are so bad, so hard, or that you aren't anybody special so there is nothing to share that could help anybody. Let's first address the idea that you have nothing to share because of the sense of hardship or failure or because things just seem so bad right now. Today's verse doesn't say we are to be prepared to give account of our hope, but only when things are good and we are off the hook when things are bad. It says **always**. In fact, I would argue that how your faith sustains you in the hard times of your life is actually one of the most powerful witnesses you have, because everybody has hard times, and people struggle trying to figure out how to handle them. When they see somebody else struggling, they often do ask the question, "so how did you get through that?" Because they need to get through some things in their own lives. You don't have to lie and say silly things like, "well, I'm a believer and with God, I never once doubted or felt discouraged." In fact, that kind of nonsense may do more to drive them away from God than draw them to Him. How much more meaningful it may be to respond with something like, "It was really hard. There were times I didn't think I was going to make it, but I always knew God was there, and He would send me little words of encouragement and hope enough to help me make it one step at a time." That, in my opinion, is a faith that is real, a faith that deals with real life and real emotions in a way that also evidences that God is real.

As for the other reasons you may think you have nothing to share, realize, God specializes in using people who aren't anything special. The ones who think they are special are the hardest ones for Him to use, because they won't get out of the way so He can have the glory. The Bible is the story of a lot of regular people facing regular situations with a _God_ who is special. Our witness isn't about us, it's about God. I'm nobody, but I have a God who truly is somebody. I've failed and struggled, but God never fails and never forsakes....He made all the difference. These are the very reasons this book exists....not because of who I am, but because of who God is and what He did for me through this hard time of my life. That was twelve years ago for me, and I am finding that life continues to have hard times in lots of different ways, but God is always there, and the experiences of my own past with God give me the courage to face my future with God as well. People are watching you these days. They wonder if you will decide that your faith is a waste of time and give up on God. They wonder what difference it makes that you are a Christian as you face these difficult times. They wonder if God really will do anything for you now. And they wonder if maybe God can make a difference for them as well. Always be prepared to share....because there are people all around you who need to know.

Day 75 Hebrews 4:16 "So let's walk right up to him and get what he is so ready to give. Take the mercy, accept the help." (<u>The Message Bible</u>)

I am not much of a sailor. I remember one time, though, as I was learning in our town's little lake, being out there alone, doing the best I could as I tried to master the techniques. I'm not sure what exactly happened, but I ended up out in the middle of the lake with a sailboat upside down in the water, mast and sail still attached underwater. I know you are supposed to detach them somehow and flip the boat, but I didn't have the strength or smarts to make that happen. I needed some help. I was very grateful when a motorboat owner came by and offered to help by towing me in. I also remember when I was in school, having times when I couldn't figure things out....and I was a pretty good student. Some of those courses, or some of the assignments in some of those courses were pretty hard....and I needed some help. I'd call one of the teachers, or I'd call a friend I knew was good in the subject until I got the help I needed. I do a lot of fixit things around the house. Sometimes, there are things I am working on I can't do by myself.... something is too heavy, too big, or I just don't know exactly how it works. At those times, I am grateful for nearby friends and relatives, as well as guidebooks and magazines or friendly helpers at the hardware store. But sometimes that isn't enough. The other day, the dishwasher broke. I called the repairman without even trying, because I am not a mechanically minded person. I knew at the start I would need help. I learned a long time ago there is nothing wrong with asking for help when you need it. If anything, the dumb thing is to not ask for needed help.

I love the way the Message Bible phrases this passage I love so much. "Walk right up....he is so ready to give....accept the help." I know lots of people who are the kind of folks who just love to help other people. But sometimes, they don't know how to help, or that help is even needed. If you let them know you need help, they would be there in an instant. God is that kind of being. Oh, I know, He does already know when we need help, and He knows exactly what kind of help is needed better than we do. But He is the kind of God who is not only willing to help, but in fact, **loves** to help His people. All you have to do is come and ask, He is just waiting for you to call out to Him. Anything in your life today beyond your ability? Give God a call, He will give you the help you truly need.

Day 76   Matthew 9:18-22 and John 5:1-9

I have shared before about a friend who, when struggling with my divorce, I had asked how long it takes to get over a divorce, wisely replied that she didn't believe one ever really "gets over" it. And now, some 12 years out myself, I know what she means. Though you can and do move on in life over time….the impact continues for many years, especially if there are children. Your financial world, your memories and traditions may feel that impact for years to come, even your social life will experience impact from the dramatic change that is divorce. Maybe you are already feeling this. I spoke with a man going through divorce the other day, who was, at the time, about 6 months from the start of his process and had just received the court settlement. That hit him hard. He was struggling, in part, with how long it was all taking and that he wanted to be able to move on in his life….the stress was taking its toll. I know another man whose state has a much longer process…he anticipates something like two years before his divorce finalizes, and he, too, is weary of it all with the stress and uncertainty. But the truth both of these gentlemen will discover is that, even when the legal process is completed, there are things that just seem to go on and on. It can be very frustrating.

I think it must have been very frustrating for the man there beside the pool at Bethesda. Day after day, year after year, he had waited for his chance at healing, and had nothing happen. Or for the poor woman who touched the hem of Jesus' robe….she had suffered years and years, trying so many solutions only to have things get worse instead of better. Somehow, though, neither of them had given up hope. And then, one day, Jesus changed their lives. I'm sure that these folks had wanted their lives to change for a very long time, that they were weary of the hard things, and maybe had even begun wondering if life would ever get better. At the perfect time, it all changed. Their encounter with Jesus may not have come as early as they had wished, but it came. God changed what needed to be changed in His timing, not theirs. Things may get difficult for you in many ways, or you may reach a point of smooth sailing soon. In either case, God remains sovereign, and will bring into your life exactly what you need, but will do it at the time He knows to be the very best....even if it means you have to wait longer than you desire. Even if it means you need to go through some more hard times to learn the lessons He has for you. When the paralyzed man and the suffering woman experienced the touch they desired, it so changed their lives they didn't waste time asking Jesus why it hadn't happened earlier. They were just grateful His healing came, and were ready to move on in their lives. God's touch will do the same for you.... if you wait for it and don't give up hope, even if things don't change the way you want as quickly as you want. God knows the best answers, and the best time to bring those answers. Trust Him to do so. The day will come.

Day 77   Isaiah 26:7-10

Hey, have you ever had any rough places in your life? I know I have had plenty of them. Some days, it feels like TOO many! I know there have been plenty of times in my life that I have had things that felt pretty rough, (although, let me be the first to say that I have not had it nearly as rough as a great number of people around this globe). In those rough times, I would often do everything I could to smooth things over. Sometimes I've had pretty good success at doing that. But more often than not, there is a huge difference between my smoothing over rough places and the way God smoothes things over. When God smoothes out a rough place, that rough place has to obey! Imagine Pike's Peak hearing God say, "level out with the Eastern Colorado plains!" What would be the response? I would guess that it would flatten itself out before it could even respond with a "Yes, Lord!" And when God starts to deal with the rough places in your life, there is nothing that can stand in the way then, either. Because we have a great God. When He makes rough places smooth, they become smooth. If He chooses to leave some little bumps, then He has a reason for doing so. It is our choice as to who we want to do the smoothing....us or God. (And sometimes we also choose whether it's going to happen the easy way or the hard way!) Sometimes I think that after I get done trying to smooth things, and finally ask God to fix it all because I cannot, He ends up having more to smooth than He would have if I had left it alone so He could act in the first place! Oh well, live and learn. But that is the key....not just to live, but to learn from what you live. Some people seem to never learn, they just keep getting in the way, when God could smooth out those rough places for them if they'd just let Him.

Now I want you to notice a bit further down in the passage, there is a pretty good clue to this whole thing. This time of God making rough places smooth included a period of time _when the person in need_ was seeking God earnestly _all night!_ And made his priority to be to do whatever would glorify God! Do you want your rough places smoothed out? Really? How badly do you want that to happen? Do you just wish he'd do it, with no real effort or participation on your part? Or do you want it so earnestly that you would seek God all night....earnestly, it says....desperately wanting, asking, begging God to show you what it is He would have you do and not do about the situation. And, is it more important to you that God be glorified, than it is that the rough places get smoothed? If you really want the rough places in your life to be smoothed out by God, the first step is to seek Him earnestly. The second step is to be obedient to whatever He shows you to do or not do. The third step is to set your heart, to the best of your ability, to desire first and foremost His glory, not your ease and comfort. And the fourth step? Well, the fourth step is God's. That is the step where the rough places get smoothed out. Look out, Pike's Peak, our God is mighty big!

MY PRAYER FOR YOU THIS WEEK

This week, I pray that God will help you know how to let go, and which things are the ones you need to let go. As you release the burdens, the cares, and the possessions to God, may you experience a new freedom in Christ that overfills the emptiness that comes with loss. May God use the letting go to create a world of healing within your heart. Amen.

Day 78   Jude 24-25

Ever feel like you are teetering on the precipice of life? Or like you walk a tightrope in some kind of balancing act, afraid to push very far to the left or to the right? Have you ever felt like enduring as a Christian is more than you can handle, like you want to just give up and yell, "What's the point?" Maybe you feel like the stress in your life has just gotten so intense that you can't take it anymore, that you are barely clinging to the edge of the cliff with your fingertips? Maybe it isn't that things feel too difficult. Maybe you just feel like maybe you made some really big mistakes, like you slipped up in your walk with God. And that sense of not doing what you know you should has left you feeling pretty badly about everything.

This verse out of Jude is really a great reminder of who it is we are in relationship with: a God who can keep you from falling. Just because you feel like you might slip and fall, doesn't mean you will. Just because you are afraid you are losing your balance, or that you have gotten tired of trying to stand for Christ, doesn't mean God is losing balance or weak. God is able to keep you from falling. God can do for us what we cannot do for ourselves. All too often we try to live our Christian lives on our own, not taking advantage of the fact that we have a partner, a helper, a God who is able to help us not fall. If you have fallen short of what you know God wants, realize that He won't just leave you lying there, but will help you get back on your feet, dust you off and get you going again.

In my life, there have been plenty of times when I have fallen.... too many times if you ask my aching bones! Like the time I walked across the patio that was covered with a sheet of ice, and lost my footing. I grabbed for the fallen tree branch to keep me from crashing all the way to the ground! Or other times when I have been walking with someone, and accidentally stepped on a rock that caused my ankle to twist and I began to fall. Not very gracefully, I am afraid, I grabbed my companion's arm and steadied myself. Or the times I have been up on a ladder, and felt my foot start to slip. I quickly grabbed a tight hold onto the side of the ladder until I was stabilized, and you can be sure, I grabbed tightly. The worst was when, as a kid, I slipped out of a tree I was climbing and scraped my back on the nearby fencepost on the way down. Ouch! Why then, in our spiritual and emotional lives do we try to manage them all by ourselves? Especially when there is someone so solid right at hand we can reach out and cling to and regain our stability.

God is there for you, just waiting for you to reach out with whatever has knocked you off balance. He can, He will, keep you from falling.

Let me share with you a story that made this image vivid for me. One time I had the opportunity to visit Mexico City. A group of friends were downtown one night, and happened across a beautifully lit old church. Now you need to know that I have been trained and worked as a photographer in my life, so naturally, I had my camera with me that night. I wanted a shot, and wanted it from a certain angle. But when I got ready to take it, I was too close. I realized I needed to stand behind the floodlights, and, as is my manner when doing photographs, I was backing up watching the image in front of me through the camera. (Those who have assisted me in taking wedding photographs will attest that it is dangerous to be standing behind me when I am shooting!) Anyway, as I stepped back behind the floodlights, suddenly I was not standing, but fell and landed on a little ledge three or four feet down below the walk where I had been. A bit shaken and bruised, I climbed back up, and nobody really had even noticed my fall. I took my shot, and then we went on. As we wandered around, I could see that where I had fallen was actually a large pit where there had been archaeological excavations of ancient ruins. What I also saw was that the pit was dangerously deep, and that, in most places, there did not seem to be any ledges....just in the area where I had fallen. That night, the image that came to me was that I had fallen, but it was the hand of God (in the form of a ledge) that had caught me and kept me from falling to serious injury or death. My friend, no matter how much you feel like you may risk falling, when you belong to Him, you fall only into the hands of God....He will catch you and keep you from falling, just as He did for me there in Mexico City 25 years ago!

Day 79   Isaiah 41:10

I don't know what your experience of divorce has been, but I remember very clearly that mine included some serious fears and concerns. I was afraid of all the things that could happen, things based in reality, and things based in imaginations of this unknown territory. Fears about financial future, fears about losing opportunities to spend time with my kids, fears this strange world called court would not be just, fears of being alone the rest of my life, fears of risking remarriage....

lots and lots of fears in wave after wave as the experience progressed. This little verse was one I had memorized years before my divorce. I believe it was one of the ways God prepared my help in advance, because when the time came that I needed the encouragement and comfort this verse gives, it was ready at hand deep in my soul. It is one thing to know a Bible verse for memory, it is another to know it in time of need.

What does the verse say to our fears? That we have a choice, and that choice is whether we fear, or whether we do not fear....a choice we make, not merely a feeling to experience! My basis for fear was all the uncertainty about the future and concern for the foundations of my life that were being threatened. The basis to not fear is given in the verse: God is with me. Again, the call to not be afraid, to select that as your choice. The basis to not fear is expanded....not only that God is with you, but that He is YOUR GOD. He belongs to you, and you to Him. He is God, your God, not just some nice guy down the street. He is the One you are to worship and trust, not your finances, not your human relationships, not your possessions, not even your future....only God deserves your worship, and only God is trustworthy.

What does the verse offer as the alternative to our fears? God promises us strength. He promises us help. He promises to uphold us through His almighty power. I don't know about your situation today, but there were many days when I needed strength just to get through the day, strength to make decisions, strength to endure the process, strength to handle the waiting and uncertainty, strength to believe it would be okay... I am sure you can fill in your own strength needs. Help? Oh yeah, I needed help. I needed someone I could lean on. I needed answers where answers were very elusive. I needed help making decisions. I needed the kind of help that only God could give, because people I trusted were letting me down and I wasn't always sure where I could turn for help. Frankly, thank God for my church. Not the church as a whole body, but a handful of good, Christian friends with whom I had long term relationships in my church, people God had placed in my life. These were the ones He could use to help me when I needed help. Finally, the promise to be upheld by God's hand. Though I might feel like I was falling, I was being upheld by God. When I could not stand on my own, I had a God who would enable me to stand. When I no longer had the strength or power to carry on myself, I had a God who would share His power to get me through. Fear not. Be not afraid. No matter how panicked you feel inside. No matter how wildly things seem to be spinning out of control. No matter how rapidly the ground is falling away beneath your feet. You have a choice. The choice God wants you to make is to not become afraid. Fear not. Be not afraid. I am with you, He says. I am your God. Fear not.

Day 80   Psalm 141:1-4

Today's passage is a challenge for any person who wants to please God. Jesus says the same kind of thing in Matthew 12:36-37 where He indicates that every word out of our lips is heard and judged by God, and that we will one day have to give account for them all. During the process and in the aftermath of divorce, there is perhaps a greater risk than at other times for inappropriate use of the mouth. People I have observed going through divorce have a variety of ways they handle their struggles in terms of their need to talk it out. There are some who prefer to use self talk, taking time by themselves to work through their thoughts and feelings without involving anybody else. There are others who feel the need to talk to a few, perhaps in a formal support group or just with a few selected friends, or maybe with a professional counselor or pastor. And then there are some who will tell their story to every person they ever meet. Especially in those early days, the relationship between talking and healing are closely aligned. I know I had various of these responses at different times, and was accused of other responses whether true or not. Maybe you need different ways to process things at different times. But as you talk, remember the biblical passage that suggests that where there are many words there is more likely to be sin involved than with few words (Proverbs 10:19). As you talk about your experience, and especially when you are working through raw emotions, there is great temptation to slander, gossip and sometimes to curse. It is in those times we need a guard placed upon our lips. If we ask, God will help set that watch upon our lips. When we start to speak amiss, the Spirit of God will prick our conscience, letting us know we are crossing the boundary. It is our job to pay attention to that Spirit renewed conscience and to be obedient. Today, imagine Jesus listening to every word you speak, and invite Him to be the guard you will need.

Day 81   Jeremiah 31:21-23

This is a really cool verse, if you understand its purpose. It refers to a time when the Jewish people were going to be carried off into exile, thrown out of their homes, and taken away as captives and slaves. Yet in preparation for that, Jeremiah buys a piece of ground in the land they will soon be leaving, and the command was issued to people to set up the ancient markers, because they would be coming back that way, under better circumstances than the slavery in which they left.

Well, if you have gotten this far into this book, then by now, you pretty well know an awful lot about me. So it is time to let you in on one more thing. It came up today because of a movie I was watching on the television, but I will get to that. What you need to know is that I am a sap. A foolish, sentimental sap. And pretty much everybody who knows me well knows that. I have flowers in my yard because they remind me of relatives who have died who grew those same flowers. I have useless things that were given to me years ago that I have retained because.... well, because I am a sentimental sap. If you don't believe me, sometime ask my wife about the 50 year old coconut head on my bookshelf. Being a sap means that I am touched deeply by music, by art, and by movies. Which is why I am writing this devotional today. There is a movie with which I have a profound relationship, if you will believe that. You see, within a week or two after my wife told me she was filing for divorce, and I saw time with my kids ripped away from me, I decided I needed to do something to help counter that loss. I made some opportunities to do some special things with my kids. In fact, I decided to come up with several things that I could do with them on a regular basis, now that my time was more limited.

Anyway, one day my teenage daughter and I decided to go to the movies. She didn't know anything about the ones playing, and I certainly didn't since I don't pay that much attention to them, so we just went to see what was on. When we were making a selection, we saw a movie starring Sandra Bullock, and she is an actress whose work I tend to enjoy, and, as far as I have seen, she generally makes quality movies. Anyway, there was a movie of hers, so we decided we would go see it. Little did we know that the movie, "Hope Floats" is about a woman whose marriage is shattered and so she spirals into depression as the divorce proceedings begin. I have never had a harder time keeping myself from walking out of a movie in my life. I was watching this wretched woman on the screen act out my life. It was awful. Not the movie. The experience. The movie was pretty good....although very difficult. And while the character in the story found that "hope floats," I was far too freshly devastated to believe it or care. My daughter apologized when we left the theater, admitting she hadn't realized what it was about. And I was able to tell her it was okay, it was a good movie, and an "accident." Although, maybe it wasn't such an accident.

Today, while the wife is away, I was channel surfing for a minute and there it was, that same movie from so many years ago. It still touched a tender spot in my heart, and still brought a tear to my eye, but now I know that the message is true, hope does float, life does move on and can move in very positive directions. Watching the bits of the movie I happened to see, there was a reminder of the pain of the past, but there was also the perspective of my returning to the same place, but with a fresh perspective. Perhaps it felt kind of like that for the Jewish people returning to their homeland and walking past the signposts they had set up as they had walked away. You will, I suspect, find your own signposts, that represent the pathways of pain for you. And one day, you will pass a park, hear a song, see a movie, something that will trigger the memories of the valley you once had to walk through, but you may see it with new eyes, eyes filled with promise of a future rebuilt by the grace of God. You will see it and realize how far He has brought you, and gratefully acknowledge His promise to see you through.

Day 82   Ruth 1:1-5

I used to be a wedding photographer, and have done some part time even after I quit doing weddings full time. So if you add my time as a minister, as well, I have been involved in hundreds of weddings in one fashion or another over the years. As a photographer, there were involvements with the couple over a long period of time, and we had some opportunities to observe interactions between them. I remember times we speculated on whether the marriage would last, based on what we observed. There were times we witnessed couples who were arguing from the first day we met them, and we anticipated their marriage would not last. Other times, some of the couples were so harmonious, we were sure they were made for each other. One of the promotions we used to do meant we would often see the couple a year later, and we were regularly surprised. I remember one couple who fought a lot, but a year later were still married and getting along very well by then, while another that seemed so good for each other were divorced within a month! It was amazing. I realized I need to speak at least once specifically to those individuals whose marriages were rather short lived, whether a month or just a few years, because you have a different set of circumstances than many.

For those of you who fit this category, I think of the story of Ruth, but not the part people always notice. We don't know too many details about her life, especially early on, but we do know a few things. She was a woman from a people called the Moabites. Living in her home country, she somehow had an opportunity to meet and marry an immigrant, Chilion, who had ended up in Moab because his parents had left their homeland during a time of famine....much like many of the Irish who came to America years ago. I suspect that she was pretty excited about her wedding, most fiancés are! We don't know how old she was when she got married, or how long she had been married before her husband died, but it was soon enough that neither Ruth nor her sister-in-law Orpah had any children yet. Granted, that is a different circumstance than a divorce, but there are some parallels. For instance, the sense of having settled one of the most important decisions in life was behind her, but only temporarily it turned out. Perhaps she wondered if she would ever be able to love again, especially if she had once thought of Chilion with high regard and deep love. Perhaps, instead, she vowed never to be taken in again, as she saw the uncertainty of life and relationships when her dreams were taken away. Maybe she felt, most of all, the dream of settling down and starting a family was now cut short...the couple would have no children.

Some of you reading this may be in the opposite situation, and find yourself suddenly having to raise your child without the father or the mother to help you make the home and family. In Ruth's case (and Orpah's), the husband she had loved and with whom she had started to build a future was suddenly gone from her life. In the ancient Near East, a woman alone was in a precarious position in society, for her legal standing often depended upon her father when she was young, and her husband as she matured, and probably her son when she was an aged widow. Ruth and Orpah were in that uncertain place, where their futures were precarious, at best. Hence, Orpah chose to go back to her family and start again from there. Ruth made the choice to stay with her mother-in-law, Naomi, because of the esteem she had for her, and very possibly because she was concerned for Naomi's security without her male guardian as well. Maybe you really relate to the situation of those women, and the decisions they faced. Where will you go, now? Will you ever love or be loved again? Has your ability to trust been permanently damaged? How can you manage with your heart and your future now in such disarray?

There are many times in the scriptures that people experience the precariousness of life, shattered dreams and difficult circumstances. In fact, I would suggest that these are the very core of much of scripture and often its purpose is to help us through those very things. By looking through the scriptures, you will find people whose stories can bring hope for your own, and promises from God to which you can cling when all else seems to be crumbling. What seems to be the end of something in our lives, can in fact be merely AN ending, with the beginning of something new just on the horizon.

In fact, I have found it helpful myself to think of life the way a friend suggested: in the form of chapters. Sometimes these experiences are simply the close of one chapter and the start of another. Orpah went back to her own family, and picked up life from there. We know nothing else about what happened to her, except the implication that by going back, she was turning from the God of Israel to once again embrace Chemosh, the harsh god of the Moabites. But we know about Ruth, and that, although things must have seemed dark, still she chose to cling to God, and God honored that choice. God even guided her footsteps so that she "happened" to end up in the field of her future husband, Boaz. The hopes that were once dashed, found rebirth in a new land, with a new husband, and a new life. And God gave her more than she could have imagined, for through her lineage King David was born, and eventually, the Messiah Jesus who would change history forever.

It is surely hard to trust oneself when things have fallen apart so quickly, and you question your own judgment. But there is nothing that happens in life that God can't restore and use for good if you will hang on to your trust in Him. In God's timing, and in God's planning, the frustration and disappointment you feel can be turned into rejoicing and hope, as you allow God to guide your steps in the future (perhaps a bit wiser and less starry eyed than you once were). As a friend of mine once said, "the dream of marriage did not die, it is still real and still out there….but that marriage died, but it also wasn't the dream." Who knows? Your next chapter might just be the best chapter!

Day 83   James 2:8-10

There are those who will tell you that divorce is a sin, and they will quote various scriptures to support their view. I believe that there are times it is a sin in the classic sense of the word, and there are times when the sin is what happens in the marriage that results in the divorce. The Greek meaning of the word "sin" was an archer's term meaning "to miss the mark." No divorced persons would ever disagree with the notion that they are divorced because their marriage "missed the mark," of the target, the perfect marriage was not what they experienced. However, many of those who like to consider divorce a sin, also follow that with a degree of arrogance as if the divorced person is somehow a second class Christian marred by sin, whereas somehow they are not. That, of course, is ridiculous. Any Christians who believe that their lives are not marred by sin are caught in the same trap of the hypocritical members of the Pharisees Jesus so roundly condemned.

I was thinking about today's text in James, and began trying to imagine what kind of analogy could be an apt illustration of the point James is making. I wondered, what could illustrate the notion that even one sin means the whole of the law is broken? Especially for those who want to consider that their sin is not as bad as another's. The image I came up with comes from my experience with dinner plates. I don't know what kind you use, but the ones we have now have places where they have been chipped, and are marred by the lack of color in those places. (And, as I am a cheapskate, we haven't replaced any of them yet!) But at other times in my life, I have had a different kind of dinner plates, ones that were supposed to be unbreakable. And, in fact, many a time I have clumsily dropped one on the floor, only to be able to pick it up and move on with no evidence of the drop. But after a while…. I don't know if it is because of age, or exposure to the dishwasher, or if I just dropped it harder, but one day, the result was far different for those plates than my current ones. When my current plate hits the ground, if it doesn't break into several large pieces, then sometimes a piece is chipped out and the dinner plate remains usable, although chipped. But James says that our sin is not like that chip. It is more like the other kind of plates I had. Those plates did not chip, when they hit the ground and broke, they literally shattered into hundreds of tiny pieces, unusable for anything. What James is saying is that when we have sinned, even in one point, we don't create the chipped plate scenario, but rather the shattering of the law, even as one drop completely destroyed those plates in my kitchen.

Someone who is looking at you or I as a divorced person, and somehow think our sin is worse than theirs has the wrong image. They have forgotten this verse in James. Breaking the law once makes us imperfect, not just slightly, but shattering righteousness just like those dinner plates. Sometimes I explain this idea by challenging people with a choice of two glasses of milk. They can take whichever they would prefer, but I inform them I am going to place 5 drops of cyanide in one glass, and thirty drops in the other. Then I ask which one they would want to drink. The answer? Neither, of course. Because whether 5 drops or 30 or a thousand, the milk is poisoned and will kill you. So it is with sin. God does not see any of our sins as slight. They are all poisonous, and have shattered our righteousness. And that is why there is not one of us who isn't absolutely dependent on the grace of God that purchased salvation for us through the redemption Jesus accomplished on the cross. Don't buy the line those folks might try to give you, they are no less in need of mercy than you and I. The good news is, the God we worship just happens to be rich in the very thing we need: mercy!

Day 84   Exodus 5:1-14

As I have written these devotionals, sometimes I have shared them with friends and family to gain an outside perspective and, in some cases, to see how they connect with individuals I know who are going through a divorce. In one of those conversations, a friend shared some wisdom that had been shared with him, a bit of wisdom that I think is well worth passing on. The text he used is today's reading. He pointed out that, at least sometimes, when God is about to do something wonderful, He first allows things to become more difficult. For instance, the Israelite people had been suffering in slavery for years. The time comes when God raises up Moses to lead them out, and as Moses begins the work of deliverance, the first impact that comes is that Pharaoh makes the work harder and their lives more miserable than they were. Now, instead of having to make bricks for Pharaoh, they had to first work to gather the straw to make the bricks, and yet still keep producing the same number of bricks! And that was tough. Tougher than it had been. Worse than they had expected, worse than they could have imagined, when they thought about God delivering them. That observation is what my friend shared as he wrestled with some of his difficult experiences.

If you take this concept a step further in the story, you can also notice that the very same thing happened to Moses himself! Raised in the royal household, when he observed an Israelite slave being abused, he was deeply troubled. So troubled, in fact, that he killed the Egyptian who was doing the harm. But the next day, when he tried to break up a fight between two slaves, he is challenged about the murder of the Egyptian, and in panic, flees the country. He then spends 40 years out in the wilderness of Sinai. Certainly NOT what he expected would be part of the process of rescuing the Israelites. And not his intention when he killed the Egyptian. What he anticipated as a good thing instead turned sour very quickly. Years later, of course, it turned out to be *very helpful* that he had knowledge of how to survive in the wilderness!!

At the time, it only seemed things had gone from bad to worse. His hopes were dashed. Even if he did not yet realize he was going to be their deliverer, he certainly had the intention of helping the Israelites out of compassion for their plight....he just didn't know it would result in his own extended exile first. *But without that extended exile:* he would not have been near the bush that was burning when God called to him, he would not have known the ways of the wilderness, he would not have had his wise father-in-law to help him know how to lead the people....probably a whole list of things that could only have happened with Moses out in the wilderness. Sometimes, there is good reason for things to become hard. One modern analogy I have heard is that the purpose of adolescence is to prepare parents to let go. And another, that a purpose of the aches and pains of old age is to help individuals be ready and willing to leave this world.

Does any of this have meaning for you? I know that in my first marriage, things got pretty tough near the end. When she filed for divorce, it certainly wasn't the first time my ex had expressed her interest in divorce. But this time, when she announced her desire for divorce, for the first time, I was willing to let her go. Things had gotten bad enough I no longer begged her to stay, nor pleaded with her to go to marriage counseling with me again. In fact, I did none of the things that I had done before. Things were at a point that I was now willing to do what I had been unwilling to do before....to let her leave the marriage without my protesting, if that is what she wanted. *Of course* that was a tough time in life, as were the years following when I tried to gain my equilibrium and start life over. However, I have since that time met my second wife, and begun with her an entirely different kind of marriage, and a chapter in my life that would never have been possible had I not first gone through those tough times. All of this is, of course, captured by the old adage, "it is always darkest just before the dawn." Dear reader, if you are experiencing tough times and your life has grown harder than you had ever dreamed, realize that it does not mean God is no longer working. In fact, it may mean He is preparing you and your circumstances for the glorious future He will create.

MY PRAYER FOR YOU THIS WEEK

This week, I pray that you will experience assurance from God. Assurance of your salvation. Assurance of how much God loves you. Assurance that God hears your cries. Assurance that God cares about your every need. And with that assurance, may you grow in confidence in God's provision for every need of your life. Amen.

Day 85   Psalm 37:1-9

One of the most frustrating and difficult parts of divorce is that there seem to be no guarantees. I know this personally from my own experiences, as well as the experiences I have seen in the divorce of friends and parishioners I have known. Part of the unpredictability has to do with the bizarre way courts can view things. For instance, I have known of a case where the children were given to the mother for the primary residence, but when she had a boyfriend move in and they were involved in drugs, the court refused to move the children. Why? The father had a good job, a stable home, but in that court and with that judge there was just one problem: he was not the mother. That particular court has been known in that state as a court that just prefers the children stay with the mother, and that seems to have overridden any other considerations. I have seen time and time again things taken to court that, logically, should have been a slam dunk, but viewed through the eyes of the court's logic, received a surprise verdict instead. The courts have a logic that is all their own….assuming logic is the appropriate word to use! You may well begin to question whether the courts have anything at all to do with justice. Yet that is not the only area where there are no guarantees. Family relationships change, too. Let's consider some of those together today, and then tomorrow we will focus on the children.

A couple of very difficult realms during divorce have to do with family and ex spouses. Let's begin with the ex, since that would be the area you would expect no guarantees. With all the varied divorces I have seen, there are times when the separation happens in such a way that you and your ex could come out as "friends," in a better relationship than you had when you were married. Of course, I know of one man in that kind of situation who indicated that it was logical she wouldn't be difficult, as she was getting significant money very regularly and pretty much everything else she wanted….which, of course, indicates that what appears to be friendship is actually self-centeredness on her part and silent anger on his part. Still, there are some who seem to do okay together. More often than not, however, people see their ex acting out behaviors they never would have expected, and frequently intense anger lashes out to a degree never before experienced as the ex seeks some kind of revenge or simply to cause pain. If this is not at all what you experience, you need to fall on your knees and give God thanks, because this viciousness is all too common. Sometimes it comes out directly, sometimes in subtle or manipulative ways, but when it comes out, it can be very difficult to deal with. You have to learn new ways and new depths of forgiveness.

Perhaps more surprising, though, are the other family members during and after a divorce. Sometimes a divorcing person's parents, siblings or aunts and uncles change their attitudes and relationship style in unexpected and hurtful ways. They may withdraw, acting as if they think divorce is contagious, or on the pretext that they have to protect their children. They may blame or condemn. I have even seen times when they have taken sides against their family member and supported the ex....although in most of those cases the behavior of the one they turn against has been so outlandish that it is very understandable. In other cases, they may overcompensate by managing the divorcing person's life as if he or she has become a helpless child. It can be very hard and very painful to negotiate these troubled relationship waters, but it is one of the necessary tasks of divorce. In it all, you will make mistakes, and you will make outstanding choices. Sometimes, all you can do is pray and, as the Psalmist says, commit your way to God trusting that He will do what needs to be done. Then, after doing that, you have to trust that what God is doing is what needs to done, even if it seems to make no sense to you. If you find yourself thinking it makes no sense, then perhaps you might want to step outside and watch the stars and planets, realizing that God's power and way of thinking are far beyond what you can possibly even imagine. Sometimes, you and I just have to trust His wisdom.

Day 86   Psalm 127:3-5 and Isaiah 1:2

Today, let us look at the ways your children can be very unpredictable and difficult in the days of divorce. (Let me mention, by the way, that though much of what I write relates to children in the home, grown children are also impacted significantly when their parents divorce. If that is your situation, don't assume they aren't affected....they are.) There are a couple of things to realize at the outset. If your children are young, then realize that until they become adults, most children are pretty self centered.... and when you add the need for survival tactics in a disintegrating family, they can become even more so. Hopefully, by the time they are adults, they will outgrow this. Secondly, children are having to deal with loyalty issues, because while your ex is no longer *your* husband or wife, they *do* remain the father or mother of the children, and children will cling to that. And they *should* cling to that! Let me say here at the outset that I am mainly seeking to encourage those who experience difficulties with their children. If this does not describe your experience, you may want to skip this, or you might read it giving thanks to God that this is not what you experience! Who knows, you might find other ways this devotional applies to you. The truth is, of course, that children can be very difficult whether there is a divorce or not, and it can be pretty difficult to sort out whether the difficulty with your child stems from the divorce, or is just a part of growing up that might well have occurred even if the marriage was intact.

I want to mention a couple difficulties that may arise. For instance, when there is animosity between the parents, as there frequently is during divorce and its aftermath, then all too often one parent will manipulate and distort things to try to turn a child against the other parent. Sometimes it is done in such subtle ways that the children can actually believe it is the OTHER parent who is doing that distorting. Years later the adult child may recognize the reality of what has happened, but it may take many years, and there are no guarantees. Another difficulty can be when children play the power game, threatening to run to your ex's home when you are not doing what they want done. Sometimes, that is exactly what your ex is encouraging to happen, maybe for financial reasons, maybe for revenge reasons, but certainly not because they have the children's best interest at heart. In these things, children view things through the eyes of a child. Later, as adults, they may realize the ramifications of what happened and begin to view the divorce no longer as your children, but as adults. It may be they will realize then that they did not truly understand, and maybe even apologize for choices they made. Unfortunately, I cannot promise that. You can possibly add to this list out of your own experiences.

In these times, you can experience such heartache and hurt. Especially if you go through a time in which your children reject you, your values, or your involvement. I wish I could give you three easy steps to make everything okay, but if I could, I would have used them myself! No, there are no magic answers to make it all better and for the hard things to go away. But there are some things I can suggest to help you through it. First, I suggest you use this time to commit your children to the Lord, asking Him to watch over them when you cannot, asking Him to work out His perfect will in their lives, even if you are not there to experience it with them. Secondly, understand that your children are people just like you. They will make their own choices; some of those choices will not be good, and some will be very good. They will also make mistakes, and then have to learn how to deal with those mistakes. Thirdly, you can use this time to gain deeper insight into your relationship with God. For instance, if your children have turned against you, you will understand more deeply what it must feel like for God when we have sinned over and again. You can understand in a different way the experience of the father in the Prodigal Son parable, or when Paul writes in Romans that Christ died for us while we were yet sinners and enemies of God. Fourth, you will be placed in a position where you are challenged to a deeper level of trust in God.... will you really trust Him with your children, whether or not they ever understand? And can you let go of your children so that God can do what needs to be done, both with them and with you? If you are a person going through this tragic circumstance, I want you to know today, that I have prayed for you as I have written today's devotional. I know it is hard...I really do know....but my prayer is that you will find great strength from God to get you through and to heal the wounds there deep in your heart. I know you love your children. God loves them even more than you do, and never forget, He loves YOU, too.

Day 87   Luke 15:11-32

Yesterday we talked a bit about children and the difficult times that come along with raising them in the midst of divorce. Today, let me mention some scenarios I have witnessed as we begin. I know of one case where the mother so convinced the child of the father's blame that the child never returned home nor spoke to the father for some 50+ years! That is a heartbreak that is difficult to handle....even more so if you know it was caused by your ex's twisting of the truth. I know of another situation where the daughter played the power game, demanding to go live with daddy. The mother allowed it because she believed it would be the only way her daughter would understand that her dad did not want her at his home. It was a hard lesson for the young girl to learn, but she did learn it and it changed her behavior immensely. Often the children do not understand what has happened, or why things have happened, or can view things from only one side and are thus led to turn against a parent (sometimes even older children). I have even seen the children turn against a parent who is actually a very good person, while clinging to one whose behavior is evil and selfish. This can happen even though that parent initiated the divorce and caused many of the problems that led to the situation.

Another hard thing can be when a parent observes the behavior of a child and, in dismay, concludes that the child has become very like their ex. That is very hard, especially if you have lost all respect for your ex because of the kind of person they have become without you. You see, raising children through divorce can be very messy. But never forget, raising children can be very messy *even if there isn't a divorce*. Even if you could sort out which things would have been there anyway, and which ones are uniquely tied to the divorce, what difference would it make for you as you try to parent? Instead of trying to trace all those threads, let me suggest a different focus for you.

Before we turn to the scripture, let me mention a couple of things. With every choice you face, do your best to ask yourself, "Am I truly looking out for my children and not just acting in self-serving ways? How will this decision affect them?" You will not always do perfectly (I didn't always manage, either), but at least you will be *trying* to keep their best interest at heart. And, in the same spirit, vow to do your best to NOT be the one who manipulates the children, or who tries to undermine their love for your ex. Even to the point of reminding them of Mother's or Father's Day, and your ex's birthday, helping them have the finances they need for those if their age makes that appropriate.

Now, let's look at today's scripture and take the image of the Father in the Prodigal Son story as the example we can follow, since that father does represent our Heavenly Father, and imitating Him is ALWAYS a good thing. Notice that he NEVER stopped loving his son, no matter where his son wandered, even if the son didn't realize the Father's love was constant. Secondly, he always kept the door to his home open to his son. Not foolishly, though. It is clear the son didn't feel he had the right to just come back and take more things to go back to his wicked ways, but he did know the character of his father was such that he could return, if only to seek his favor as a hired servant. Focus on **your** consistency of character. Do your best to make sure your children know who you are, and what you stand for. But, perhaps hardest of all, this father had the courage to allow his son to find his own way. Much like the wise mother above, he didn't demand that the son had to stay at home, or try to forcibly prevent him from his foolish experimentation in the ways of the world. Though it had to grieve his heart, he knew the son would have to discover the truth for himself. Are you willing to use the same attitudes as your children seek to find their way through the years ahead of them?

I have often thought of the power of the story called, "the binding of Isaac," in Genesis 22. Isaac was the great promised blessing of

Abraham's life, and he must have loved him immensely. Yet he knew that, before God, he had to lay Isaac on the altar, trusting that God would work things out for good. That may be exactly where you are in your parenting life today. It is a very difficult, but very powerful thing to do. Remember I told you yesterday that God loves your child more than you do? If you are struggling with issues concerning your children (and what parent doesn't struggle over that?), then I invite you today in your mind's eye to come before the altar of God, and lay your child upon that altar, that God may have His perfect way. You may even want to go to your church, and do this before the altar there in some symbolic way. Love the child, keep the door open for them, allow him or her to learn the hard way if they must, but give the child to God and let go of the idea that you can control how everything turns out. Then, perhaps you, too, in God's perfect time, will receive your child back as if from the dead. And, even if they don't return, you know that you have placed them in the best of hands.

Day 88   Psalm 27:1-2 and Matthew 6:25-26

It is amazing how fear can grip you in the process of divorce. Especially in those early days. Fears about your future. Fears about the court process. Fears about what will happen with the kids. Fears about whether you will ever be loved or able to love again. Fears about financial disaster. Fears about losing all the things you have worked so hard to get. Fears of losing the security you once had. Fears that things will never be the same. Fears about what people....maybe certain people....will think. Fears because your life is spinning out of control, and you don't seem to be able to do anything about it, nor do you know where it will lead. These fears can be haunting, overwhelming, and sometimes even paralyzing. But there is a fatal flaw in the logic that leads to all these fears.

The flaw is this: thinking that you had things in control in the first place! The truth is, you have never really known exactly what your future held anyway....only God knows that. The people around you, whether in court or with your own children, have never been fully predictable to you....but their lives, plans and decisions are an open book before God. As for love, nobody has ever loved you the way God loves you, and, if you are to be in a relationship again in the future, God can guide you to that person, just as He has guided you in other areas of your life. Financial disaster? The warning in the Hebrew Scriptures was that thinking we made our own wealth is a serious error, for it is God who gives us both the opportunities and the abilities to earn income. If you are fearful of losing your security, then you need to remind yourself that your security is in God, not in the things of this world. And certainly things <u>will</u> never be the same....but they never would have been the same, anyway, for life is full of changes and nothing ever gets fully repeated. If you are afraid of what people will think, then, again, your focus is in the wrong place....we are to be God-pleasers, not people pleasers. Jesus, Paul, Peter, Stephen...the believers in the New Testament lived their lives to be pleasing before God....what people thought of them paled in comparison.

And finally, you may feel like your life is spinning out of control, but it is merely spinning out of YOUR control....which you never really had, anyway (think about the last natural disaster you saw, did you control that?)....it has never been outside of God's control and power. He still sits on the throne, He still reigns, He still works, He still plans, He still redeems....God has not lost control of the universe, nor of your situation. Trust Him to be in control, not only of your situation, but yield also to Him the control of your life, your decisions, your future. If, indeed, God is your God, your light, your salvation, and the keeper of the birds of the earth, what is there of which to be afraid? God is bigger and more powerful than anyone or anything that could come against you in life. When the fears arise, then you arise, too, and remind yourself of the great God who speaks the assurance that you are worth more than many sparrows, you need not be afraid. Turn your fears into faith as you focus on the One who will make all things right in His time.

Day 89   Genesis 18:9-15

What do googly eyes and beagles have in common? Well, actually nothing....except to me. In the early days of my divorce, some of my friends were concerned for my emotional well being (and thank God they were!), and suggested I should get a new dog (the dog we had was left with my ex). Turned out that somebody had some little beagles, and I could get one for free. Since I had always thought those were fun dogs to have, I decided to take up that opportunity. That little puppy's love brought a special joy to me as she licked my face with her tail wagging as puppies do. I was choosing a name for her one day as I was driving my son to a school music festival a few miles down the road. I was thinking of the joy, the hope and the love she brought into my life, and was considering something like Hope as a name....which my son thought was ridiculous for a dog's name. Then he reminded me that I had always said if I got to name a dog, I would name it "Notspot". That way, if somebody asked the dog's name, I could simply say, "Well, it's not-spot" and have a demented little laugh!

So he and I began kicking around possibilities, and somehow ended up on the old "Who's on First" routine of Abbot and Costello, and I decided to name my beagle "what" so that if somebody were to ask, "What's your dog's name?" I could respond simply, "You are right! How did you know?" Same demented laugh, just a different punchline. However, I created a unique spelling of the word (which I'm not going to share) for when I have to write it down for veterinarians and such, but basically, to this day, my now aged beagle is named a form of "What," and my stupid joke persists. And I can never tell her name without remembering the day my son and I laughed ourselves silly with those potential dog names. And, as far as I can tell, my beagle has never really been troubled by her name.

Now googly eyes, that is another story. In the midst of the garbage of the divorce, one evening I took my daughter, a friend of hers, and her exchange student friend, and we went out for an evening of miniature golf. We had a lot of fun....especially since the exchange student had never done it before. Then we played a little skee ball....which my daughter loved....and ended up winning some stupid little googly eye things that you hang over your mirror in the car....at least, those were the prizes I received (not because I won....they gave me the leftover tickets they had won). Anyway, I have those googly eyes to this day, and they sit on the knobs of my desk, and each time I see them, I chuckle over the silliness of that evening of miniature golf. In a dark time of life, these two things brought smiles to my face, and pleasant memories to my heart. Memories that I still treasure to this day.

When God told Abram that he and Sarai would have a son, Sarai thought it was ridiculous, and laughed, since she was far too old to be raising any babies. As a result, the angel told them they must name the child "Isaac".... "laughter." That meant that every time they called their son in for supper, they were reminded of the day she laughed at the idea of having a child. Every time they wrote his name as they were teaching him to read and write, they surely had a smile come to their faces. With their child named, "Laughter," they would never forget the time they shared a laugh with God over something special He did in their lives. In these difficult days of divorce, when so many things can drag you down, I want to encourage you to find something outside of yourself to bring some joy into your life. It could be a pet, it could be special time with children, it could be a lot of different things, but find something. And then, once you have found or done that something, find a way to create a tag that you will always remember, something that can bring a smile to your face each time you encounter it in your daily life. There have been many times I have enjoyed the silliness of a dog named What, and the googly eyes. Those memories bring back a happy day in the midst of many difficult days. I feel like God has brought these moments of joy for me to remember when I sometimes need to be reminded of His hand. Make that same kind of opportunity in your life, something that you and God will be able to look back upon and laugh together over a shared joy.

Day 90   2 Kings 6:8-17

There are events we experience that are life changing….the kind of events that open our eyes to something we never thought possible, and, as a result, we never see the world the same way again. Today's scripture describes such an event in the life of Elisha's servant. He had always thought he understood how military engagements are structured. Perhaps there was a West Point or other military academy for Israelite soldiers of the day. In our time, those who study to prepare for military leadership often spend significant time studying things like the battle strategy of Leonidas, the conquests of Alexander, the overthrow of the Babylonian empire, the Trojan horse, the conquests of Napoleon, or the Battle of the Bulge to name a few. In those days, perhaps the course would have included the defeat of the Egyptians at the Israelite crossing of the sea, the conquest of Jericho under Joshua's leadership, the defeat at Ai—also under Joshua's leadership, perhaps Gideon's tremendous defeat of the Midianites. Surely it would have included the wonderful strategy used by David to defeat Goliath and thus, the Philistines. The lessons modern military students might learn would be the importance of protecting your flank, the dangers of maintaining a war on multiple fronts, or the fact that bomb raids alone will not conquer an enemy without the aid of troops on the ground to complete the task. But in those days, the strategy would have included things like when backing yourself into a corner by a sea, you can trust that God will open the way for you, or that you can defeat a city by marching around it for seven days and blowing trumpets....if that is what God tells you to do. He would also have learned from Gideon and David that military strength does not lie in numbers or earthly power, but in the power of God, and, from the battle at Ai that the servant fighting God's battles had best do things the way God describes.

Elisha knew these lessons. His servant didn't. But that day, he learned. He learned that God's army is mightier than any earthly force. And he learned that, just because he couldn't see how God was working, didn't mean that God wasn't working. I believe that this servant never saw the world the same way again. Every time he passed by a mountain, he must have wondered what kind of beings God had stationed up there. Whenever he saw a group of soldiers passing by, he must have peered at the road ahead straining to catch a glimpse of the angelic entourage accompanying the force. And he must have developed a different appreciation of God's direct involvement in the affairs of His people on a daily basis.

Your divorce will be one of those life changing events for you. You will be forever changed....even if you and your ex reconcile, you will never forget what you have experienced and learned in this time. Some of the lessons may be hard ones to learn, like the frailty of relationships, or the things about yourself that need to change. Some of them will be very encouraging things to learn, like the value of good friends or that God never abandons the one who truly seeks Him. You will see people who have been divorced, and may notice a pain in their eyes you had never seen before. You will realize how precious each moment you have with a child truly is, as there will be too many moments with them that will be denied to you.

So, how are your eyes being opened, not in a negative way, but in a way that causes you to see the hand of God in places you had never seen it before? How will what you are learning alter your perspective so that you will never again fail to see the way God is positioning His troops to fight for you? Lifechanging events are few and far between. Sometimes they can be devastating. Sometimes they can be faith building. The difference is often whether or not we learn how to see God at work.

THE SEASONS OF DIVORCE: WINTER

Will the beauty of life ever return? Will these dark days end? Supposedly the ancients actually believed that the sun was somehow dying as the days grew shorter, and feared that eventually there would be nothing left but darkness. In these hard and bitter days of life, you, too, may fear that soon nothing will be left for you but darkness and despair. Where there once was the warm feeling of love and the comforts of home, all too often there is a coldness that chills to the bone. Or maybe your home wasn't so comfortable and love was not what you experienced within its walls. But, in the midst of divorce, you have discovered that the process is much harder than you expected, more pain, more uncertainty, more loss, more impossible decisions to make….just more than you anticipated would come with a divorce.

While the ancients may or may not have feared that winter would stay and spring would never come, we understand today that winter is a function of the tilt of the earth and the revolution around the sun, and that spring will naturally follow as the earth continues in its orbit. During the winter storms of life, we feel emotions that may be difficult to handle or work through. We may desperately long for the warmth we once had in our lives. It can seem that the darkness is closing in around us. And yet….

Bitter though winter may be for those of us who live in places where the climate changes drastically, there are benefits that come through the nasty winter weather that we should not forget. For instance, the bitter cold impacts the life cycle of some of the most troublesome insects that spawn in our waters and soil. The moisture that comes with snow and ice is absorbed into our soil and water table differently from the rains that come in other times of the year, and so helps replenish the aquifer. There is a gentle soaking as the snow melts into our fields, lawns, gardens and ponds. And, as an uneducated fan of those flowers that grow from bulbs, it is my understanding that those beautiful tulips, jonquils, crocus and hyacinths need the dormant time of winter's cold to prepare them for the warming spring sun that signals their time to grow and bloom. Without winter's freeze, they would not bring their gift of spring beauty into our world.

So, as you pass through this winter storm of your life, realize that even in the cold, God's creative hand is at work. He will move you forward, whether rapidly or slowly, to a time when warmth and beauty will once again lift their heads in your life. There are good things He will accomplish that will require this hard time to prepare the beauty ahead. So bundle up, find warmth where you can, turn your head away from the bitter cold of the winds that are blowing, and endure your way through to springtime. But let me give you one more thought.

There are people....I am not one of them....who love the coming of winter and the snow piling up on the ground. While fully aware of the dangers that exist, these people don't focus on the treacherous icy roadways or the threat of frostbite. Instead, they haul out the sleds, the ice skates and the skis. They bask in the sunlight as they race down the mountain slopes. They boil the hot chocolate to enjoy when they come back from the sledding. They love the feel of the wind on their faces as the speed around the ice, laughing when they slip and slide across the glassy surface. And when they come back inside, hot chocolate in hand, they curl up with a book in front of a roaring fire, content with the wonderful day. It isn't that they don't experience the same harsh winter weather that I do. It's that they find ways to make something good happen out of the things that others find frustrating. In your winter, I want to encourage you to not only experience the hardships that come, but find a way to make something good out of the events. Maybe it will be capitalizing on the freedom to do as you please by taking a jaunt to a nearby town, or attending a movie, or calling an old friend you haven't seen in years. Don't merely trudge through the muck winter brings, ski some slopes as well. Don't let the external events dictate everything in your life; make some fun for yourself.

Day 91   Colossians 3:8-10

It is interesting to hear how those who observe the breakup of a marriage perceive the various interactions that take place. I have learned many years ago to be pretty careful about deciding whether one side or the other bears more of the blame. Many times I have heard people talking about marriages that are breaking up and explaining how one of the spouses has done this or that, but because of my more intimate conversations through counseling sessions, I had the awareness that sometimes the observers are clearly deceived since they didn't know a lot of the private details that I did. One time I heard about a divorcing parent telling the kids that the other parent was way too angry in the process. When I heard that, my immediate thought was that, *of course* the other partner would be more angry: that complaining ex had committed adultery multiple times, had abandoned the family, robbed the finances and left the family in an extremely vicious manner. OF COURSE anger is going to be a natural emotional response! Of course that partner might be more angry than the other....after all, who left whom?...who cheated on whom?...who stole and behaved badly toward whom? Although, it was kind of funny—I know both spouses, and the one making the accusations about anger acted in, from what I observed, a far more angry manner than the accused! It is actually hard for me to imagine that a spouse who would treat the other so evilly as they broke up their marriage, would honestly be baffled at receiving anger as the response to the bad behavior! Probably it was simply a ploy to get sympathy.

Maybe you are the one who has been making choices that intentionally inflicted pain in the life of your ex. And even if you aren't doing that, the process creates such friction, that to think there aren't going to be at least moments of anger is not very realistic. Some people just perfect the art of being angry, while others seem to land more in the realm of extreme sorrow and sadness.

The truth is, there is plenty to get angry about when you go through the divorce process. And quite frequently, one partner does suffer significant injustice at the hands of the other. Anger can cause us to do some pretty crazy things. And it can tie us up in knots inside as we simmer and stew, or plot revenge and nurse grudges. I don't know about you, but when I read this Colossians verse, I am amazed at how the instruction is so simple: put away anger, malice and slander. Like it is no big deal. Are you kidding? Obviously, whoever said that never had anything to be angry about! Oh, wait, Paul **did** have things to be angry about. He had people lie about him. He had people drag him to court over false charges. He had people verbally abusing him. He had people who beat him and who tried to execute him and who hounded him from town to town to town. Maybe he did have things to become angry about....maybe he wasn't so out of touch as we might think. Maybe he had learned that anger is a dead end street. Maybe he *realized* that he did NOT have the right or wisdom to judge others for their deeds, as he had once believed he did when he was headed to Damascus. Maybe he *realized* that he was better off spending his life nurturing the positive thoughts, feelings and moods rather than allow anger, malice and slander to take over his life. He says it is a matter of choosing to put them off. So, what have *you* realized lately? What do you want to hang on to? And what do you think it is time to lay aside for the sake of cultivating a better you for today and tomorrow?

MY PRAYER FOR YOU THIS WEEK

This week, I pray that the love of good and faithful friends will surround you. I pray that God will send the right people to you in the right moments of your life....even if those moments seem to you not to be the right ones. May you have the courage to reach out to them for help, for encouragement, for counsel and, most of all, for love. May those friendships become cherished treasures as you share with those friends this troubled time of life. Amen.

Day 92   Isaiah 30:15-17

It has been said that, in heaven, we will perhaps be most grateful for all the times God didn't give us the answers we sought from Him in prayer. At least, that's how I remember C.S. Lewis' writings....and others who think like him. I cannot explain why God makes the choices He does. I know there are scriptures that discuss the importance of praying in line with the revealed will of God so that we have assurance when we pray, and promises that what we ask in Christ's name will be granted by God. However, I also know that many times people of great faith and obedience have offered petitions to God that were not answered in the way that was requested. You have probably had that experience. I know I have. But today's passage is not about times when somebody didn't get what they asked in prayer. Rather, the people were so persistent in desiring things that were NOT what God wanted, that God told them He was going to let them HAVE what they thought they wanted. But the rub is, once they get what they think they want, they are going to find out it doesn't accomplish what they think it will accomplish. In fact, they are going to be very surprised and very sorry when God lets them have their way. They boldly announce they are going to speed away, and God replies that they will, indeed, speed away, but it will not be a proud moment. Instead, it will be a moment of fear, defeat and captivity. Not that it had to be so. It was so only because they wanted their way more than they wanted God's way. Does that ever describe you?

I believe that we have two options in how we handle our relationship with God, much like we have those same kinds of options in life experiences. People talk about those options in life experiences as learning things the easy way or the hard way: that if we are smart enough to learn from the mistakes of others, we don't have to suffer the consequences ourselves. In terms of our relationship with God, the wording may be phrased differently. It might be said that we can let God guide us as we make our choices, or we can insist on our own way until we beg for His guidance to get us out of our messes. It might be said that God's plan for our lives is the best, but if we are strong willed enough that we won't submit to His plan, He will let us experience the devastation our own plans bring. It could even be worded similarly to Paul's statement in 1 Corinthians, chapter ten: we can learn the lessons God wants us to learn from the teachings and examples of scripture, or we can learn them through the school of hard knocks and end up learning the hard way that the scripture was right all along. The difference, of course, is the level of guilt, shame, regret, unnecessary suffering and loss of valuable time.

You are in a situation where you will be making lots of choices. How will you handle the call to be a giving person? What about whether you continue to attend worship, continue to serve in your church? You will face questions about following God's guidance in jobs, family issues, responding to difficulties in the divorce process....lots of different arenas. Even consider the possibility of a future mate, will you submit to God's will as He reveals it to you as to whether or not you remarry? Will you accept scriptural restrictions on that relationship.... like whether you date only Christians, or the boundaries you set in dating in terms of private activities as well as public ones? And how will you decide God's guidance, or how to apply the scriptures to your own situation?

The key to all of it is, I believe, humility. "God, I am not going to insist on my own way, I will submit to whatever you desire, even if it means choosing a harder path than I would prefer walking." Don't insist on speeding away if God is telling you to stay put. Because if you insist long enough, God may just let you speed away....but He won't be pleased about it. And ultimately, neither will you.

Day 93   2 Corinthians 1:3-5

You are in the midst of a mess, very likely, or just come out of one. You may be wrapped up in a deep pity party. You may be depressed, barely able to get through the next week, the next day, or even the next hour. You may feel isolated, betrayed, useless and hopeless. And, hopefully, as you are turning to God for strength, you are finding Him responding in little ways here and there. Today, I want to challenge you to something very specific....I want to encourage you to begin allowing God to redeem your situation by letting Him use your experiences and learnings to make a difference in the life of at least one other person. You at least have this devotional book. You may have a verse God has given to you. You may have friends, a church family, a family of origin, or a support group that surrounds you and helps shore up your weakened being. But there is somebody around you who does not have those things, or does not have enough of them. God will get you through this, but not just so that you get through it. Just as He fashioned the awful execution cross into something that transforms the lives of those who believe, so He wants to fashion the awfulness of your experiences into something that He can use to touch the hearts of others. The only reason you have this book to read is that God has done that very thing time and again in my own life, and this book is one of those ways.

There is a great truth that can bring great encouragement and hope into the lives of believers. That truth is that there is nothing that can come into your life that God cannot use for His glory somehow. When we need comfort, He teaches us how comfort is administered, and infuses compassion into us for others who need comfort. When we struggle to find answers for our dilemmas, we find answers that can be helpful for others who are in similar dilemmas. There are things you will learn that, even though it may not seem like it now, will be helpful in future situations, things that will bring into your character abilities and insights that God can use and which, someday, you will come to appreciate. It just doesn't seem like it now. But if you pay attention, you will hear people around you say things that you realize you can relate to and will be able to assist. While it may not be your desire to have to learn what you are learning, or to go through what you are, it is some encouragement to know that all this pain, all this uncertainty, all this devastation will not be entirely wasted. God will find a way to use it, if you will give Him the chance by offering yourself as a vessel He is welcome to use.

Day 94   Isaiah 42:1-6

Today, just take some time to reflect upon the One to whom you are coming in this time of need: the gentle, merciful, loving God. That is not to say God is not also the God of vengeance, justice and might. He relates to us from that part of Himself which best meets the needs we are experiencing at the time. It is very likely that if not now, at some point in the divorce process, you will feel like that dimly burning wick, that bruised reed that is about to break. The image for Isaiah was for things that no longer were worth keeping, things that most people would have discarded. These things have become useless. You may feel that you are now useless. Useless because you have been rejected by a spouse, and therefore think you are defective and unlovable. Useless because you no longer feel effective with your children. Useless because at work you can no longer concentrate on the tasks at hand. Useless because you feel like your future has just disappeared. Useless because you think God cannot use someone who has been divorced….somehow you have come to believe that is the ultimate, unforgivable sin. But the characteristic of God that appears in this passage is that of the God who reaches down and tenderly nurtures, holds and restores that which is broken, fragile, useless by human standards.

Though your spouse has rejected you, God has not. Though your friends may distance themselves and reflect an awkwardness in your presence, God does not. Though some family members may even turn their backs on you, God will not. God comes into the brokenness you experience deep within, and gently, patiently will nurture you back.

Today, find some way to make time to just sit in the presence of the God who wants to restore you. Listen to some worshipful music. Sit in a sanctuary or watch a sunset. Open your Bible and read a Psalm or two. Or just sit and listen. Let the tears flow out if they need to. Let the rage find voice before Him. Whatever it is that for you will mean a few personal moments with God, make that happen. Imagine yourself as that little wick, as that bent and dying reed. Feel His hands tenderly take yours and hold you close. God is so near, even if you cannot sense His presence. In the fragile moments of our lives, in the midst of devastation, in the depths of despair and heartache, we can experience the personal ministry of God's Spirit to ours in a way that we experience no other time in life. Open yourself up to God's Spirit right now, and let what will happen with Him happen.

Day 95   Ezra 3:8-13

One of the hardest things for me with my divorce has to do with the changes that inevitably occur around special days and traditions. Thanksgiving, Christmas, birthdays, Father's Day, Mother's Day....all are permanently altered in a moment. You may have always celebrated Christmas on Christmas morning, but now, you may only get to see your kids on Christmas morning every other year. You may celebrate Mother's Day within certain time constraints, having to take your children back by a certain hour, if you even get to see them at all. And the sad thing is, you can never go back to what had once been the normal celebration. In all likelihood, you will never again celebrate Christmas the same way, and there may always be a twinge of pain at the loss of those traditions that mean so much to you. You are relating well to the elders in Ezra's day who wept at seeing how dramatically things had changed. No longer were they going to see the glory of Solomon's Temple, the gold was gone, the magnificence was gone.

But then, there were also the younger folks there with Ezra. They realized that, while the glory of the legendary temple was gone, they now had a temple again after all those exile years without one. And they began to dream, to hope, to imagine, and to plan. From now on, they could make the journey to Jerusalem for the annual festivals, and arrive at an actual temple for God....something they had never gotten to do before. That beginning of a temple that was built, was enhanced time and again, notably by the Hasmoneans and then, by Herod, to the point that the disciples in Jesus' day marveled at the temple… the temple that was the replacement, the temple that began with the elders weeping.

The point is this: while you, like those elders, may well be mourning the losses due to the dramatic changes that have overtaken you, don't forget to also dream, like the youths in that day. You have lost what was, but have also been given a clean slate opportunity to create what will be. And it is entirely up to you. A simple example from my experience was that at Christmastime, after my divorce, I no longer used an artificial tree, but instead made a new tradition of annual treks to the Christmas tree farm to select and cut our own tree. One of many NEW traditions I began to create. You have that same opportunity, to start some new traditions, to create some new memories. Real tree, or artificial? Thanksgiving turkey or ham? Celebrations at your home or at the home of the grandparents? Prayer requests included before Thanksgiving dinner and offered in a different way? Maybe even choose to make the way gifts are given a new tradition….by adopting a family in need, or focusing on handmade gifts, or spending gift money on some special mission need instead of presents at all. The possibilities are endless.

Day 96   Matthew 1:18-2:6 and Luke 2:1-14

Did you ever wonder how the Christmas stories ended up in the Bible? I mean, none of the disciples were there to witness these events firsthand. And none of the Gospel writers were there either. So where did they learn these stories? Some might say that God just revealed them to the writers. Well, I certainly believe God could have done it that way, and there is no evidence to say He didn't. However, there is a hint in the beginning of Luke's Gospel that suggests he did his research. Luke talks about the angels, the shepherds, and the arrival at the Temple with Anna and Simeon. Matthew speaks about dreams, the star, the wise men and Herod's slaughter of the babies. How did the writers end up with their different collection of birth stories? I wonder if it had anything to do with Mary and Joseph. Not that I am saying it did, but it's kind of interesting, isn't it? Maybe Mary remembered the angel speaking to her as the highlight of that time, while Joseph remembers his dream that led to their narrow escape into Egypt. And I can just imagine the two of them talking years later, laughing and remembering different parts of the story about the time Jesus was twelve and talking with the Temple leaders.

One of the things that divorce does is obliterate those shared memories. I can no longer turn to my spouse and ask, "Was my daughter's first word mama or ball?" Or any of the multitude of other details that come our way day by day. Of course I have my own memory bank with all of the special memories I have. But every once in a while I run across an item, or a picture, and I know it was given by somebody significant, or there was a good reason we had kept that picture....but I can't for the life of me place it. Even in my present marriage, we have an awareness that we don't share memories of when our children were born. We share memories from a certain point in our lives and the lives of our children. But we can't sit together and recall together the anxiety we had over our first born as a shared experience, but only as a private memory we share with one another. Perhaps you might want to journal memories now, as they come to you. Many of mine came as I was sorting out things like Christmas ornaments and school papers or pictures. The saddest thing of all in this is that memories that used to bring such joy, now have a bittersweet taste as the divorce takes its toll on my heart.

Day 97   Genesis 7:11-19; 8:6-12; 9:8-17

Perhaps there are times you feel like Noah, as if your whole world were flooding and you are being cast about from one stormy wave to the next. Today, I want to offer you some hope. The flood was certainly a terrible time....all the evil that led up to it, and then all that time sitting on the ship and waiting....Noah and his family certainly had a unique experience. Imagine, stepping off that ship into a world washed clean, all pristine with no civilization or sign of life around them save what they chose to make of it. And then the rainbow, that great sign of hope....the promise of God for the future.

There is also hope for a new world for you, after the floods of divorce subside and you begin, as they did, to pick up the pieces and start afresh. But what I want you to notice today is the hope. Noah was looking for hope. He sent out the first bird, but it returned without anything, restless to be back on the ark. The next bird also flitted about, but when it returned, there was a sprig in its mouth. And then, of course, there was the bird that simply did not come back, but went out into the newly washed world to start over, as soon Noah and his family would do.

The same kind of experience may be true for you these days. There may be days you look for hope, but all you find is restlessness, that the time is not ripe for your future, and you remain in the tossings and turnings of your ark. There may be days when you see a sprig. Something gives you a bit of hope. You see a smile on your face, or you think about making a job change. It may not yet be that your ordeal is over, but you catch a glimpse of hope. And then comes a time when, like that last bird sent forth, you have a sense that your future is just around the corner, that the time is quickly growing ripe. Or it may be a day when your own personal rainbow pops up, maybe in the sky, maybe somewhere else, and you realize God is still smiling on you and there is a tomorrow worth hoping for. Rejoice in your tidbits of hope, in the little sprigs that are brought your way, in the colors of the bow in your clouds. Everything may not be finished yet. You may not feel like you have come to a place of rest, or that you are ready to come out of your ark. But watch for and treasure the little pieces of hope, the little bits of sunshine, as promises of the tomorrow you cannot yet see. God is faithful. God will get you there. Trust. Receive. Rejoice.

Day 98   Luke 22:54-62

One of the hardest feelings to handle during divorce may well be the feeling of failure. Failed as a marriage partner. Will I also fail as a parent? Could I ever be a good enough spouse for someone? What did I do wrong? Sometimes those questions get taken clear to the point that we can convince ourselves that the success or failure of our marriage depended entirely upon ME. Or that since my marriage failed, then I am a failure in all the other areas of my life. Maybe the marriage did fail. But remember, just as it takes two to make a good marriage, it also takes two to make a divorce. Own your share of the marriage problems, but acknowledge the share that belongs to your partner. Or, for some people, it may need to be said, acknowledge the share that belongs to your partner, but also own your own share of the responsibility. But failures are not the end of the world. Failures always bring with them the opportunity to learn, and the opportunity to grow.

Perhaps nobody in the Bible felt more like a failure than Peter. I cannot imagine how he must have felt when he uttered his third denial that he even knew Jesus, only to see Jesus looking at him as the words came out of his mouth. Peter wept bitterly. He was so sure it would never happen to him, that all others might disappoint Jesus, but he never would. And yet he did. It even happened to him. Maybe that is your story, too. You knew lots of people who went through divorce, but you just knew you would never be there....it just wouldn't happen to you. And yet it has. Perhaps you, like Peter, have wept bitterly. I know I did. But today's scripture reading reminds us of something important. Just because we have failed at something, does not make us useless to God. Just because one area of our lives has fallen apart does not mean we are failures as people. As a good friend of mine once reminded me, we are more than just a person walking around with a big "D" engraved on our forehead....there is much more to who we are. And God is in the business of taking people, even with their failures, and accomplishing mighty things through them. After the resurrection, Jesus came to Peter and spent some personal time with him by the Sea of Galilee. We don't know what all was said, but we do know part of it, the part where three times Jesus made a point to let Peter know that He hadn't given up on Peter, that there was still a place for him in the leadership of the kingdom. People have done a lot of interpreting of that passage; here we merely focus on this simple act of restoration that Jesus did personally for Peter. And Peter came away, perhaps a bit more humble and less cocksure of himself, but ready to be used by God however God would lead. He went on to be one of the most significant leaders of the early church.

Today, I want you to hear the same thing that Peter heard after his moment of failure. Jesus wants to restore you. The Kingdom of God still has a place for you to serve. God has NOT given up on you, but because He is faithful, will stand by you through it all, and on into the next chapters of your life. Read the passage again, slowly. Let the tenderness, the encouragement, the kindness of Jesus sink into your troubled soul, and know that Jesus still loves you, and it is His desire to help, heal and restore you.

MY PRAYER FOR YOU THIS WEEK

This week, I pray for your choices. Many in your shoes make choices that are not honoring to God...I pray that you will not be numbered among them. There will be pressures to make choices based on expedience, angry emotions, greed and many other things....I pray that your choices will be made not because of pressure, but because of the teaching and guidance of God. Amen.

Day 99   Job 1:13-22

So, we think about Job once again. Can you imagine what Job must have felt. His house, his fortune, his children....all gone in an instant. Surely he must have been experiencing utter shock and disbelief. We know from the rest of the book that he just couldn't understand why all these things were happening to him. I'll bet he walked around in a daze as the reality of what all had happened began to sink in. Is any of that something you can relate to? Have you been dealing with times of shock? Maybe you feel you have been blindsided and walk around numb and dazed yourself. And, how many times have you asked yourself why? Why, God, is this happening to me? Why did I ever marry that person to begin with? Why didn't I see it coming? Why didn't I go talk to somebody? Why, why, why? The most amazing thing about the book of Job to me is that the dominant question of the book is WHY.... and yet.... Job keeps asking why all these things happened, and his "friends" keep explaining to him why they think it happened. And their suggestions only lead him into worse despair as he knows their answers are nonsense. Does any of that make any sense to you, too? In the midst of you wondering why it has all happened, have you had friends come in with their attempts at good advice or good explanations, only to leave you feeling more frustrated and confused than you were before they came by? I think Job's friends meant well, they just didn't know what to say, or what they really were saying. And probably you have some well intentioned friends in the same boat.

Anyway, back to the amazing thing. The dominant question is why, and yet God never explains to Job the WHY. Instead, along about chapter 39 and 40, God helps Job to catch a glimpse of WHO. A glimpse of who God is....who God REALLY is, and also a glimpse of who Job is, especially in comparison to God. Job is brought to the point that he realizes that God understands things that we simply cannot, bound as we are by space and time. And once Job realizes God does understand, he also realizes that it is okay that he doesn't understand. It is sufficient for Job that God understands, and since he believes deep in his soul that God is good, Job simply comes to the point of trust as he acknowledges that God can run the world as He chooses, and that God's way is indeed the best way. Then, Job comes out of his shock into a deeper level of trust. How about you? Are you still asking why? You may ask for a long time to come. But it may be more important that in this time of questioning, you gain a better understanding of who. Who God is, who you are, and who God designed you to become. Because when you really understand the whos, you can truly trust that the why is the best possible why of all....whether you understand it or not!

Day 100   1 Thessalonians 4:1-7

Let's take a day to talk about the opposite sex. Divorce brings up all sorts of feelings about the opposite sex. I remember thinking I would never get married again. That was a part of the painful and emotional struggles concerning women and marriage that I experienced just after my divorce. I have known a lot of others I have known who feel just the opposite. It's like they decide their problem was that they just had the wrong member of the opposite sex and everything will be great with a different person. A grass is greener sort of approach. And so, sometimes even before the gavel falls, they are in the arms, and maybe even the bed of another. They don't allow time to reflect on who they are, to heal up from their wounds, or even to think through how they got where they now are.

There are two central things I would like to communicate to you in this area. First, God has purpose for the opposite sex, and that may include a purpose for your future. You may feel anger or disappointment or even fear of the opposite sex, but it is important to realize that not every member of the opposite sex is like your ex, nor would they treat you as your ex did. Each person is a unique individual, with unique attitudes, abilities and desires….don't assume that every member of the opposite sex is the same; there are those who are completely different from what you have experienced.

Secondly, no member of the opposite sex can heal or fix you; finding that "perfect man or woman" will NOT solve all of your problems. Sure, the right kind of mate can make a huge difference for your life that can be incredible and valuable. It can be a wonderful feeling to have a member of the opposite sex who adores you, and the fun of a relationship can be exhilarating. But the issues that belong to you….and there are issues, for none of us is perfect….those issues belong to YOU. The solution for those issues is not going to be found by replacing your mate with another, nor by rejecting all members of the opposite sex. They are going to be solved when you examine yourself before God, perhaps with the assistance of a pastor, counselor, or trusted friend. Allow God to bring into your life the growth, maturity and change that He would seek to accomplish in this time. And, do your very best to keep godliness at the center of your attitudes and actions toward members of the opposite sex. If you follow these guidelines carefully, God can prepare you for whatever relationship with a member or members of the opposite sex awaits you in the future God will shape in the days ahead.

Day 101   2 Timothy 4:9-18

I was sitting at the computer one day, and my Siamese cat was sleeping on the bed. Now, let me first lay to rest any nasty rumors. I also own a beagle, and my wife has a dog and another cat. So I'm neither a cat person, nor a dog person….maybe just incapable of making a decision one way or the other. Anyway, now that I have laid that inane tidbit to rest, let's go back to my computer and cat. After sitting there a few moments, the cat got up and jumped into my lap, expecting me to pet him. Of course, I obliged for a few moments, and then turned back to writing. The cat was not impressed (they never really are, you know). The cat turned and rubbed his head against my chest, and then nestled up closely insisting that I wasn't done scratching his fur until he decided I was done when he'd had enough.

Of course, again, as the obedient house guest I am, I stroked his fur until he was content to go back to his own domain, part of which he allowed me to occupy a bit longer. And suddenly I was struck by something about cats in general that I think divorcing people can benefit from emulating.

My cat had the courage to come over to me, express his need for caring, and did not give up until his need was met. Sometimes when we are struggling in divorce, we need to have the courage to express to those who care about us, that we are in need of something. In other words, to just ask for help. Or for love. Or whatever assistance we need. In today's passage, even Paul asked for help! I remember a friend who was so struggling that she realized in the middle of the day that she hadn't fed her toddlers that day, and yet didn't feel she had the strength to do so. Instead, she called another family member and asked if they would mind coming over and making something for the toddlers to eat. Of course they were willing, because sometimes those who care for us want to help and want to be supportive, but don't know exactly how. A request like that gives them the opportunity to express their concern in appropriate ways. Or I remember a time when I was sorting through some of our more sentimental things, and was concerned I might not divide them with the fairness I desired, so I called a good friend and asked if she would be willing to come over and help me sort through those things. She did, and I felt much more confident about how that task went. It helped ease my conscience. And sometimes it may be simply telling a good friend, "You know, I could sure use a hug today."

I realize there is a danger in this, because I also knew a person who was so needy, that he just wore out his friends. I probably did, too. In fact, I know I did. And I thank God so much for those friends who were willing to give of themselves so generously when I needed them most. Perhaps the trick is not to put the entire load upon one person if you need something. But, remember what that friend of mine said: "If you believe that it is more blessed to give than receive, then if you don't let me give of myself, then you are robbing me of a blessing!!" So don't let those who care for *YOU* get cheated out of a blessing, just because you are hesitant (or maybe too proud) to ask for help.

Day 102   Proverbs 15:13; 17:22

One of the best suggestions I was given during those hard days was that I needed to do something fun for myself each day. Well, I don't think I did that very well….for a lot of reasons. However, I knew I needed to intentionally bring some joy in to counterbalance the hard things. For me, that meant taking time to read through my entire collection of "Peanuts" cartoon books. And "Far Side." Or, God blessed me with friends, good friends with whom I could enjoy some fun activities….a movie, a play, a museum, a soccer game….anything that was just something enjoyable in the midst of all the things I didn't enjoy. It was "good medicine" for a heavy heart.

What things brought a smile to your face in your past? Make time to include some of those things into your daily schedule. Something that can take your mind off all the hard things you have to deal with, and instead give your mind, give your stress, a rest. For some, it may be exercising by walking or jogging through scenic byways. It might be walking on the beach, or watching the sunrise or sunset. Maybe it is playing with the grandkids. One of my best things was always when I got to do something fun with one or both of my kids….a vacation away, miniature golf, whatever. But, I needed more than just fun with the kids, because the time with the kids also reminded me of all the other time I didn't get to be with my kids. If you had diabetes (maybe you do have), you would not think twice about the fact that you have been prescribed insulin to keep you on balance. Consider this your prescription for a heavy heart, the antidote you need to take, whether you feel like it or not, whether you want to or not….make a place for joy in your routine.

Day 103   Luke 11:9-13

Sometimes when one has gone through a divorce, there can be an overwhelming sense of, not only failure, but unworthiness and unlovableness. And when we feel those things, we can even attribute that attitude to God….as if God sees us as a failure, as no longer worthy to be in His presence, or as someone who cannot possibly be objects of His love. And, sadly, far too often good Christian people in good Christian churches reinforce those feelings by telling divorcees that they can no longer serve, or I have even known a person who was told that she was no longer welcome at her church until she remarried. I never did figure out what that was all about….it made no sense at all to me.

First, you need to do your best to distinguish between what people…. even God's people….may indicate by their behavior, and what it is that God Himself actually thinks. But let me ask you to consider a different perspective. If your child received an F in math at school, would you then decide that your child was nothing but a failure and give up on him? Or would you take her aside and give her a hug and encourage her to try again, or to celebrate the fact that she received an A+ in another subject? If he had been at little league, struck out every time at bat, and missed every fly ball that came to him, would you then lock the door and keep him from coming home, because he would no longer be worthy of being part of your family? I would hope not, although sadly, I know it happens. Or what if your daughter breaks up with her boyfriend, and he tells all her friends that she is simply an unlovable person, would you then decide they must be right and no longer love your daughter? Doubtful. Jesus' way of expressing this is found in the phrase, "If you, then, being evil, know how to give good gifts to your children, how much more will your Father who is in heaven give what is good…." (Matthew 7:11, NASB)

Just listening to those examples, even if our personal experience with our parents or children was different, yet deep down there is the awareness of what it OUGHT to be like….and that OUGHT is the reality of what God actually IS. Even if the child received the F by being disobedient and not studying when you asked them to, while you might be disappointed at the choice they made, you are not going to disinherit him. If only you can get deep down into your soul just how much God loves you, muck and all. When we say we love somebody, we realize that there may be some unlovely things about that person of which we are not aware….so we love them with some lack of knowledge. But when God said He loves you, He already knew everything there is to know about you…good and bad, lovely and ugly, past and present, successes and failures….and with that full knowledge He looks you in the eye from His place there on the cross and says, "I love you. Now, and forever."

Day 104   Psalm 147:1-6 and Revelation 21:3-5

If you are a person struggling with your divorce, feeling pretty down and out, or brokenhearted, then there in those blues, there are special promises for you. The one I want you to see today is that in a time of brokenness, God is nearby in a way unique to those times. It is when we are the most weak, that we most need His strength....and He knows that. It is almost as if God Himself knows that we need a hug. Can you imagine Him wrapping His arms around you, wiping your tears with His tender hand and offering you words of encouragement in your darkness. Can you imagine Him taking your broken heart and touching the wound with His healing hand? There is a tenderness about God that is most experienced in times like these. Today, I don't want to say much to you. Instead, I want you to take the time you would normally spend reading, and sit quietly in God's embrace. Weeping, praying, hurting, giving thanks....whatever is going on for you....let His embrace touch your broken heart today.

Day 105   John 6:52-69

We often hear all the stories about the times Jesus called to people and they left everything to follow Him. But this story is just the opposite. It is a story about a time when people responded to Jesus' teaching by choosing to walk away, and Jesus asks if His other disciples want to leave as well. Instead of asking if they'd follow, He asked if they'd leave. Peter has one of the most marvelous statements in scripture as his answer. And his answer reflects more insight than perhaps even he realized. After all, once you have experienced the touch of the Son of God, and the call to become His for all eternity in glory, what could compare? And yet.... there were those who walked away. Other New Testament scriptures also mention people who leave the faith. What would it take for YOU to abandon your faith?

You may well be in one of the toughest times you have ever experienced in your entire life. The pressures are great. You may feel like God has let you down. Or you may feel like being a believer doesn't do any good, because it didn't even save your marriage. Or maybe even feel like God deliberately misled you....maybe you prayed asking God to guide you before you got married, but then it fell apart anyway. Why would God have led you into that kind of a mess? This may be a time when it would be very tempting to just give up. Just walk away. Quit trying. Stop believing. Don't worry about living right, because it doesn't pay. Maybe just chuck it all and go have some fun for a while. There may be lots of opportunities around you right now that may look very tempting. Things like getting plastered or high just to escape and let off steam. Things like becoming a party girl or good time guy. After all, so many of those people seem to be having so much fun, while you are so blue. Why not go for it?

If you are feeling any of those things, let me suggest some alternatives. First, take Jesus' question to His disciples personally. In this time, visualize Him asking you, "Will you walk away, too?" Secondly, think seriously about Peter's answer....where WOULD you go? Jesus is the only one with the answers of eternal life....is anything else you might choose to pursue really worth jeopardizing eternity? You may say to yourself that it will be okay, you can always turn back later, Jesus will forgive you again, later. But do you really want to create rejection for Christ, after you are experiencing rejection yourself? In addition, think about the things you are considering running toward, what are they? Will they really result in what you think, or will they actually create more problems than you think? The glitter of the world never has the substance it pretends to offer. It always leads to hollowness, regret and disappointment. So again, in this time of great duress, will you walk away, too?

MY PRAYER FOR YOU THIS WEEK

This week, I pray that God will show you vistas. That looking across the horizons of your life will take your breath away, just like the first view in morning light of the splendor of the Grand Canyon. That you will see possibilities like the dazzling rays of the sun in the most glorious sunset. That the potential will appear as endless as the panaromic scenery from the top of Pike's Peak. May God give you a glimpse of the glories yet to come into your life. Amen.

Day 106   Hebrews 10:19-25

So yesterday, we examined the question of whether you will walk away in this time. Most of us would say (especially if you are a person reading this devotional), "of course I won't leave God....not me." And we truly mean it. However, it is not as simple a question as it would appear. In most of the divorces I have seen in the churches I have attended and served, it is almost the norm that at least one of the partners will end up leaving that church...hopefully for another....and often both partners just seem to drop out. Why is that? Well, if you are in the process of divorce, I suspect you can answer that question as well as I can. You know....the feeling that people at the church with whom you used to be so comfortable just now seem so uncomfortable around you....like they don't quite know what to say. Or how hard it is to sit in the worship service surrounded with smiling couples, often one partner with an arm around the other, while you struggle with the question of whether "family friendly" includes you or not as a family of one adult, regardless of the number of children. And when you go back to your church for worship, even walking in the sanctuary feels odd, because the seat you used to occupy with your spouse now feels so empty and awkward sitting there by yourself. In addition, if you happen to be attending the church in which you got married, just looking at the front of the sanctuary brings back so many overwhelming memories. What do you do?

Well, first I would suggest that the devastation you have experienced is a chink in your armor that Satan will be more than happy to attack in hopes of pulling you away from God and from the church. Satan will do his best to make sure you overhear somebody talking about how unchristian and irresponsible people are who get divorced. Or make sure you end up in very awkward situations where being alone just feels awful. Remember that just because you are getting divorced does NOT mean God has thrown you out of the ranks of His believers, so you are still a target for the attacks of evil. Since you have not been kicked out of God's church, then you are still an important part of the community of God and your role still matters even as it changes. However, I remember the feeling of the awkwardness well. In my case, I found myself not feeling comfortable sitting in the sanctuary as I had always done. Instead, my church had a little chapel at the back just off the sanctuary, and that chapel became a sanctuary within the sanctuary for me. I started sitting back in that chapel where there were a handful of people....families with young children who might need to slip out, individuals who for other health reasons needed to be mobile, some who knew they had to leave early and some, who like me, just simply felt more comfortable sitting there for who knows what reason. It took a long time for me to feel comfortable moving back into the sanctuary itself, so my little chapel of refuge and the friends I sat with back there was an important bridge in my clinging to the church I loved.

Perhaps you will need to make some other adjustments yourself. Like my chapel, your church may have a similar space you might try out. Or maybe you will simply move to a different part of the sanctuary. Maybe your church has other services that you could attend as you make your shifts. Or maybe there is a small group you could become part of to carve out your new niche. But the scripture is clear in its warning: do not forsake the assembling together. You may tell yourself, "It is only temporary, I'll just take a break for a few months and then come back later." But that is a dangerous choice to make. It is actually harder to come back to a church you have dropped out of than it is to start into a new church in the first place. Don't take that break....it can become habit, and that habit will lead you to disobedience as you DO forsake the assembly of worship. If you cannot make a place for yourself in your church, then perhaps your answer is to start afresh in another church....we'll talk about that tomorrow. But whatever you do, do not forsake the assembling. Awkward though it may be, uncomfortable as you may feel, don't quit....be faithful. Even when it is hard. Especially when it's hard.

Day 107   Hebrews 10:19-25

Let us pick up again where we left off yesterday. Let's assume you have committed yourself to not letting your worship and Bible study attendance diminish during this time. And yet it just doesn't feel the same, and you just can't seem to sense God's presence anymore during worship. (If this doesn't apply to you, read it anyway, we'll talk about the rest of you another day.) What can you do? The key thing is not so much WHAT you do, as HOW you do it. That is, you may decide you need to start afresh at another church. If so, do it in a healthy way, not slinking out the back door. Here are my suggestions for your consideration. First, remember, this church has had meaning for you and is (hopefully) a significant support network for you....be very careful in considering casting it aside. One of the things you might try is to attend different church activities than you have done before as a way to carve out a new niche: a different worship service, a prayer meeting you neglected before, a different study group, or even just a different location in worship.

But real life is that for many of us, and for many different reasons, we just cannot find another niche into which to fit. Then there is a second level: maybe this is the opportunity God places in front of you to CREATE that new niche. That is, there may be other people in your congregation who just don't feel like they fit in very well (odds are very good that there are), and maybe you can be the instrument to start a group where you and they can belong. Maybe a new Bible study group. Maybe a divorce recovery group. Maybe a singles club. Maybe a prayer warriors time. Maybe a dinner out after church group. There are lots of ideas. If you are feeling these things, BEFORE YOU DECIDE TO LEAVE, I want to encourage you to make time to talk to two people. First, visit with another person in your church who is single or divorced, and ask them if they ever felt the same thing, and how they handled it. Get their advice, their insight. I have seen people end up being best friends just because of this kind of commonality. Secondly, visit with your pastor or whoever is the appropriate church leader. Tell them how you feel, tell them you are considering moving to another church, have the open conversation so that if you leave, you can leave with the blessing of the church leadership, rather than the awkward embarrassment of simply disappearing. If you end up moving to another church, you will then be able to do that without guilt or feeling like you let somebody down. And if you end up moving to another church, please remember....it simply will not be the same as your previous church.... don't expect it to be. And don't expect that it is all their responsibility to make sure you feel welcomed. You take some initiative to show up at some of the events or small groups and meet the people to build your new support group. I know there may be a temptation to just disappear into a big church where you can be anonymous, and, temporarily, that might be helpful....but God didn't plan us to be anonymous. Not only do you need other people, there may be a person there who desperately needs what YOU have to offer. Fulfill your part of the body to the best of your ability at this time, wherever that part may lead.

Day 108   Psalms 41:4-13; Zechariah 13:7; and Matthew 26:30-32

When you read the story of the passion of Christ, one of the prophecies is the one you have just read. It refers to Judas Iscariot, the disciple who had traveled with Jesus, who was trusted with the money they used, and who ultimately turned Jesus over to the authorities for 30 pieces of silver. When it was penned, I suspect David wasn't thinking about a someday prophecy so much as he was thinking about his own son, Absalom, and his accomplices who had rebelled against him. (This is called double fulfillment, and occurs many times in scripture.) But it makes no matter. Either way, the story is one that is a common theme in human experience: individuals you trusted, individuals you considered friends, even intimates do not always remain true. In fact, it is such a common experience that the psalmist warns us against trusting in princes….in fact, in any human….because people can and do let you down. Perfect faithfulness is the attribute of God alone. And yet, it does hurt, to think that somebody so close can turn into a Judas.

There is a wonderful song by Michael Card that addresses the issue of betrayal with the line that only a friend could ever come so close to cause such pain. And that is true. Nobody else could hurt you as much turning against you as not merely a friend, but even a spouse. Someone with whom you trusted your secrets. Someone with whom you built a home, a life, a dream. Someone you pledged to stand beside for the rest of your life, as they pledged to you also. But now…. Now, you have a different, perhaps more intimate insight into what Jesus suffered for you. You also have a deeper insight into the scripture that says He can sympathize with our weaknesses because He has been tempted just like us. He, too, understands the intense hurt. He understands the anger, the desire for revenge. He understands the feelings of failure, of disappointment, of rejection….and you understand His. Except you don't understand really….your sorrow is just a hint of how much it must have hurt to come to your own creation, and to your own specially called people for the purpose of showing them how much God loves them….only to have all the world turn against Him to the point of viciously torturing and killing Him. While your ex may, indeed, have rejected you, I doubt that you have experienced the level of rejection that Jesus did….and, in fact, that He continues to experience from people in our own day. But for today, know this: Jesus really does understand. He understands at an intensely deep level. And so pour your heart out to this One who knows exactly how you feel, the One who went through rejection Himself, but came out victorious on the other side….just as He will help you to do if you let Him in.

Day 109   2 Samuel 10:1-5

One of the things you might need to face, is the issue of pride. You may not want to hear it, but the truth is, one of the things that hurts most in your divorce is, that it hurts your pride. You may have been proud of the kind of wife or husband you were. You may have been proud of a stable marriage while others around you were falling apart. You may have been proud of how well life was going. Or you may have been proud of how hard you worked to make your marriage work. And there is nothing wrong with taking pride in one's work, one's character, one's accomplishments. Unless excess pride takes up residence in you, because the Bible clearly warns of the dangers of pride. Foolish pride can cause us to boast unrealistically, and to do things we would never do if we were thinking straight….and that can set us up for failure. Even if you aren't a proud person in the sense that the Bible refers to in these instances, it is your pride that gets hurt when your spouse rejects you, when you feel like you are a failure as a spouse, and when you feel like the most important relationship in your life has fallen apart. It hurts your pride. And you feel the embarrassment of "being a third wheel" in various social settings. Again, as a friend of mine said: "You may feel like there is a scarlet "D" branded on your forehead, even though there isn't." But your pride being hurt is not necessarily a bad thing. I remember so well that person who said to me, in reference to a couple she had seen getting divorced, "but for the grace of God, there go I." That is a statement you will no longer make….at least in this case. You have been forced to face the fact that you, too, are a fallible person in a frail, fallible world. And that creates for you an opportunity.

One of the promises of scripture is that God opposes the proud, but gives grace to the humble. You have been humbled. Maybe until this point everything in your life was going great....according to the world's standards. But now, you have come face to face with a failed marriage. Regardless of who is at fault the most, it is a very humbling experience. To see things like your name in the paper, or to have people into your transitional home, or to feel some days like you are such a basket case.... these are very, very humbling. Just like the men in our story today, but God cares tenderly for the humble, just as David was careful to protect these returning men. God makes plain in scripture that humility, not pride, is the virtue. In fact, pride is one of the seven deadly sins of old. And humility is one of the seven heavenly virtues! But humility means you are acknowledging your own failure, your own lack of strength, your own lack of perfection, that you are a person who could use some help from God. And that is the best place in the world to be....because only the people who know they need help ever seek help from God. The neatest thing of all in it is this: God delights in helping, in giving grace and strength to people who are humble. Yes, you may have been humbled....count that a blessing, and start seeking the hand of God who delights to come to you in this time.

Day 110   Luke 19:1-10

Today, I want to address forgiveness from another angle. If you are the one who feels wronged because your spouse has left you, cheated on you, filed against you or otherwise bears the responsibility for the divorce, then you need to understand some things about how God views these things. But if you are the one who is on the other side of that fence....that is, you know that the breakup is due to choices and actions of your own, then this lesson will especially speak to you.

If you are carrying a load of guilt due to actions that have led to your divorce, you may be asking yourself whether there is any hope. You may carry a heavy load of guilt, as you see the devastation you have brought upon your family. Many a person has stepped out into the world of divorce it was going to solve all their problems, only to find that the grass was not greener after all, but that the choice resulted in creating more problems than it solved and complicating even the most simple pieces of daily life. And maybe you have even come to believe that God can not possibly forgive you. I have known of people who have pointed out that such an attitude is, actually, pride. That you and your wrong are bigger than God, and that you know better than God whether or not He can forgive. In fact, you have placed yourself above God, because you have determined that what is and is not forgivable is yours to decide, not God's!!!

The first thing you need to recognize is that God is God, not you, and God is the only one who has the right to decide what can be forgiven and what cannot, to decide what is just and good, and to decide to whom He wants to show mercy. God. Not you. Not me. God. So the first thing you must decide is whether you are going to acknowledge that these questions are in God's domain, or whether you are going to somehow usurp God's authority in your life and decide for yourself what God is and is not able to do regarding YOU.

Assuming you are willing to acknowledge that the choice on forgivableness is God's, the next issue is to examine your own guilt. Plenty of people try to tell us these days that we shouldn't feel guilty. But the truth is, when one is guilty, OF COURSE they feel guilty, guilty is what they are. Maybe that is you. You know you are guilty, and you feel it intensely. One of the most incredible statements of Jesus is found in Luke 19:10, where He says that He did not come to call the righteous, but sinners to repentance. If you are aware that you have sinned, the good news is this: you are in the category of people Jesus came to call. If you have not done so yet, take time today to come before your Heavenly Father as that son in Luke 15's Prodigal Son story did, asking God to forgive you for the wrongs you have done. God promises He will do so. Now there may be more to it than that. The son in the story could not undo what he had done….the money was squandered, never to be his again. It may be that you, too, will not be able to undo damage you have done. You may need to ask forgiveness not only from God, but from those you have wronged, and in some cases, that may even mean you and your ex starting over to give the marriage another chance, in other cases, it is already too late for that. But the apologies may still be the path you must take as part of your return to the Father. Forgiveness is ours when we honestly seek it in repentance before God.

Day 111   Luke 15:11-32

Let's reexamine today's passage from a perspective that may be different than you are used to: that of the son, and what he expected would happen. He knew that his actions had created most of the mess he was in. He knew that he should have listened to his father in the first place. He knew that he deserved whatever punishment or lack of consideration his father chose to give him after he had wasted all his inheritance. What he didn't know, though, was what his father was really like.

Today, what is it you know? Maybe you actually feel like God doesn't want you. After all, your marriage has "failed." Or you didn't come to Him when things were going well, why would He want you now that things are falling apart? Or maybe you have decided that God is like your spouse….loves you to a point, but now is ready to give up on you. You really wonder if God can possibly love you, with your life all screwed up, and your hopes all dashed, so in your brokenness you are convinced you are worthless. How amazed that son must have been when he didn't even get the chance to give his prepared speech to his father, because his father was so excited to have his son back, he ran out to meet him, brought him a new robe, the family ring, prepared a feast, celebrated exuberantly over the restored relationship he now had with his son. The son had no idea that his father was that kind of person. He had concocted the idea that his father was a taskmaster, who might grant him a job, but would never forget how his son had squandered the opportunities given to him.

I do not know how you are feeling today. Nor do I know how you are feeling about your relationship with God or your sense of responsibility for the marriage you have lost. No matter what the case in regard to those issues, I would like today to help you enlarge your vision of God. It may even require you closing your eyes and daydreaming a bit, seeing in your mind's eye an image of a father, running out to meet his son with gleaming eyes, profuse kisses and great joy….and in that daydream, realizing that you are the one God is celebrating! It may be you have wandered so long and so far, or are so deep in despair that you have no sense that God notices or cares. As a father myself, let me assure you, you never forget your children. When they make mistakes, when they misbehave, when they yell as teenagers are prone to do, even if they turn you out of their lives…the fact remains….there is always a special place in a father's heart for his children….confused though they may be. You are in the Father's heart….always….even when you know you are far away, and even when, among the pigpens of this life, you feel absolutely alone and unlovable. Spend some time soaking in the depth of God's love for you as you read once again this marvelous story of a father, running with joy to meet a troubled son.

Day 112   Mark 10:17-22

In this midst of all the circumstances in which you find yourself, there are lots of opportunities for examining your life....sometimes it seems like TOO many! Of all the things Jesus did, perhaps the most profound was the way He challenged people, no, almost forced people to examine themselves. He let no one get away with self-deceit. Time and again, He made people uncomfortable as He challenged their self complacent lives....and He knew they were better off having had the chance to confront themselves than they would have been to go on with their lives of deception. When so much of your life feels like it is falling apart, as often accompanies the experience of divorce, God can use that time to help you confront yourself in ways that you might have just let slide by without this tragedy. If you can, take a moment now to look at yourself in your mirror....to really look.... not just at the outside, but what you can see deeper within. And I want you to consider some questions.

First, have you truly given your heart, your life to Christ? Do you really believe that your eternal salvation is secure, because you know that your sins have truly been forgiven through the blood of Christ? What about that commitment, when you gave your life to Christ, what did you promise? Have you been faithful to that promise? Is there something that you know God has asked of you at some point in your life, and yet you didn't do it? Maybe there was a time you thought God wanted you to go into pastoral ministry. Or maybe to work with teens as a youth leader at church. Maybe you have longed to go overseas, to help someone in need. Or maybe you have always thought it'd be rewarding to work at the local soup kitchen. Or maybe it is a more personal issue that you have neglected....like not being as faithful in your giving as you know God desires of you, or not being as regular in church attendance as you think you'd like, or maybe you just don't spend time alone with God you want to spend. Is there some way that you know God wanted to use you....at least at one time in your life? Look long and hard. Have you been completely faithful to what God called you to be? Now, you have an opportunity, unencumbered by the wishes of a spouse, to revisit your commitment to God. Granted, your finances may be creating some limitations....such as not being able to afford an overseas mission trip. Or as a single parent, you may feel you have even less time to spend alone with God. Surely, this time of life changes does have its impact. But that is no excuse to avoid taking a serious personal inventory of your life with God. Look hard. Find an area where you are willing to take on a challenge that you know God desires for you. Turn this time into an opportunity for growth. Don't make the mistake the rich, young ruler made....don't walk away from the challenge God has for you at this time.

MY PRAYER FOR YOU THIS WEEK

This week, I pray that God will help you to learn, experience, and embrace contentment, as Paul learned that secret so many years ago. May contentment keep you in tune with God no matter your situation, and may contentment be yours as you look to your future. Content whether single, or divorced or remarried. Content whether financially secure or struggling. Content with all that God has allowed into your life, trusting that God does have your best interest at heart. May contentment override all temptations to complain, to dwell on self pity or to despair. Amen.

Day 113   Acts 16:16-27

Nobody likes me, everybody hates me, think I'll go eat worms. Hors d' oeuvres anyone? Everywhere you go, there are people smiling. It may seem like every song you hear describes someone in love. Every place you look, there are happy families, husbands and wives who love each other while making enough money to live comfortably. And then there is you. You may feel like life is falling apart. You may feel like a total outcast. You may be in a mood where everything for everybody seems so much better than anything in your life. Of course that is not true, but it still may be how you are feeling. Which is okay, but it can become consuming. You can sit around moping, feeling nothing but how bad YOUR life is and how much better everybody else has it (which isn't actually true by the way), and how all your dreams are now shattered and you have nothing to look forward to. But is that really what you want to dominate your life? I understand those feelings.... it IS a tough time....don't think I am saying it isn't. But those feelings and thoughts can become a vortex if you let them. You have to balance them with the opposites of your life....and there are opposites.

Get a pen and paper, and make a list. Is there a roof over your head? Does your heat or air conditioning work? Is there food in your refrigerator? Do you have a friend? Do you have a Bible? Does your heart still pump blood? Can you see? Can you walk? Can you hear? There are a lot of things in your life that are still good and functional. Parents, children, job, bank account, health, church, your country, whatever those things are, you need to make a point to focus as much time on what is *right* in your life as you do those things that are painful and troubling just now. Make that list. Find the things that are good. Make the list. Add to the list. Don't just focus on the things that are hard, painful or wrong. Find those things in which you can take joy, and then rejoice in them. Remember, Paul and his companions were very likely in worse shape in Philippi than you are now....and they sang songs of praise, because they were unwilling to only see the prison bars and the wounds of beatings. They also considered the God they served, the salvation He offered, and the strength He gave. Can you find a song to sing, as well?

Day 114   Joshua 1:5-9

This is one of the great scriptures in the Bible. What a promise! What a challenge! Do you manage to meditate on the word day and night? Is it what you wrap your life around? Or, do you squeeze in only a few minutes here and there? There is such a promise here, if only you will make the scripture a priority in your life, then God will make sure your way is successful and prosperous. Guaranteed. Now, perhaps we should take a second to define these terms. To succeed and prosper from God's perspective may not be the same as the world's, or maybe even what you yourself think. It doesn't mean every time you have to go to court you will win. Nor does it mean you are going to be the CEO of some Fortune 500 company. It may not even mean that you have that lovely house out in the 'burbs. It means that you will have a life that is successful because the goals you are aiming at are godly, not worldly.

I think of Jesus' challenge in Mark 8:38, where He asks what profit there is in acquiring everything the world has to offer, but then losing your own soul eternally. That certainly must play in here. The word translated "prosper" is the root word "shalom" in Hebrew, which means peace, prosperity, wholeness, well-being….a whole bouquet of blessings. You will succeed and you will prosper because you will be taking on the tasks that you know are what God wants you to do, and so you will not be doing those tasks alone. Tradition has it that Isaiah was executed by being sawn in two and Peter was crucified upside down. The scripture tells how David won conquest after conquest, building a significant empire, and then his son, Solomon, was king of an empire wealthy beyond anything on earth. All of these prospered and had success, whether it seems that way to us or not. Because they were seeking to do what God called them to do. Except maybe Solomon. Although he did many great things and God used him in many ways, he later allowed himself to be distracted by worldly influences, so that by the end of his life, he seems to have lost track of where he had started.

But for our purposes, the point is that being successful and prosperous is not measured by possessions. It is measured by assurance of God's hand and blessing upon you. It is measured by looking back, as Paul did in 2 Timothy, and knowing that you have lived your life following Christ to the end, fulfilling the purpose for which you were placed here on earth. So many people seem so lost, not ever knowing what their lives were really about. Don't let the world trick you into thinking that success and prosperity are measured by the glitz that is projected in the media. I hear story after story of people who are rich, famous and powerful, whose personal lives are a disaster, don't you? I wouldn't trade places with any of them. So rest assured, God will make sure you are successful with the things that matter. You might remind yourself of what those are, by reviewing the Lord's prayer in Matthew 6—daily bread, or further down in the chapter where He warns against fretting over clothing and food. Ah, to be at peace in the midst of your upheaval. To know that God will give you that sense of satisfaction of knowing it has all been worth it. Doesn't that sound good just now?

Well, the primary purpose of today's devotional is to challenge you to make sure you are sowing the seeds that will get you there. Those seeds, according to the scripture, are sown first by time spent really wrestling to understand and know the teachings of the word. Night and day? To me, that implies it is the first thing you dwell on in the morning, and the last thing you think about at night. I have even heard of folks who always end their day by reading aloud a scripture verse to reflect upon as they fall asleep. But, realistically, how can you do your work and daily chores if you are off meditating on scripture? You can't. But then, you aren't told to. It says nothing about leaving all your responsibilities and getting away off somewhere to meditate. In Deuteronomy 6, the challenge is to reflect on scripture when you walk and when you sit, when you leave and when you arrive, in your home or out of it.... Everywhere, the word is to be with you. You might object that you cannot take your Bible with you to work to sit and read it. Later on, I will give you some tools to help you in this very area.

Day 115   Matthew 5:4 "You're blessed when you feel you've lost what is most dear to you. Only then can you be embraced by the One most dear to you." (The Message Bible)

I ran across this verse in the Message Bible the other day. It's really striking, isn't it? It talks about being blessed in the loss of something precious....that is not what we would normally say at all, is it? It surely doesn't feel like you're blessed. Instead, it feels like the blessing was when you HAD what was most dear, not when you LOST it! And what would be more dear than losing a spouse you had once loved....maybe even still were in love with up to the day they filed for divorce. I know I didn't want a divorce, and I didn't believe that is the way to solve the problems in a marriage. I believed the obligation of marriage vows is that you do everything possible and make it work, because the vow was for better or worse. But staying in a marriage requires the decision of two people, not just one. So a divorce may very well be the time when this verse applies to you....you lost your spouse, perhaps a significant portion of the time with your children, your marriage, your home, your financial security, perhaps a hunk of your retirement funds, perhaps your church home....have you lost something dear to you? Perhaps what you have lost is what you have held to be the most dear in this world. That loss may have impacted you so severely, you have fallen into a deep and painful grief. Mourning. Not just the Bible, but Jesus Himself uttered the very words that you are blessed in that circumstance. Not because of the loss, but because of the opportunity that loss creates: the opportunity to be comforted by the Almighty.

In your life, when you had times that brought tears, who have you turned to for comfort? I remember a time when my current wife was going through a tough time in her divorce process, before we were even dating. I was beside her when things just overwhelmed her and she started crying, and I literally said to myself, "this woman needs a hug." I was concerned about giving mixed signals at that time, but I felt she so needed a shoulder to cry on, and so I gave her a hug and let her cry. But she is a woman of faith. I was there at that one moment, but her real comforter was her Savior. And, if you know Jesus as your own, He is your real comforter as well. This time of loss has created an opportunity for you to draw close to Him and to let Him wrap His arms around you. It is an opportunity for you to sit before Him and let your tears flow upon His shoulder as you pour out your heart to Him. An opportunity to experience the tender compassion and care of God. Simply having that opportunity is a blessing, because you can experience God in an intimate and special way you will experience at no other time. And it IS a blessing, because being embraced, comforted by God, is one of the greatest blessings any human can ever experience....perhaps second only to experiencing salvation and forgiveness in Christ Jesus.

Day 116   Acts 6:12-7:22

What a story of courage and faith. Here is Stephen facing trial and needing to offer his defense. And he has to offer that defense before the great theologians and religious leaders of the day, many of whom knew the books of Moses word for word memorized. Stephen has the audacity to use the very scripture they know as his defense for his belief in Christ. How in the world could he have done that? If he got the facts wrong, they would have called him on it instantly. But no one does. Because he recounts the story accurately. How? I believe it is because he did exactly what Joshua 1:8 said...he immersed himself in the scripture, and did so in such a way that, when he was under the gun, he could access the scripture for instant use.

I would suggest that the best way for the word to always be there for Stephen or for you is to memorize scripture. I would encourage you to memorize some verses to build up your storehouse so that when you face *your* trials, you will have plenty to access. I would encourage you to begin right now, while you are really sensing a need for God's strength, for this could be the most opportune time to do so. When you do, the Spirit has a tool always ready for use at any time right there in your heart, in your memory. Ah, but you may think you are not able to memorize verses. One question and two suggestions. First, can you complete the following: Twinkle, twinkle _____? Of course. Why? Because you repeated it so many times that it became familiar. That can work for Bible verses as well. The suggestions are that you don't worry about memorizing Bible verses, instead, find one verse or one passage that is important to you and then just concentrate on memorizing it….just one verse at a time is sufficient. And, secondly, place it where it is a regular part of your day. My wife keeps a special verse on the inside of the medicine cabinet, so every day when she goes to brush her teeth, there is that special verse that speaks power to her. Do something like that, and just concentrate on making it a part of your daily meditation….and then God can use that dedication to speak to you and guide you toward the success He has planned for you.

Now, let me be clear. This challenge has nothing to do with you being able to impress people with how many scriptures you know, nor to make you into super-Christian who is more holy than everybody else. It also isn't so that you can become the instant answer person for everybody's problems because you can quote all the appropriate verses. This challenge is for only one purpose….to be a tool to enhance your relationship with Christ by saturating yourself with His word so that He can teach you, guide you, speak to you and reveal Himself to you no matter where you are or what you are doing. If that's not enough, you might want to read Psalm 119:11 as another good reason. May God take whatever passage is meaningful to you, that you adopt as your challenge today, and press it dearly upon your heart in such a way that the voice of God speaks through it to you. For what it's worth as an encouragement, many of the verses that are being used in these devotionals are ones that God has used in my own life to speak to and guide me, in part because some were memorized. You CAN do it, and God WILL bless you in your efforts.

Day 117   Romans 8:26-39

This is an important passage to have as a foundational truth throughout this devotional, as well as during this tough transition time of your life. Go back and read the passage again. Death. Life. Angels. Principalities. Present. Future. Powers. Height. Depth. Nothing created. That's a pretty exhaustive list, isn't it? In fact, as I read it, the only thing I can think of that doesn't fit in those categories would be God—Father, Son, Spirit. But even God could be considered to be in some of those categories.... Heights, powers, present, future. What can you think of that does not fit in these categories? Think about some other things that you might want to list, and examine to see if they are possibly excluded... some things that might be very real to you right now. For instance, how about divorce? Or your ex? Or the heartache you feel? Or the court? Or the judge? Or loneliness? Or separation from your kids? Or depression? Or moving to a different house? Or....I suspect you can think of a whole bunch of other things that right now might be making you feel like God is far away. But the truth is, nothing can separate you from His love. Nothing.

In a time when everything in your life feels transitory, shifting, uncertain, maybe even like it is collapsing, it is important to remember that there is one thing that is NOT changing, and that is the fact that God loves you. Some of your relationships are falling apart, or are feeling strained, and you may not know exactly how it all will turn out. But there is no strain on God's love for you. Nothing can alter it. Nothing can faze Him. Nothing can make God change His mind about loving you. You may do things that keep you from experiencing that love, or that cause you to question it, but that is about you, that is not about Him. He is constant. His love endures forever.

Today, I want you to just soak that fact into your spirit. Read the passage again, slowly, listing for yourself things that are in each category....and hear the message that none of these things can separate YOU from the love of God in Christ. And after that, go back to Psalm 136 in a translation that uses "steadfast love" or "lovingkindness" as the translation of the refrain, rather than "mercy". And then, end your session with John 3:16, followed by going back to Romans 8, but this time focus on 8:32. Do you get it yet? Feel free to reread this devotional as many days as you would like, because the bedrock of your life needs to be the assurance of God's love.

Day 118   Ephesians 3:16-19

Let's go back to the concept of the love of God for you. Does this passage remind you of what we considered yesterday in Romans 8? Here, Paul prays for the Ephesians, for the readers of the letter, which includes you. In that prayer, his desire is that God would enlighten your heart to be able to comprehend the incomprehensible....the love of Christ. You may feel like this is overdoing it, but if you are going to come through your divorce experience closer to Christ than when you entered that process, it needs to begin with a broadening of your understanding of God's love for you. Especially if you are feeling unlovable right now.... which so often happens in divorce.

Today, I want you to do something very tangible to imprint your soul with the vastness of God's love. If you live near the ocean, then go to the beach when you can spend a few minutes there. If not, I want you to go where you have a decent view of the sky. In either case, study the horizon. How far do you think it is to that horizon line? Do you think the ocean ends there? Or the sky? If you could go over to that horizon line, wouldn't you see that the sky and ocean extend to the next horizon line? I don't know how many times you could do that before you'd reach the opposite shore of the ocean, but whatever it is, that is only a fraction of the breadth of the love of God *for you!* Tonight, if you can, go out where you can see the stars. Look up toward the stars....how far do the astronomers say those stars are? And as you look at the stars, look to see if you can see the edge of space out there....the point at which the universe ends. You know, as well as I, that you cannot see it, because it is described as infinite. Select one star and focus your attention on it. While staring at that star, let that begin to make you realize the image of the height of the love of God, because the distance to that star is but a fraction of the height of the love of God *for You!* My prayer is that the Spirit of God will well up within you to impress upon you the greatness of God's love for you, the immenseness of it, the awesomeness of God's love. If only you can catch a glimpse of this truth, you will be able to trust this same God during all the dark and difficult days ahead. God really does love you. Don't forget it.

Day 119   2 Kings 6:8-13

It is a weird feeling being in a separate home from your spouse after years of marriage. Especially when you have kids. So much goes on in their lives outside of your purview. And the inconsistencies of standards between one home and another can drive you nuts if they exist. "Dad lets me drive by myself." "Mom never makes me go to bed before 11:00." There is also an odd experience of being excluded from the life of a person with whom you have shared years together previously. Then there is the flip side of it....feeling like everything you say or do in your own private space is no longer private, like your ex is now trying to find out what is going on in your life. All too often, the children end up being used as spies, or feel like they are. "So what did you do at your dad's this weekend?" "Who is that man I saw leaving your mother's house the other day?" And you try to make plans for vacations or holidays, maybe even buying birthday presents, and no longer feel that it is just between you and your children. Now you have to take into consideration a schedule at the other house or with the other side of the family, a schedule of which you are not informed. You may begin to make plans, only to discover after the fact that your kids are tied up with plans made by the other family in the very time slot you were using. Kids often end up in situations where they have to negotiate to keep both sides content, a situation that may actually be impossible. Sometimes these invasions are done with malicious intent, sometimes done as an act of revenge, sometimes just by happenstance, but regardless of the cause, things that once were simple are now suddenly complicated. And a person who has taken on the role of an adversary intrudes into so many aspects of your life, an invasion of privacy. Some ex-spouses are worse than others. Some make a point to peer in windows and doors, drive by the home to check who is around, interrogate the children....others aren't so interested in the lives of their exs, instead they simply plan their own lives.

The king of Syria felt like his private spaces were being invaded as well. He responded aggressively, counterattacked in hopes of taking captive the prophet behind the information. As a result, a lot of soldiers died unnecessarily. The cycle stopped only when some of the soldiers were smart enough to bow their knees before God's prophet. While it may not have solved all the problems, it certainly made life less threatening for those soldiers. If you are feeling trapped and invaded during this time, bow your knee before God with your concerns, and do your best not to be the one upon whom destructive fire descends, or who causes it to descend on others.

MY PRAYER FOR YOU THIS WEEK

This week, I pray for your tender heart. In the brokenness of divorce, a vulnerable heart can be easily enticed, quickly misled, sadly deceived. May God put a guard around your heart to protect and keep you. May God keep you from following after quick love, that the perfect future He has for you will be the experience of your life. Amen.

Day 120   Psalms 57:1-11

What an incredible person of faith the psalmist must have been. To be able to come before God and declare, "my heart is steadfast" is quite the confession. What a great thing to aspire to as your goal. I remember when I was going through my divorce, how sorely tested I felt. I remember times it was tempting to skip worship....just so I didn't have to face people in the awkward situation that inevitably seemed to create. I remember other times it was tempting to blame God....after all, He could have prevented the whole disaster if He had warned me way back when. There were times when the temptation was to simply give up, to quit trying....especially when I grew weary of the process and just wanted it to be over. In my case, I did my best in those hard times to find ways to turn back to God to seek strength, hope or direction. I don't know that I could say that my heart was steadfast, because there was such upheaval and hurt. But what did happen was that I found myself coming back to God time and again as I struggled through the experience. Maybe that is what steadfastness actually is. Not that you don't struggle or find your feelings wavering. Not that you don't mess up, make poor choices or stumble along the way. Not even that you are always at church, always in the Bible, always praying. Maybe it is more that, when push comes to shove, you always go back to God. David was called the man after God's own heart in the scripture....and if you know his life story at all, you know there were lots of times he messed up, sometimes in very big ways. But he always came back to God. He always ended up confessing his sin to God, taking responsibility for the poor choices he made and the consequences of those choices. He didn't always do it immediately. Nor did he always do it without prodding from people like Joab or Nathan. But, he eventually did come back to God and get things right with God. This Psalm was penned by that very David. What about you? Will you choose to keep coming back to God? Bounced around though you may be, and even though you may make some poor choices along the way, I urge you today to bow before God and ask Him to strengthen your heart toward Him, so that when push comes to shove in your life....and it certainly will....you will consistently find yourself coming back to God.

Day 121   Jeremiah 17:7-8

This is a fairly well known passage, one I have known and loved for a very long time. There are so many things to learn from these little verses that apply to so much of life. First, it speaks so clearly about the importance of where you are planted. Turns out realtors are right, it's all about "location, location, location." The critical factor here is being planted by the water, and that water image is so important in scripture. And that criticality was well known in the world in which Jeremiah lived. If you ever go visit Israel, or any area that has significant desert areas, you will understand what Jeremiah means. If you travel to western Oregon, the trees are thick and tall, because there is so much moisture for them to draw upon as they grow. But in Sonoran desert of Arizona, the only "trees" are saguaro cactus. There may be an occasional mesquite tree here and there, but they are small and scrawny....for they have no water. When you visit Jeremiah's Israel, not only trees, but settlements were made in the places where water is nearby. If the well was dry, the people moved on....and the wasteland was left just that, a wasteland. Only when irrigation of some sort was accomplished could a community thrive. At Qumran of Dead Sea Scroll fame, or Jerusalem or Megiddo, all in Israel, or Petra in Jordan, communities thrived because of elaborate cistern, aqueduct and tunnel systems for the purpose of water.

So, the parallel is vivid for Jeremiah's hearers....be smart about where you are planted. Jesus promises that those who come to Him will have rivers of living water flowing from within. The image is strong in Revelation 22:17 as well, where the invitation for all who would come is to come and receive the water of life. The location is to be planted in Christ, keeping Him close at hand. Anywhere else is a wasteland that bears no genuine eternal fruit. But I want to go one step further with you.

The image as the passage describes it is that the tree is planted by water, so as a seedling it has a source of water to keep it growing. While the water flows, the tree flourishes. But when drought comes....as it does in desert lands...it still grows, because the roots are sent out to the source of water. It has prepared. The image is an important one for God's people: make your roots deep while times are good, and they will stand you good stead in times of drought, your deep roots will get you through. So many times, though, Christians only run to God when they are in trouble, and the panic that sets in....sometimes even failure....can come because their roots were never established. So the first question to raise is to ask, "How are your roots?" If you are doing okay right now in your life, then now is the time to dig deep down to establish roots for your relationship with Christ, roots in His love, roots in the scripture that will get you through when your drought hits. Today, take some time to reflect on your own sense of rootedness.... tomorrow we will pursue this just a bit further.

Day 122   Jeremiah 17:7-8

So here we are again. Let's go the next step. Probably most of the people reading this do not feel like they are in the well watered times of life....it probably feels more droughtlike. If you have a sense that you have dug deep roots of faith over the years, then realize that this is the time for which you have been preparing. Those roots will get you through. Draw on them. Let the nourishment well up from deep within. Absorb every bit of life giving moisture from the water of life Christ has placed deep within. Let the verses well up within, much like artesian wells that continually refresh themselves. Perhaps take time to look back through prayer journals if you have them. Take time to reread some old favorite passages of scripture. Maybe go back to a place where you had a special encounter with Christ, and linger there to reflect and relive those times. Call an old spiritual buddy, and share some memories and prayers. Maybe even take time to write out your spiritual biography, recalling all the ways you and God have walked together to this point in your life. Whatever will help you get back in touch with those roots, now is the time to take advantage of it....the roots are there for a reason.

But there is still another possibility to consider. What if you have decided that your roots aren't so good, that you have just coasted in your spiritual life for the past years, and now that you are up against the wall, you don't know what to do? Well, it is best to put the roots down when things are going well and you can do so leisurely....because plants all show us that roots take time to generate, they don't grow overnight. However, there is also a sense in which a tough time, like a drought, creates the necessity of deep roots, and so survival mode sets in. Either you get roots down, and get them down now, or you wither. The urgency demands energetic growth. That may be you. You may not have the deep roots from before, but that doesn't mean you can't get them down there now....if you get with it. Do what it takes to get close to God. Find someone to disciple you. Develop a new prayer habit. Memorize a new verse. Read through the Bible....especially some passages you might not know as well. While it is a good thing to have your roots in place in advance, a time of drought can push you to get those roots down now. Tough times make us develop stronger roots, or fail. God promises to help us through if we lean on Him and trust Him through it all, so it is a guaranteed outcome if we make the right choice. Dig those roots, and dig them now. Come to God and seek that living water afresh.

Day 123   Jeremiah 17:7-8

Truth is, I actually intended to only have one devotional on this passage. However, as I reflect on what has helped me in life to share with you now, I realized there is so much here that you would end up with either a very long devotional reading, or I would shortchange the passage if I only left it as one day. Today, I want you to notice something that is not what you would normally expect to hear during this time of your life. I remember struggling so hard, sometimes just to get through the day. I called on some friends to help me through. I leaned on old roots, and sent out new ones, all trying to make sure I survived the drought that had come upon me. But there is a problem with all of that, and I had to learn it by experience. If you pay attention to this passage, you will notice that the purpose is not sending the roots out so that the tree will come through the drought strong and healthy. The roots ensure not only that the tree survives. The roots also ensure that there will be fruit. Remember John 15? God's goal is to help us bear fruit in our lives. This tree does not cease to bear fruit. In John 15, there is the image of pruning that increases the fruit. God's desire is to use this drought time in your life to produce fruit in spite of the drought, and perhaps to prune you back so that even more fruit is produced.

Instead of simply looking to find ways to keep standing, to survive, look for ways God can use you, that God can prosper the kingdom through you at this time. Now, there are lots of interpretations of what is meant by fruit, and for our purposes here, I encourage you to find some definitions of your own. Some look at fruit in terms of winning souls for Christ....and this time will certainly be a time when your life can be a witness to the role of Christ in your life. Others look at all the good things they could do as the way God brings fruit out of our lives....so they work soup kitchens or church nurseries, and in this time, it is good to remember to not just focus on yourself, but how you can be of service to others. Another interpretation that I think can be very useful just now in your life, is to see fruit in terms of character development....that the fruit is to be more like Christ. These folks often like to refer to the fruit of the Spirit in Galatians 5, where the primary fruit is love, with all the attributes tied with it. This can certainly be useful in this time. For example, is your divorce a really rough time for you? Well, the attribute of longsuffering can only be learned through suffering. The practice of gentleness can only be learned in times when not being gentle is the temptation.

The point to consider and remember now is that God has a purpose, even in this time. As we have said before, this is a time when God can strengthen you, temper you, demonstrate His glory through you, establish you, prepare you for tough times ahead, and yes, even USE you….all because of a drought.

Day 124   Luke 15:11-32

Let's revisit this great story, okay? Today, I want to use it to help you think through where you are at in life. As I have said before, many times people go through a divorce thinking it will solve the problems they struggle with and make life better, only to find out later that they have abandoned some very precious things and life didn't become as wonderful as they had thought. Sometimes, after a few months apart, the filing partner decides they are making a mistake, and seek restoration. In these kinds of scenarios the prodigal story becomes a very important one. Let's look first at the father, who in our scenario represents the person who has been abandoned or filed against. Notice that the father does not go trailing after the son, begging him to come back home, telling him he will do anything to make him happy if only he will come back. At the same time, he scanned the horizon each day, hoping for the return of his son, already having decided that if the boy came back repentant, he would welcome him into his arms. If your spouse has left you, you need to think through what your reaction will be if they return. Notice that the father restored the boy, but only after he saw the boy was truly repentant. He welcomed the return, but full restoration only took place after the boy expressed his repentance. To welcome somebody back who has learned nothing or changed nothing means that nothing will change. But once there is evidence of a changed heart, then the father was more than willing to let bygones be bygones. Are there certain evidences, certain signs that you will be looking for if your spouse returns that attest to you that both you and your spouse have truly changed, and you can together begin the process of restoration and forgiveness? If you are going to welcome your spouse back, you need to welcome them not merely back, but forward into a new kind of marriage that won't lead to the same results again. If nothing has changed, what makes you or your ex think anything will work any better? At the same time, don't disappoint yourself by creating silly, fantasy notions of your apologetic ex running back into your arms and about how wonderful everything will be. In most cases, there is a very high chance that he/she won't be coming back. God may make that happen for you, and He may speak restoration to your heart. If that is the case, hang on and trust. But don't mistake your own wishful thinking for the voice of God.

Now, let us consider the young man who had run away so brashly. He, like so many of us, had to learn his lesson the hard way. I like the phrase that says that he came to his senses. Sometimes that is what it takes for us....we just have to come to our senses. What he learned most in the pig sty was that what he was running away from was far better than he had ever realized. There is no record in the story that the prodigal decided a few years later things were the same and he was ready to leave again. That is because the son who came home was not the same son as the one who left. He was a changed young man, and in humility, ready to do whatever it took to make things right. Expecting nothing, he received everything. Deserving humiliation, he received exaltation. And life began anew as expectations, demands and the daily responsibilities of relationship were renegotiated. Perhaps that is what will happen with you and your spouse. That is what real reconciliation is about. I have known of some who have gone back to reconcile, but instead of truly reconciling, they just went back to the same old same old. In some cases, that may not be such a bad thing, because sometimes it seems a person seeks divorce due to having unrealistic expectations of what a marriage "ought to be." Those people, out on their own, realize they had misunderstood, and go back to reclaim what was right to begin with....but they still go back a changed person. Others I know have gone back, and nothing is changed, nobody has learned anything, and so it is much like a boxing match, where they simply have moved from round one, to round two...that kind of same old same old is NOT true reconciliation.

If reconciliation truly comes into your divorce to restore or renew your marriage, that is perhaps one of the greatest blessings that could come your way during this time. For the rest of us, it is important not to settle for something that pretends to be reconciliation, but is not. That kind of "reconciliation" accomplishes nothing, except a delay until the next moment of crisis arises. Examine yourself, observe your divorcing spouse, and then follow the leading God gives to you, not what God gives to somebody else.

Day 125 John 14:1

This is another one of those sayings of Jesus that I find absolutely amazing. It is about choice. We have discussed this same notion at another time looking at Philippians 4:6. But here the words come out of the mouth of Jesus Himself. And they come at the time when His disciples are about to face the greatest temptation to have troubled hearts they will ever face....they will observe the trial, condemnation, torture and crucifixion of their beloved teacher, Jesus. In preparation for that, Jesus tells them to not let their hearts be troubled. What I think is amazing here is the choice factor: in the midst of the circumstances of life, we choose whether or not our hearts will be troubled. And if that admonition applies to the despair as awful as what the disciples would experience from Maunday Thursday until Easter Sunday, then how much more does it apply to the other circumstances of life on earth.... including divorce.

This world contains a lot of difficult things to experience. Famines, earthquakes, floods, hurricanes, fires, wars, murders, cancer and other illnesses, financial collapse....you can make the list as well as I. This is a dangerous place to live, and some of those things are so traumatic they can leave you reeling. Often tied in with the crises of life is the element of uncertainty: Will I survive? Where will I go? What will I do? How will I make it? In the midst of those times, hear the voice of Jesus say to you, "Let not your heart be troubled. Believe in God, believe in me." Don't let it get to you. Things on the outside need not control your inside....don't let it hurt your heart. Believe. Trust. So many things in this world are not stable....buildings collapse, friends disappoint, even Christian leaders turn out to be less than honest. In fact, the truth is, the only thing that is absolutely trustworthy and stable in not only this world, but in all the universe, is God. And when things fall apart in your life, whether through divorce or any other tragedy, an opportunity is created in which to trust God for that which you cannot control, for that which you cannot see and trust that God can and will use all things for His purposes. With whatever is going on in your life....believe. Trust. Not just any and everything that calls for your trust, but believe and trust **GOD**. It may mean different things to you at different times in your life, but it is always the antidote to a troubled heart. Take time to assess your heart....what troubles you? What keeps you awake at night? Can you take these things to God, and believe that He will take care of you? Can you trust that God knows exactly what He is doing? God really does desire the absolute best for your life, even in the midst of tragedy. There are just things about this fallen world that are not good, that are difficult and scary. But God can use even them for His greater purposes. Believe. Trust. Jesus may be speaking those very words to your heart even now. With all the troubles you may be experiencing in your life, don't let your heart be troubled, too. Believe. Trust. God is *for* you.

Day 126   Hebrews 11:1-12:2

I was visiting with a gentleman one day who was going through his second divorce. He shared with me some things in which he was contrasting his first divorce with his second. He was devastated that he was going through the experience again....not at all what he desired. He talked about the ugliness of the experience, and that things with his first ex had become amicable over time, so much so that he had forgotten how ugly things had been back then. The whole experience was unsettling for him. I remember thinking, in the midst of my dark days, that I was not sure I would ever marry again because I sure didn't want to go through the hurt and pain I was experiencing ever again. I am sure that gentleman felt the same way during his first divorce. But here he was, once again facing the turmoil, the pain, the frustration and uncertainty of another divorce. Perhaps that is you. Perhaps you are reading this because you, too, are once again in that awful place you never wanted to be again. Or, perhaps you are where I was, in the midst of your pain, vowing to never get into this kind of experience again, even if it means you will never get married again to accomplish it.

One of the interesting things that Jesus said was that the rain falls on the just and the unjust. There are those who would try to tell you that if you follow the Lord, then nothing bad will ever happen to you, and certainly not divorce. But when you read Hebrews 11, the chapter that lists the great heroes of faith, you do not find that all of them, because of their relationship with God, were spared hardship. In fact, some of them experienced intensified hardship because they were Christians. That only makes sense, because Satan cannot keep you from turning to Christ, nor can he prevent God from answering your prayers for salvation or protection....so instead, he does everything he can to make you miserable enough that maybe you would give up on God. And if you don't, it certainly must pain God's heart to see His beloved children suffer. So the war goes on. Life has few guarantees. Some people say it has no guarantees except suffering or death, but that is not true. God offers other guarantees. Like if you call on the name of the Lord Jesus Christ, you will be saved. Or that no matter what happens in life, God will never leave you nor forsake you. These are promises that nothing in life, and no spiritual force can take away from you, because they are guarantees from God.

The point is, whether you are one going through another divorce, or one wanting to make sure you don't by considering not marrying again, there are lots of risks in life, and sometimes those risks end up in hurt, other times they end up in surprising joy. The old adage is "nothing ventured, nothing gained." Everything in life can teach you something. Everything in life can be used by God. But not everything in life works exactly the way we think it "should" work, partly because we live in a fallen world. You may be frustrated over what has happened, or frightened of what might happen in the future, but God is the constant who will always be there. Add your name to Hebrew Eleven's "Hall of Faith" by trusting that God will get YOU through, too!

MY PRAYER FOR YOU THIS WEEK

This week, my prayer is for your financial life. May you see God's hand at work in your checkbook and bank account. May you find new ways to give, to be stretched in your faith and filled with generosity. May you become a blessing to those in need around you. May you experience God meeting your every need, according to His riches in glory, and according to wisdom beyond this world. Amen.

Day 127 Hebrews 11:1-12:2 (since we already read this, why not try a different translation today?)

Isn't it incredible to read all those stories of all those people who served God so powerfully for so many years, leaving behind their stories as a testimony to give us encouragement? One of the fascinating things about this chapter is why they were listed here as heroes. Not because they were famous, not because they were smart, not because their lives were perfect, not because everything always went their way, not because of all they suffered, not because they prayed all the time. They are included in this chapter for only one reason: their faith. All the different personalities, all the different struggles, all the different victories, even all the miraculous things that happened are not the reason they are included in this chapter as examples for us. It is because of their faith. They were people who believed. They believed in God, they believed He cared for them, they believed He would meet their needs, give them protection or grace, guide and provide....they just believed. And because of that, they were included in this chapter. Even some folks who didn't always believe, but struggled with doubts of their own, were still included because the overall testimony of their lives was that they always came back to God, they always believed, that ultimately, God was the answer they needed. It wasn't what happened in their lives, it was how they responded to those things.... they believed in God.

You and I, too, are writing the chapter of the testimony of God's hand in our lives, and the kinds of responses we choose. No matter what happens in our lives, we, too have the opportunity to write a testimony of faith by choosing to respond with faith that God does know what He is doing, and that God will get us through to victory.... either victory here or ultimate victory in glory. Now, let's be honest with one another, shall we? Sometimes it is hard to believe. It is hard to believe God can work things out when we cannot see how it could possibly work at all. And it is hard to believe that what we can see, touch and hear are not the most important things, that God can supersede all of them. When things are hard, it is sometimes hard to believe that God has placed limits and we are not facing more than we can bear. On the other hand, when we work hard and see things go well, it is hard to believe sometimes that it is God's favor that achieved those things, not merely our own sweat and blood. Faith, however, gives us the eyes to see the hand of God in our lives....no matter what happens!

Day 128   1 Corinthians 4:1-5

During the time of divorce and the subsequent life arrangements, there are many temptations and many choices. There are temptations toward revenge and manipulation. There are temptations toward selfishness and dishonesty. There are temptations for shortcuts and immorality. There are temptations toward gloating over victories won and unforgiveness of defeats suffered. God is looking over all the areas of your life, all the choices you are making, all the ways in which you conduct yourself and the values you hold dear to measure you by one standard: faithfulness. It is the characteristic of faithfulness that God is seeking in you. Now that you are being tested, now that you are on your own, now that you are cut free while also being pushed to the extreme in some areas of your life, will you sell out, or will you be faithful? It is the old "when push comes to shove" sort of thing. From my years as a pastor, I cannot even guess the number of times I have known of a couple divorcing, and then one or the other of them quietly drops out of the church, given up on the Lord, or compromised the way they are living their lives. Choose to NOT let that become YOUR story. Instead, let these times prove that YOU, by the grace and strength of God, will be faithful. Because THAT is pleasing to God.

Day 129   Mark 4:1-20

Jesus says so much in this little, beloved parable. So much of life is contained in the nuggets of these verses. For instance, the fact that the only thing that really matters is the fruitfulness in the long haul.... the plants that make it to harvest are the only ones that count. Today, I want to focus on just one of the soils upon which the seeds fell, and the evidence of the soil that is contained in the life of the plant. Generally, whenever we read this parable, we always see ourselves as the good soil....we are the ones who heard. It may be wiser to examine the ways in which our hearts are represented by all the soils at various times and various ways. The soil that is rocky is soil in which God's word can take root when the seeds are planted. I have known people whose entire spiritual life is demonstrated by this soil. Something from God comes along and they get very excited, respond immediately, and would appear very devoted. And yet, if you watch their lives for more than those moments, you see the changes quickly wither away like a cut flower out of water. Maybe they wither because they get discouraged. Maybe they wither because hard things turn their attention elsewhere. Maybe they wither because the opposition is just too great. But the core of the matter is that they wither because they have no deep roots. I have known far too many people who have seemed to wither away in their faith, and a fair number of them withered during the time of their divorce. The embarrassment or sense of failure kept them from attending worship or Bible study. Their financial struggles led them to take multiple jobs and crowd out the time they had for God. The fact that things didn't go how they thought they should caused them to doubt and turn away from God. And they wither. Their roots don't keep them nourished in the time of real testing. Of course, the hard thing is that, for these plants of the parable, the time of drought is a little late to be deciding to send out roots deeper. That should have been done when things were going well....but all too often, people doing well take it for granted, instead of taking it as the time of preparation. Still, if you are questioning whether your roots are deep enough to get you through, there is still hope.

When the sun beat down hard on the little plant in the parable, it was in an emergency situation. If it didn't immediately force its roots down in search of water, it had no chance of survival. Granted, it would have been better to have done it ahead of time, but that time has passed, and now is the time that has become critical. If this is you, you are going to have to choose how badly you want to endure, and what price you are willing to pay to make sure you do. Falling away and withering begins with one step. The one morning you tell yourself it's okay to skip worship....just for today. The one day you decide you are running late and you can get by without any daily prayer time with God. Or the day you are feeling so down, you just don't want to face all those fellow Christians with all their happy lives (but if you only knew what we pastors know!). The first time you do these things, makes the second time easier, which makes the third time even easier, and so on until you discover that your faith has withered. The challenge to you is to take the crisis seriously. If you feel like skipping worship one Sunday morning, then make a point to go to both morning and evening services instead. If you are tempted to skip the personal Bible reading, then read for an extra ten minutes instead. Do the opposite of the temptation. Do the hard thing. You are choosing to go after water, rather than let the sun sap your strength.

Day 130   *Genesis 31:4-16 and 1 Samuel 19:1-18*

What a time these two Hebrew leaders had in life. They were followers of the one true God, and, in Jacob's case, had learned that his conniving ways would backfire. But both of them were in experiences with troublesome people who made their lives miserable. Laban had tricked Jacob so that he married the wrong woman, before Laban let him also marry the woman he loved. Then he changed his wages, and apparently wanted to get rid of Jacob. David has served in Saul's army, defeating Goliath as Israel's hero, and then won battle after battle in Saul's behalf. But Saul grew to hate David, and sought time and again to hunt him down. David's nobility is that even though he was being wronged, he would not raise his hand against Saul, because he knew that Saul had been called and anointed by God. (That is a lesson a lot of church folks could stand to learn concerning how they treat their pastors, by the way.) Anyway, both David and Jacob had been wronged....seriously wronged. And there was no indication that there would be a change of heart in the one who wronged them....that is what they could expect in the future. They endured. They stayed faithful. They trusted that God would take care of them anyway. And they responded with action when the time was appropriate, waiting for God to open the doors and take care of the circumstances first for them.

Have you been wronged by your ex? Is there any indication that you can expect anything different? Both my wife and I have experienced some of that ourselves, and probably our ex's would claim the same about us....divorce just makes things pretty skewed and cloudy. But I will say that I did try to be considerate when it mattered. Like Mother's Day, and mom's birthday....making sure the kids knew it was coming up, and had money if they needed it to purchase presents. Do these things whether you feel like the consideration is reciprocated or not (and odds are, they won't be); because it isn't about reciprocation or your ex...it's about who *you* are and what *you* want to teach your children. But like David and Jacob, God never promised to get the difficult people out of our lives. He promises to get us through the trials. He promises to take care of things His way in His timing. The difficult people remain. And often they remain difficult. Of course, you could never learn how to endure if you didn't ever have to endure anything. You could never learn how to forgive if you were never wronged. You could never learn to love your enemies if you never had any enemies. So, like it or not, the difficult people....perhaps including your ex....may be in your life for a very long time. Learn the lessons of Jacob and David as they sought to do what they knew was right in spite of how they were treated, and as they trusted God to take care of the things they could not. Maybe you are one of those whose divorce was entirely amicable. God bless you. Help others you know who are divorcing to learn how to handle things amicably. But in all the divorces I have known, I have known very few that were anywhere near amicable....the hurt and rejection are just that powerful. At the same time, I know that many, over time, are finally able to lay aside their hurt and anger and develop a somewhat cordial relationship. Because difficult situations teach you difficult solutions. Jacob and David came through the difficult times with difficult people to become leaders and patriarchs in God's plan of redemption. How will you come through?

Day 131   2 Samuel 15:1-6

Absalom was a dreamer. He imagined what life would be like if he got everything HIS way as he told the people what he would do if HE were king. And in so doing, he connived his way into becoming king. But that wasn't what he really wanted. What he really wanted was his dad to love him in such a way that he knew personally his dad's love. What he really wanted was for his dad to have stood up for what is right by charging Absalom's half brother Amnon with the crime of raping Absalom's sister, and doing something about it. These were two of the things Absalom wanted in life, but he didn't get because he pursued other things or pursued things his own way instead in a godly way. That led to nothing but heartache and tragedy for everyone concerned.

David didn't get after Amnon like he should have. Probably never did, which may in fact have led to the crisis in the first place. Absalom may have wished his dad would have handled Amnon differently than he did, but David didn't. Right or wrong, that wasn't who David was. Absalom couldn't receive David's love, it seems to me, partly because he had a false understanding of who David was, which meant that the love David gave, Absalom probably didn't recognize as love anyway. Not that I am just letting David off the hook here, but we are talking about Absalom, not David. When Absalom ran away after killing his brother, what he really wanted was David to take him back in, to forgive him. And so he connived to force that to happen, too. And David did let him move back, but he didn't welcome Absalom with open arms and seat him next to David at the supper table. In fact, he kept Absalom at arm's length, refusing to see him face to face. Absalom failed to understand the depth of the pain he had caused his father. Absalom failed to understand that actions have consequences. Absalom failed to understand that if you are going to be welcomed back after committing heinous sin, you need to come back in humility and repentance, not arrogantly assuming you deserve restoration. And if David was anything in his life, he was a man who understood the importance of humility and repentance…. he had to do it over and again himself! Anyway, Absalom responded to all of it by conniving again to make himself king. He connived to kill his half brother, he connived to become king, and his conniving ended up costing him his life and accomplishing none of the things he desired most: justice and love. What a wretched ending.

What is it *you* really want? What are the areas in which you have decided to force things your own way, and ended up with your head tangled up in trees because of it? How have you tried to get in touch with *your* Father, and ended up estranged instead because of your lack of humility and repentance? We can't manipulate everything in life like we sometimes think we can. And when we do, sometimes we find out that we don't know so much after all, because we don't end up where we really want to be. I am going to leave this one very open ended. What is it you really want? And how have you tried to get there that hasn't worked? And where do you need to just swallow your pride and get back where you need to be, before it's too late?

Day 132   2 Samuel 15:1-12

I have found in my work with divorcing people down through the years that very often the person who files for the divorce becomes very angry in the process at what they perceive to be the injustice of it all.

Of course, the people who did not want the divorce would feel some of that as they see so much of their lives being stripped away, but the other person, after all, was the one wanting a divorce, why would they be angry? The answer is the same as what we observed about Absalom yesterday: unintended consequences. The filer wanted a divorce, but didn't think about the fact that a divorce might impact their own retirement, their own credit rating, their own opportunities with their children. They didn't think about the fact that the court would not only grant protection for them in the divorce, but would also grant protection for their ex as well. They didn't think about the fact that it is the court, not themselves, who was in charge of making and approving decisions and choices. They certainly would have input, but so would the ex, and as a result, it may well be the court is the one who needs to decide what is best after making considerations for both sides, when the filer expected things would go just the way they wanted. I have seen it time and again. When they filed for divorce, they may have felt like they were taking control of their lives as they sought to get out of the marriage, when, in fact, it may be more realistic that they have given up that control....at least temporarily and in certain areas....to the court.

Again, I want you to consider your life and your life choices. What are the areas in which you feel mired down and trapped? Rather than shift your anger and blame at your ex or the court or whoever and whatever else, take a long hard look at the choices you have made yourself to see that some of those consequences are of your own creation. It is part of being a healthy person to accept responsibility for our own choices and consequences, so that you can learn from them and grow into a better person able to make better choices. It may require you to apologize to some people you have brought pain to, people you have disappointed. It may require you to take some action that is stronger than apology, to make things right with somebody through repayment, or through changing your attitude or agreement. If there are things you need to face, you are also, then, faced with a choice of becoming a better person, or continuing to be less than what you could be. It is a hard choice to make, and even if you choose to ignore it all, you are making the choice to be a person who ignores issues you need to face. Take the challenge and become a better person by facing what you need to face. In the long run, you will be glad you did.

Day 133   2 Samuel 18:31-19:8

How David's heart must have ached. A daughter raped by her half brother. That son murdered by *his* half brother....the daughter's brother. And *that* son turned against him and was eventually killed in revolutionary battle. Certainly the picture perfect family every believer desires, right? I am always encouraged when I find that somebody God used to lead a nation, to write scripture, and who is venerated some 3,000 years later by his people as the greatest leader they ever had.... had a life and character that were far from perfect. I can relate to that part more than the other, can't you? Anyway, I cannot imagine what it must have felt like. Oh, sure, I've had heartaches aplenty. And sure, if you have kids, you are going to get hurts as well as joys. But the depth of pain David must have felt over those things.... I have known people who have lost children in a variety of ways, accident, disease, even murder, and I have seen the pain on their faces. I have known victims of rape, and witnessed their heartbreak and struggles. I simply cannot imagine. If you can because you have been there, I am sorry, I know it must be hard. I have no words, I have only a God who cares.

I simply cannot imagine what it must have been like to be David the day he was told that Absalom was dead. I certainly can understand the weeping he did. Sure, his son did some terrible things, but he was still his son. Sure, David must have been disappointed, he surely had hoped for more, but he was still his son. And David wept. That was okay....for awhile. But in his grief, David lost his perspective, as most of us probably do. Yes, there was the need to mourn, but the day came when Joab knew David needed to move on. He knew David felt loss, but David had lost touch with how much people loved him, and how much they had risked for him, and needed to know that he appreciated them, too. I have heard of times when a child died, and a parent so obsesses over the child they lost that the remaining children not only feel neglected, but begin to believe that the parent wishes they had died instead of the other one. That's kind of what Joab was trying to get David to see. I'm sure there was no love lost between Joab and Absalom, but Joab never said David didn't have the right to feel grief at the death of his son. What he said was that David didn't have the right, especially as king of the people, to make that grief the only focus of his life to the neglect of the other people and other tasks he had. And he wanted David to get back to realizing the work God was doing in David's life, and in the kingdom.

In divorce, grief can be overwhelming. It can become an obsession. But there comes a time when you need to heed the advice of Joab. You need to choose to not let the grief dominate. You need to focus on the other people in your life who love you, not just the one who has turned against you. You need to focus on what other people need from you, not wrap yourself selfishly up in your own grief. You need to start seeing what God is doing now, in your life, and in His kingdom around you. Mourning has a place, just make sure you keep it in its place rather than it keeping you in your place. Is it time for you to move on? If not now, when? Moving on does not mean the grief isn't real, it simply means there is more to who you are than merely a person in grief. And it means that you are important to more people than merely the one you have lost. Is it time?

MY PRAYER FOR YOU THIS WEEK

This week, I pray for your endurance. Perhaps some things in your life have become tedious and drudgery. Perhaps they have become too burdensome and have weighed you down. Perhaps you cannot see the end of your struggles, and the path has become dark and discouraging. I pray that God will flood your soul with the light, hope and strength you will need to finish the race God has set before you, whatever may come. Amen.

Day 134   Jeremiah 32:17

Life can be very exciting and joyful, but it can also be very challenging and difficult. There are sorrows just as surely as there are joys. Sometimes the hard things we face in life just seem too hard. Sometimes we reach the end of our rope. Sometimes we just don't feel like we can go on. In those times, we need to remember who our God is. Our God is a great God. Our God is a mighty God. Our God is an infinitely wise God. He is a God of strength, power, majesty and glory. Things that seem hard to us are simple to Him. Things that seem huge to us are but specks of dust to Him. Things that appear to have no solution can be solved by the all wise God for whom nothing is too difficult. In fact, He may take special pleasure in solving the unsolvable, revealing His glory to the world, and His power in your life and mine. It just once again proves how incredible God is. Nothing….absolutely nothing….is too hard for God. One of the silly theological questions people like to play with is whether, if God can do anything, God would be able to make a rock so big that He cannot move it. When somebody raises that question with me, my answer is simply this: of course He can make a rock so big He cannot move it….and then He would move it anyway!!

What is the biggest struggle you face? What are the unsolvable problems you have? What are the unanswered questions of your life? Whatever is the biggest thing weighing down upon you, it is nothing that God cannot handle. It is only a problem for you if you are choosing to try to handle it by yourself. If you partner with God, it suddenly is no longer beyond you. Remember when Jesus invited us to take His yoke upon us, as recorded in Matthew 11:28-30? If you can imagine yourself with half a yoke upon your shoulders and neck, and the other half on Jesus' shoulders and neck walking at your side….what is so big you cannot plow through it with Jesus at your side ?

Day 135   Isaiah 49:13-16

I don't know whether you have ever been around a mother with her newborn child or not. Dads love their kids, too, but biologically, we dads serve a different role, we don't have the ability to nourish our children through nursing like the mothers do. Have you heard the cries of that hungry little baby, the cries that never cease until the child gets what it seeks….the nourishment of milk. Once they get wound up, they are very hard to ignore….loud, insistent, piercing in their cries…. they certainly can get your attention, can't they? God asks whether a mother could ever forget her nursing child. If you have been in a room with a baby acting as I have described, you know that it would be hard for *anyone* to forget that child, least of all the mother. But the mother has a special interest in the child….because it is HER child….even if everybody else would forget the child, she wouldn't. I like the image of what I have seen with young mothers these days, who often have their children in slings across their chests. That baby rests its head near the mother's heart. That is the image I like, that as she goes about the tasks of her day, she is keeping her baby close to her heart. With the baby there, do you think she could forget that child? No, that mother won't forget, because she loves the child, it is hers.

God goes even one step further. He remembers us more than that mother!! He says that even if a mother could forget her nursing child.... and, tragically, in a number of news headlines in recent years we have seen stories of some mothers doing some pretty terrible things to their children, so we know it could happen....but God says His love and watchcare are beyond that. He will never forget you. In the midst of hard times, or uncertain futures, or times of loneliness, it can feel like God has forgotten you. But He hasn't. Pay attention over the next few weeks as you go through the routines of your life. Every time you hear a baby cry, or see a mother with a child at her side or in a sling, let that be a reminder that God keeps you close to His heart....always. Not only is He ever mindful of you....He has even engraved you on the palm of His hands! How intimate is that? No, my friend, you are never forgotten by Him. Never.

Day 136   Galatians 2:11-16

Divorce is an experience that affects most of its victims rather deeply, I believe, even though it is hard to see in some people. Some just seem to go on their merry way as if nothing significant happened. But many people go into deep depression, or even become murderous and suicidal. As you see yourself in the midst of this, you may wonder what will remain, what kind of a person you will be when you come out. The answer is, you will be who you are, with the addition of the things you have learned and the ways you have grown through the experience of divorce.

Look at the life of Peter in the scriptures. Time and again we see his impulsiveness, his willingness to jump into something without thinking it through. He leaves his nets to follow Jesus the instant he is called. He puts out to sea when Jesus tells him, but when he realizes what kind of a person Jesus is, he panics and begs Him to go away. Later, when he sees Jesus on the water, he tells Jesus to allow him to walk on the water, too....and then realizes what he has done once he is a few steps away from the boat. He is the first to say he would never deny Jesus, even though he is the one we remember as having done so three times. And then, after the resurrection, there at the Sea of Galilee, when he recognizes Jesus at the shore, he jumps overboard to get to Him. I wonder if he thought he would be walking to shore. And I wonder if it occurred to him to evaluate whether or not he was within swimming distance, or if he just jumped and then thought about it. Later, even though he had become a great church leader used by God many times, when some more legalistic believers came around, he jumped tables without even thinking about what he had learned at Simon the tanner's house. Paul had to confront him about it, and they apparently got things straightened out. But I want you to notice, Peter was impetuous before Jesus called him, he was impetuous as he followed Jesus, he was impetuous after Jesus rose from the dead, and he was impetuous after the Spirit of God filled him and he was a significant leader in the early church. He had learned things, he had grown, he had matured, but his core personality remained, because it was who God created him to be.

Today, I want you to know that God created you a unique and precious individual to be and do what He designed for you. And when He designed you, in His incredible foreknowledge, He knew you would be going through a divorce. While that does not mean it was what He desired most for you....that "perfect will" notion....it does mean He wasn't surprised, and will be able to incorporate important things out of your experience to help make the "core you" into a greater and better instrument for His use. As such, you will handle things in a different way than some others may....you will make your own mistakes, your own good choices, and handle many things in ways that are unique to you. Remember, in all of this, you are a unique individual, and nobody can give you the exact guidelines that will be the "right" way for you to deal with things....you will have to deal with them based on who YOU are, and on the basis of YOUR relationship with God. And God will make sure the guidance He gives fits YOU!

Day 137   Ruth 1:11-18

I knew a person...actually have known several....who was so devastated by their divorce that they could no longer see a purpose for their lives, no longer find a reason for living. You know, I suspect that this was the same kind of heartache that Naomi and Ruth experienced. With all that they had lost, with how radically their lives had been altered, and with all the hardships they had already experienced and yet knew even more were ahead, they must have been overwhelmed. The one daughter-in-law, Orpah, does go on back home as Naomi suggests. Naomi decides that is what she must do herself....go on back home. Nothing much awaits her there, but nothing much awaits her where she is at, either. So she decides to at least go back among her own people. Ruth determines that Naomi needs her, and so she decides to go with Naomi to this other land. And, perhaps too, it is that Ruth decides SHE needs what she saw in Naomi....a different kind of faith and a different God than she had known before.

Somebody needs you, too. Oh, you may think you are not important, but that is not true. There may be a parent of yours who is deeply concerned, and longing to see you again. There may be a grandchild who would be without a grandparent if you weren't around. There may be a co-worker who is going to have some rough times ahead in which only you can minister....and if you aren't there, nobody will be. I sometimes think about the people who make cars. So much of what they do is so unseen. Like the guy who makes sure the lug nuts are screwed onto your wheels, to keep the tires on the vehicle. If that guy didn't do his job right, your test drive would be a disaster. Or the guy who puts together the air bags for safety. Most of the time, most people will never know if he did the job right or not. But for those who do end up in an accident, his job becomes very important. You have no idea how important some of the things you do really are. My grandmother would probably be very surprised to know how much it meant to me to be in her home, and hear her cuckoo clock. I was only there once or twice, as she lived too far away. But now, 40 years later, a cuckoo clock still reminds me of my grandmother. And she probably paid no attention to it. Nope, you don't know all the ways your life touches other people. But it does. And the more you invest in them, the more difference you make. Ruth decided that somebody needed her, and so she chose to go wherever was necessary to help make that difference for Naomi. I encourage you to consider how you can do the same thing.

Day 138   Galatians 5:22-23

This is certainly one of the best known and loved passages in scripture, this list of the fruit of the Spirit of God. Love, joy, peace.... such wonderful things. But then there are also these other words.... longsuffering or patience and self-control. These indicate something else. These indicate a person in circumstances that might require some patience, or, if you use the translation "longsuffering," then the implication is someone suffering a long time....how else could you even know this is your character if you never suffered for long? It would be okay to have patience, if only you didn't have to deal with the circumstances and individuals that require you to have patience! And then, self-control. That suggests you have some temptation that would make you lose control....but when this characteristic is part of who you are in Christ, you keep your cool, resist that path, stand strong and stable. The same is also true of the ones we normally focus on in this passage. Peace is great when everything is good, but to experience God's peace when there is no visible cause for that peace? Or joy, when everything inside tells you to weep instead?

Today, instead of giving you a lot of reflections on this passage, I want to challenge you toward your own reflections. Read over this list once or twice again. How does each item listed apply in whatever your current situation is? How do your actions reflect or not reflect these characteristics? And as you consider these things, then consider also, **the source is the Spirit**, NOT YOU! So what can you do to open yourself up to a greater experience of God's Spirit during this time of life? The passage does not limit the characteristics to particular times of life....instead, it connects them to relationship....relationship with the Spirit of God.

Day 139   Matthew 28:20

Look around you, wherever you are. Jesus is there. Maybe you want to visualize Him sitting beside you, standing in the corner, His hand on your shoulder, holding you close in comforting embrace....any of these, all of these, Jesus is with YOU. ALWAYS. Perhaps the greatest promise God gives us for our life in this world is this one. No matter where you go on this planet, Jesus is with you....to the end of the age. No matter what you are doing with your life, Jesus is always close at hand. No matter how you feel, Jesus will stand with you....even if it doesn't feel like He is there. No matter what happens to you, or how others treat you, Jesus is with you. No matter who else might abandon or discard you. You never have to go through any experience on earth alone. In fact, let's change that wording a bit. Not only do you not have to.... YOU DON'T! Christ is always there. Always. Every moment. Every breath you take. Every stumble you experience. Every smile on your face. Every tear on your face. Every accomplishment you achieve. Every medical procedure you face. Every conference with your attorney. Every shattering court decision. Every timid step forward into a new life. Every headlong mistake that is impulsively made. Jesus will always be with you. Nothing you have to handle do you have to handle alone. He knows things have impacted you....He was right there when they did. He knows the precariousness of your situations....He was with you when you realized it yourself. Life on this earth is far from easy. And there is a lot of uncertainty. Satan, of course, seeks to use those things to knock you out of action, to keep you away from God. But he cannot. Because Jesus refuses to leave. He is with you always....even beyond your earthly life. Take some time to just enjoy His presence. And tell Him know how you feel about knowing He is with you.

Day 140   Genesis 9:12-17

Okay, I guess I am in a rut. Yes, we have talked about rainbows before, maybe to the point that you think it is an obsession. So forgive me, but I had a fresh reminder yesterday, and just have to share it with you. A friend and I had gone out to eat in a town a few miles away. When we left, there was an impending thunderstorm, with threatening winds, although no warnings of tornadoes, so we went. Most of the storm passed through either as we were driving, or while we were eating. On the return trip, we were seeing some sprinkles here and there, and discussing the great variety in the clouds, as well as the line of clear sky just a few miles away. (For those of you who live in mountainous areas like my Kentucky friend, it might help if I mention that in some places in Kansas, you can literally see storms thirty miles away as they are approaching.) Anyway, it was kind of fun seeing the shapes and colors of the dark, low hanging smaller clouds change as we passed under them to the other side. When we arrived back in town, my friend looked back and pointed out to me a very bright and intense rainbow. Suddenly, I was struck by something that I believe is worth sharing.

The rainbow in scripture is God's promise that He will never flood the earth again to destroy it, right? But as I looked back at that rainbow, it occurred to me that the reminding rainbow was not visible on the opposite side of the clouds, BEFORE the storm hit, but only on the back side, AFTER the storm had passed. (Maybe rainbows aren't always afterwards, but it was that day.) Forgetting the physics involved, I think it is significant from a spiritual point of view. The rainbow does not remind us before the storms that it is only going to be a shower and relatively local, instead of a storm that will destroy the whole earth. We might think that "before" is when we need the reminder, though, mightn't we? That is, to be reminded as life's storms are approaching, not after they have passed? But apparently God didn't think so. Why not?

Well, I certainly will not claim to know why God does everything He does the way He does it, but this is what occurred to me through this experience. The rainbow reminds us AFTER the storm what we should be remembering BEFORE and DURING the storm. It's almost as if the rainbow is God saying, "Didn't you remember, I promised I wouldn't destroy the earth with the flood again? This rainbow will help you remember FOR NEXT TIME!" We might prefer rainbows would come at a different time in our experience of life's storms. Times such as when the storm is impending and clouds looming overhead, or while the storm is raging. But without the rainbow, those times become opportunities to trust, to walk in faith, to lean on the promises, to see the unseen. And if you are doing that, then when the rainbow appears after the storm, it almost becomes a private joke between you and God. It is as if the two of you are saying, "That's right, we knew it was only temporary, didn't we? I told you it would be okay."

There are lots of storms in my life when I feel like I would sure like to see some kind of rainbow NOW, but that isn't how faith works. Sometimes breaks in the clouds here and there give me hope, but the rainbow, the assurance, comes AFTER the storm. My job is to remember the promise when the storm is approaching and when it is raging. Then, when God's handiwork and purpose become clearly evident after the storms, I can say with God, "We knew it was temporary, that you would not let me down, didn't we, God?"

MY PRAYER FOR YOU THIS WEEK

This week, my prayer for you is that God would grant you the wisdom you need for the situations you currently face in your life. God promises to give that wisdom freely, but not when we seek only our own ways. May you be filled with wisdom as you encounter the apparently insurmountable, that you may find God's way through or around it. May His wisdom guide your every decision, every choice, as you experience daily events, selecting which to respond to, and which to simply walk away from, trusting God to handle what you cannot. In the name of the only wise God, Amen.

Day 141   Isaiah 58:13-16

When you are single, or when you are struggling and discouraged, it is perhaps even easier to skip worship on Sundays. You have so much to get done, and so little time to do it. You walk into the church and see all the happily married couples sitting with their children as a family, and feel the empty seat of your spouse and the seats where your children might have sat, and it is very awkward. The offering plate comes around and you struggle with how little, if anything, you have to drop into the plate. The truth is, Satan is always trying to create situations that will cause people to give up on their church involvement and worship. And he is looking for <u>your</u> vulnerable point to make you consider quitting. The truth is, though, this is a time in your life when involvement in church and regular participation in worship is absolutely critical.... even if it doesn't feel that way. It is important to continue to stand for the Lord. It is important to make opportunities for you to hear God's word proclaimed. It is important to create opportunities for you to serve and be used by God in the lives of others. It is important to maintain a habit of faithfulness, rather than to inadvertently begin another habit of absence.

It is tempting to think that not attending worship will give you more time to accomplish the overwhelming tasks around you, or keep you from feeling embarrassed at being alone or being broke. The truth is, you can never really gain in life by neglecting God and His instructions. Oh, you can try to rationalize it away, by saying that you can keep your relationship with God strong through private worship at home or out in nature, and it is true you can spend that time with God. But you cannot be continuing to assemble with other believers as He instructed while by yourself. You cannot be encouraging other Christians, or fulfilling your role in the body of Christ if you are absent. And you are not putting God first or keeping the Sabbath holy if you are instead putting priorities on housework or chores or any of the other things that claim to be so important that you need to skip worship to deal with them. While so much of your life is being restructured and reassembled, make sure that your obedience to God for the day of worship becomes established more solidly, not disassembled along the way. You will find that God is right, it DOES make a difference in how everything else in life goes, and how you are able to handle everything that comes your way. If you have children, your choices set the example of what you believe is important about church. And besides, somebody there may need you....don't let them down.

Day 142 Jonah 1:1-17

We don't know that much about Jonah. Not really. But somehow, for some reason, the word of the Lord came to him, and instructed him to go to Nineveh. Wouldn't you like God to speak so clearly to you that you always know what the word of the Lord is in your life choices? Of course, many of those choices he has spoken very clearly about, in the scriptures, but there are those times when we sure would like some guidance.... However, that is not the topic for today. Instead, today we think about the fact that Jonah knew what he was supposed to do, but chose to go the other way. It's called, "disobedience." Not a term we like to apply too often, because we really don't relate that well to the master/servant/slave relationship of the scripture....but the term does apply....it is disobedience, in Jonah, or in you and I. I selected Jonah because he was clearly and deliberately disobedient. Sometimes maybe you are, too. Other times, we just mess up, make dumb choices without intentionally trying to be rebellious. However, often the results of disobedience are the same whether we act that way intentionally or unintentionally, and usually those results are not very pleasant. There are lots of folks in the Bible who make bad choices by rebelling, by turning away, by falling victim to temptation….lots of folks mess up in the scriptures. Just like we do in life here in our modern world.

Jonah became convinced he had really messed up, and stood up to take the blame instead of passing the buck, even to the point of suggesting the sailors throw him overboard. I suspect he thought this would end his life….he certainly didn't expect to be rescued by some kind of big fish! But God does rescue him, and Jonah realizes his need for God and for obedience, and when the fish ejects Jonah, he ejects him at the location where he was supposed to go to begin with. It is God's way of giving Jonah a second chance, as He does so many of His people time and again in the scriptures.

Maybe you have days when you feel like you have really messed up your life, like you can't do anything right. You need to learn the lessons of Jonah. First, accept responsibility for what you have done wrong. Not responsibility for everything and everybody, but responsibility for your own mistakes. Then recognize that even those mistakes are indicators of the fact that you need God. You need Him for forgiveness, you need Him for guidance, you need Him for strength, you need Him for salvation….you just need God. And then, like Jonah, stand up, dust yourself off, and head off to the Nineveh of your second chance. God is not done writing the story of your life and testimony yet. If He was, you wouldn't be reading this, you'd be standing in His presence in heaven. Nope, there are missions ahead for you, and God will give you second chances in more areas than you can imagine. So maybe you could join me in saying, "Nineveh, here I come!"

Day 143   John 15:1-11, 16:19-24

So, today, let's move to some reflections on rejoicing and joy. The key factor in this discussion relates to the source, the wellspring of our joy. Our joy is not to be based on our circumstances, no matter how wonderful those may be, for all circumstances are but *temporary*, and God's desire is for us to have joy *that lasts*. You may experience a burst of joy upon finding a gold coin worth a few thousand dollars, but a few months along, that money will have found uses and your mood will return to its normal state as the joy ebbs away. You may even find joy in doing ministry for the Lord, and seeing people come to Christ because of your testimony to them, or you may experience God's hand of blessing upon other tasks you undertake as you serve Him. But just as the early disciples found out, sometimes there is a special blessed time of God's moving, and there are other times the same actions result in opposition and persecution. Joy needs to not be based upon those things, either. No, the admonition is that we are to rejoice *in the Lord*.

One of the ways this might apply can be found in comments I have heard from many people going through a divorce or experiencing the death of a loved one. In these times, I have often heard Christians say, "I don't know how somebody can go through these things without Christ." These people know how to rejoice in the Lord. Their joy holds firm when their life is in upheaval: "Yes, many things in my life have been upset, but I have a God to see me through. I have a God to give me strength. I have a God to turn to for guidance. I have a God who will never abandon me, no matter who else I lose through divorce or death. I have a God who has given me eternity with all the glories of heaven, no matter how bad things become here. In all this assurance, I have cause for joy." Each of these IS a cause for joy. That you are not alone....rejoice. That you have One who understands and loves you... rejoice. That you have a God who will never fail nor forsake you. That none of the difficult things in this life can jeopardize your eternal salvation. Rejoice in these things, for these are eternal treasures found in your relationship with God. These are not subject to change. They are not subject to decay. They are not subject to the vicissitudes of life. They are not subject to your emotional mood swings. These are more secure than the mightiest fortress on earth. And they are the cause for rejoicing, for God is on your side.

(Not that God is choosing sides between you and your ex. That is not yours to say, anyway. It *is* true, though, that He is choosing sides between you and Satan's efforts to destroy you.) This joy from God dwells deep within. Sometimes it bursts forth in the form of happiness and laughter. Sometimes it abides in your soul as a sense of secure peace. Sometimes it impresses itself upon you as you stand awestruck at all that God has done for you and the depth of His love for you. Sometimes it serves as a deep, stabilizing force when all around you urges despair.

This is the joy that the world can never take away, the joy that comes directly from Christ, the joy that is available to you in the darkest moments of your life. Rejoice, my friend, God is still on the throne, and His love for you is secure.

Day 144   Daniel 3:18-30

The stories in Daniel are quite fantastic, aren't they? And what faith is exemplified by the individuals in the book. Especially Hananiah, Mishael and Azariah (Shadrach, Meshach and Abednego). They said, in effect, "Whether He saves us or not, we aren't going to worship anything but God." Pushed to the extreme, they declared themselves for God. Job said much the same thing when he said, "Though He slay me, yet will I trust Him." (Job 13:15a, NKJV) There are those critical moments in life in which one experiences extreme testing in terms of one's faith. It is easy to hang on in good times, in easy times, in times that fit your preplanned paradigm of life. It is another when everything you are and everything you believed in and stood for are challenged and attacked, whether that attack is by individuals or a spiritual battle within your heart and mind.

If you have never read any of the stories of those who have faced the ultimate test in their faith, this is not a bad time to get familiar with some of the stories of God's martyrs. The scripture records some of those stories, not only in Daniel or Job, but in the records of Jeremiah's life, the story of Stephen and the early church, those recorded in the Hall of Faith in Hebrews 11, and even Revelation records the role of the martyrs. There are also stories of Christians throughout the history of the church who have suffered and died for their faith, from the earliest of days up through modern times around the globe. Reading those testimonies reminds us that we are truly in a spiritual battle, and must continually make our choice for God. They encourage us to hang on and stand strong when we are tested and tempted to quit.

There are plenty of books and websites that can help you know the stories of suffering and martyred Christians, not just of days gone by, but there are Christians suffering persecution and martyrdom *even while you are reading these words*. Spend some time with those stories. If nothing else, these struggling brothers and sisters need your prayers. But odds are, it can help you have the courage you need to face what you are facing during this time of life, and might even make you realize how small your problems truly are compared to what others are being asked to do.

A divorce is, indeed, a time of life that tests believers and their faith, although it is not the ultimate time of testing. In Job 23:12, Job confesses his belief that through the time of extreme testing, God is purifying him like the smelting of fine gold, and that God will see him through the testing time. God can use this time in your life for the same kinds of things: to give you a testimony to the faithfulness of God, and to burn away the dross that has accumulated in your life and cluttered your faith. Remember the words of Jesus in the Sermon on the Mount? Jesus said that when we face these hardships, we can rejoice because we are in good company, the company of prophets and martyrs throughout the years. So hang on, God is working and your stand for Him will not be in vain.

Day 145   1 Kings 11:1-10

Solomon apparently did nothing in a small way. I tend to believe one wife is plenty. Solomon, on the other hand, seemed to think it was better to have a different wife (or concubine) for each day of his life! Or pretty close to that. And because he allowed himself to get caught up with so many women, many of whom worshipped other gods than the God who had appointed Solomon King of Israel, his faith was slowly eroded away, led down the path of the gods of his women. It isn't that the loving relationship between men and women is a bad thing. It is about excessive infatuation with the opposite sex, to the point that he or she is more important than God.

Have you ever thought about Solomon's kids? We know that when Rehoboam succeeded his dad as king, he decided he wanted to be just like dad...only tougher, and that decision resulted in the division of Israel into two kingdoms. We wonder how he could have so misread the needs of the kingdom. But when you stop to think about it, the truth is, all of Solomon's kids were probably pretty confused about things, especially in terms of their direction in life. Surely they had heard the stories about how their father was chosen by God and blessed with great wisdom from God. But then, when they looked at his life, he sure didn't seem to be very wise in terms of his religious faith and his values. Torn between the God of his fathers and the gods his wives worshipped, Solomon was unable to keep true to his calling. Certainly that would have left his children totally on their own in figuring out what to believe and what not to believe.

Perhaps your children are facing the same kind of dilemma. With their family environment changing so radically, they may not know where to turn, or what to believe about life, God, whom to trust, lots of things may have them uncertain or confused. At a time when you are sorting out afresh lots of things in your life, it is important that you remain faithful in the midst of it. Your children, as well as friends, coworkers and a host of others, need to see a consistent example of what it means to be a Christian. Maybe your ex is not living that example. Maybe you are tempted to give up on the faith or your moral convictions just as Saul was. In my ministry as a pastor, as I have often said, time and time again, I have seen Satan use divorce as the stumbling block that turns people away from Christ and His church. (And, tragically, I have seen Satan use it to cause churches to turn their backs on divorcing people who desperately need the church's encouragement and support.) Sadly, sometimes the people who leave are folks you would not have suspected could ever turn away. I have seen some of them leave the church and move in with a lover. I have seen some fill the emptiness with other things, such as work or alcohol. Some have been so tossed into depression that they simply give up. Maybe they no longer feel like they fit in. Maybe every time they step foot in the church it reminds them of their past marriage. Maybe their friends at church have let them down one way or another. Maybe they are unrestrained for the first time in their lives. Maybe they no longer feel worthy to be in church, like they no longer belong or are no longer welcome. These are just a few of the reasons, and a few of the resulting behaviors.

Don't YOU join their ranks. Choose to be the one who holds to God no matter what, and be the kind of influence and example in the lives of your children and the lives of your friends. Solomon's kids and friends were probably very confused about who God is and what He requires, because of what they observed in the life of Solomon. Don't let *your kids and friends* be confused when they examine *your* life. Don't let your life become a stumbling block for them. God **will** get **you** through, if only you will give Him the chance and the time to do it. Cling to Him as if your life depends on it, because ultimately, it does.

Day 146   Exodus 17:1-7 and Philippians 1:29-30

"But God, I prayed for guidance, and I am doing what I believe you wanted to the best of my ability. How come things are such a mess? Why has everything seemed to have fallen apart?" Yet the truth of today's passage is that Moses _was doing_ exactly what God wanted…. even though things were hard. The Israelites were in God's will, _even though_ it seemed like they would have nothing to eat or drink. Perhaps you are looking back over your life, and maybe are now struggling with how things are turning out in such unexpected ways. Perhaps the prayer above could be yours. And yet, it is a theological mistake to make the assumption that hard times means God is failing us or that we have misunderstood God's will.

Jesus Himself said that we _would_ have tribulation in this world (John 16:33). He was so right, wouldn't you say? In Acts, we read of lots of hard times for Christ's followers. Peter and John were arrested and beaten. Stephen was executed by stoning. The church was persecuted viciously. Paul was multiple times arrested, beaten, shipwrecked and otherwise thrust into difficult circumstances. This is so true that in 1 Peter we find the admonition that we are not supposed to be surprised when fiery ordeals come to us. Why then, **are** we so surprised or unsettled when we experience hard things in life?

Maybe we struggle with hardship because we have misunderstood the promises of God. God never says everything will coast along easily in life. The scripture actually teaches just the opposite. It teaches that because we are trying to live life the way God wants us to, we are like fish swimming against the current of the world, and things will actually push harder against us. It teaches that there are spiritual enemies who do not like that we are following Christ, and those enemies will seek to undermine, discourage and destroy our faith. It teaches that our true life isn't found in this world, but in eternity as we journey purposefully through this life toward Christ. In fact, the implication is that the hardships we face should be a cause to rejoice, because they can be evidence that we are, indeed, following Christ, otherwise we wouldn't be meeting such opposition. Not that all hardship is simply because we are believers. Some hardships, we know, are just the way the world works. Some of it is of our own creation. But when we know we are following exactly what God has led us to do, and in the midst of that following meet hardship and opposition, we can rejoice because we have become more like Christ, who suffered for us and was *extremely* persecuted because of his stand for God.

Is there something difficult for you just now? Are there things that have not turned out as you had hoped or expected? Do you know that you have done your best and are continuing to try to do your best to follow Christ? Then rejoice in the opposition. And keep your eyes open constantly so that you will not be duped by the evil one, and so that you will be quick to see the mighty hand of God working in your life for good. Not necessarily for easy, but always for good.

Day 147   Exodus 5:1-23

You know, I just hate those times when life gets difficult. In those times, two things happen in my life. One thing I do is spend lots of time and energy trying to understand how I got into that difficult situation and what I can do to solve it. The other thing I do is to ask God to help me out of the hardship somehow. And sometimes, I am sorry to say, I sound just like those Israelites after Moses first appeared to Pharaoh. Moses had come back to Egypt, and it seems folks were excited that they were finally going to get out of slavery. But when Moses confronted the Pharaoh asking for three days so the people could go out and worship in the wilderness, the response received was that Pharaoh considered the people lazy, so made their work even harder. Boy, did that make them mad. They grumbled at Moses. They grumbled to Pharaoh. "It isn't fair. It's an impossible demand. Why is this happening to us? Instead of getting better, things have gotten worse. God, where are you, and why are you allowing this to happen?" And probably a few other choice words expressing their anger and frustration.

But if you stop and think about it, if Pharaoh *had* granted Moses request that first time, or even some of the later times, what would have happened would have been that they would have had a three day weekend attending worship services, and then back to the slave camp. Not much of a deliverance, huh? Not nearly as good an answer as escaping from slavery in Egypt carrying with them treasures from Egypt, which is what eventually happened. The deliverance that did occur is remembered and celebrated every year to this day by Jewish people around the globe during Passover. If they only got their three day weekend, OR if they had only been in slavery for three days followed by an easy time prior to deliverance, I wonder if anybody would have remembered. Somehow, I think God didn't want to do half a miracle for them, He wanted to do something mighty.

I remember when I went to seminary in preparation for ministry, following what I believed was God's call and God's timing. We put the house on the market, and moved to an apartment in a new town to start classes. But the house didn't sell. In fact, it never sold the entire time I was in school. We managed to get it rented out, but that meant we still had to make house payments as well as our apartment rental. It was only after I completed my studies and started at my first church that the house sold. That church had a parsonage, so I was able to put the money into an account, which was then available when the time came to buy another home. Frustrated though I was to be paying rent and making house payments while trying to study, I later realized that had the house sold, the money probably would have all been frittered away on expenses during the time in seminary and thus not been available when we needed it for a down payment on a new home. God could see much further down the road than I could.

Are you struggling with something in life just now? Could it be that God is not answering the way you think He should because He doesn't want to do a halfway deliverance for you, He wants to do something more than you know for reasons that you don't yet know? Grumbling is natural when you are waiting for deliverance. Faithful trust is supernatural. If you are like me, sometimes you bounce between the two. But hang on, let your faith keep you strong when you feel frustrated and grumbly. God's deliverance will be worth the wait, it will be something worth remembering.

┌───┐

MY PRAYER FOR YOU THIS WEEK

This week, my prayer is that you would be filled with God's love to overflowing, so that God's love will overflow from you to the people in your life who need a greater sense of being loved at this time. May God grant you the sensitivity to family, friends and strangers to be able to discern who needs your special touch of love, and when to give love, and the manner in which to love that it may be well received. Amen.

└───┘

Day 148   Psalm 18:1-6, 27-43

Yesterday we talked about God's method of delivering His people out of Egypt. Today, let's take that one step further. Today we find David describing a time when he cried out to God for deliverance. We can look at the stories of David and Saul, and find some of the kinds of situations where he needed deliverance. We may not know exactly what happened that spurred him to write this, but we do know some important things. Some hard situation of his life cast him upon the arms of God. He found himself boxed in not knowing where to turn, and turned to God for the help he needed. For him, God was his rock and refuge, and all the other things David confessed in this Psalm. Therefore, it was part of David's practice to turn to God for aid. When he turned to God, God answered his prayers and David received the deliverance he needed.

As a result, David wrote this Psalm of praise in which he declares the wonder of God's mighty power, proclaims God's ability to give David the strength he needed to defeat any adversity, and, perhaps most importantly, describes God's ways as perfect. Perfect. Probably not what he would have said when he was first crying out to God trying to get out of the difficult situation. But, once he experienced the deliverance God granted, he was able to see the perfection of God's ways, much like we discussed yesterday. And now he had a story to tell, a story of God's faithfulness and power, a story he would not have had if he had not been in a tough situation to need God's help. Not only David, the rest of the scripture recounts stories of people in need of God's aid in tough times, and the stories are recorded describing how God came to their aid. People like Jonah in the fish, or Daniel in the lion's den. People like Peter in a Jerusalem prison, or Paul in a Philippian jail. And those are just a few of the many deliverances God accomplished for His people in the scriptures. Do you notice what is the common theme of these events? Believers found themselves in very tough situations, they called out to God, God accomplished what they needed, and then they have a story to tell about God's power in their lives.

Can you look back over your life to some of the tough times you have experienced? Maybe it was the time God rescued you out of sin's grip in the first place. But there are likely other stories in your life, other times when God was working to meet your needs as you cried out to Him for help. Those stories are your testimony, just as surely as Psalm 18 is the testimony of David to God's deliverance. If you find yourself in tough straits now, and it is likely you do, let those stories of the ones who have gone before in scripture, as well as the stories from your own life, give you the assurance and encouragement you need to call out to God now, knowing that He can work on your behalf. In fact, the only way to gain such a story, often called a testimony, is for you to be in a situation in which you DO need God to help you. Difficult as those tough times might seem, they actually are a great thing if they push you to call out to God. Sadly, sometimes we only think to call out to God when things do get tough, or we call out with more zeal than we do when things are not so difficult. If you are going through a tough time, take time to recognize that your tough time is an opportunity to cry out to God and see how He can meet your needs, just as He has so many others for so many years.

Day 149   Hebrews 11:1-3

Trusting God is kind of a tricky thing. So often we want to trust, but find it difficult when we just can't see the results we want to see. But that is the definition of faith given by Hebrews 11...."the conviction of things not seen" (NASB). You may not be able to understand why these things have happened in your life. But, faith is the conviction of things not seen. You may be convinced that your life will never get better, or there will never be a second chance. But, faith is the conviction of things not seen. There may be bills that you simply cannot imagine how you are going to get paid. But, faith is the conviction of things not seen. Maybe there are other things that trouble your mind....where you will live, how your children will turn out, if your job will be sufficient to provide for your kids and yourself, or even whether you will ever be able to love or be loved again. In each of these areas, remember, faith is the conviction of things not seen.

What is it in your life that you wish you could see right now? Maybe it is how things will ultimately turn out. Maybe it is that you are going to be okay. I can't even begin to make the complete list of the things I would like to know and don't, so I doubt that I could effectively create YOUR list for you. Take the time to consider all the uncertainties of your life, all the matters you wish were settled, all the problems that seem insurmountable to you these days....and then remember, faith is the conviction of the things NOT seen. And, more importantly, remember that just because YOU can't see how everything is going to work out for you, does NOT mean God doesn't see it. He sees the end from the beginning, with a view of everything in between. Like that old song, "His eye is on the sparrow....and I know, He watches me."

Day 150   Genesis 42:35-38

When Joseph's brothers plotted against him, then sold him to the Midianite travelers and brought back the falsified bloody coat, they probably thought their problems were over. Oh, sure, Rueben was upset, because he was going to rescue Joseph. And when their father heard about it, perhaps he was more upset than they expected. But having a little extra cash to spend helped soothe any guilty feelings they might have had. Not only that, but they finally wouldn't have to listen to Joseph's obnoxious dreams anymore. However, the tough times they were having didn't end just then. Getting rid of Joseph didn't accomplish everything they thought it would. Because it seemed that every time they turned around, their dad was still missing their brother....like they had broken his heart and didn't know how to make things right. I suspect that there were days they wondered whether things would ever be the same again. When they saw the tears on their dad's face, they probably wished they could have gone back and undone the damage they had done. If only they could have had a second chance, another opportunity. If only they hadn't done what they did. If only they knew how to make it all okay again with their dad. But they didn't know how. And, they couldn't go back and redo things even if they had wanted to do so.

The Bible is full of stories like that. Like I suppose Jacob's brother, Esau, wished many times over he had not sold away his birthright so rashly. And I suspect there were days when Jacob was out in the fields working for Laban, knowing he was being cheated, that he wished he had never run away from home. I bet Moses wished he hadn't acted so rashly as he stood on Mount Nebo looking over the river to the Promised Land he would never enter. I can't imagine that Samson didn't live with a lot of regrets about his whole affair with Delilah.... especially as he sat in a Philistine prison with his eyes gone. Surely Naomi must have questioned the wisdom of leaving Israel after so many family members died there in Moab. And how many times did David get himself into messes with his poor choices, wishing he could take back his actions and start over. But they were in the same boat that all of us experience at some time in life....the issue of regret over poor decisions that we wish we had never made. For the family of Jacob, once Joseph was sold, things never would be the same again. Life just isn't like that. They couldn't go back, they could only go forward. They simply had to make the best of the situation they had created, and repenting before God, try to start again from where they were. When they did go forward, they actually ended up doing okay, because God provided for them during a famine by having Joseph in Egypt ahead of them to pave the way.

There may be days in your life when you wish you could go back and change the choices you have made. That is not an option God has granted in life. There are ways you may be able to go and make amends and reconciliation in relationships, but you cannot undo the past. The good news, though, is that the biblical stories of individuals who made poor choices they could not go back and change, very often demonstrate that God does not end His work because of our poor choices. Instead, He can even turn the poor choices into something very good, such as Joseph rising near Egypt's throne. But only when an individual is willing to go forward. Pining for the past, living in regret, longing for the good old days accomplishes nothing. Allowing God to start where you are at, and then to guide you into what could be, brings the promise of God into the realities of life. Make what amends you can or feel you should, leave your regrets behind you and walk toward tomorrow with God.

Day 151   Job 2:11-13

Some people have observed that, although Job's friends offered not terribly helpful words that sounded more like accusations than consolation, *at least they came and sat with their grieving friend for seven days BEFORE they spoke a word!* Most of us today are more likely to mail a card or drop off a casserole! However, in the Jewish community, this example of the time commitment one extends to friends in grief is called "sitting sheva"....which means sitting for seven days and is a core concept tied up with the Jewish traditions for those in grief. Other American cultural and religious traditions in times of grief include the sending of flowers, gathering of families, holding wakes, bodies lying in state for visitation and, of course, the memorial or funeral service itself. But those ceremonies only apply to times of death. There aren't those kinds of processes available to those who grieve losing a job, losing a home to a fire, hurricane or foreclosure and not, as relevant for us, for the loss of a marriage through divorce. But, as we have said before, the grief is *just as real.* Today, I want to reflect just a bit on the grief that results from divorce, because it is more complicated than many people imagine it to be.

It is patently obvious that the grief in a divorce is tied in with the loss of a marriage. But the tentacles of that grief extend into many arenas beyond the marriage relationship, and it is that I wish to consider today. For example, at least one of the divorcing people will *also* be suffering the grief of losing their home. You both may experience grieving the loss of some time you might have had with your children. You may grieve the loss of the normalcy you once had, and it may surface in such things as feeling awkward going out with a couple whose company you used to enjoy frequently when you were married. It can show up in the things that you sense may never be for you. Things such as when you see a couple smile at each other when their child acts cute at the school play, or when you attend the 50th anniversary celebration for friends, realizing that you probably won't have one of those anniversaries yourself. I remember being at the home of some friends, and admiring a beautiful potted tree they had. They told me they had received it as a present for their 25th anniversary.... not realizing that their words would make me consider that I had just lost the 25th anniversary I would have celebrated in a few short years, and felt that I might never have the opportunity to celebrate a 25th anniversary in my life. Grief can strike you in unexpected moments, like children's graduations, weddings, or even when you attend concerts, movies and the kind of sporting events that were part of your past. Especially if you used to watch your kids in those events. There can be this pervasive emptiness, and an overwhelming sense of loss that pops up in the most unexpected places. Since there are no clear ceremonies for the process of grieving a divorce, and no clear recognition of the grief process, you can feel very alone and troubled when these moments catch you off guard.

I have no big answers for what you will experience, no little formulas to make it all okay. What I do have is the suggestion that you add to your information bank the knowledge that your divorce process involves a lot of grieving, even beyond the initial loss of the marriage. I suggest that you take heed of the Jewish tradition of sitting sheva, recognizing that the grieving process isn't going to resolve itself in a few short moments over a casserole and a card. And recognize that sometimes the things you are grieving are a reflection of the richness of your life....you wouldn't be bothered over that time you felt awkward with your friends <u>if you had no friends</u>! Finally, let me suggest just a few thoughts. First, find yourself some good friends you can count on to "sit sheva" with you when you need someone. Secondly, recognize that grief is a function of the loss of something important and valued.... so if you are grieving, it is because of the values you hold dear. And finally, never forget that, even though you may be blindsided by unexpected grief, God was not, and that these odd little quirks may in fact be intentional prods toward healing that He has placed along your path. He will guide you all the way through as you move forward to healing and hope....even if that forward movement takes much longer than you think it "should." God will continue to walk with you, no matter how long it takes.

Day 152   Luke 10:1-6, 17-20

It is so important to keep in touch with those God has placed in authority over us. I am one, by the way, who believes that scriptural authority comes through servanthood, not the might of power.... those who are called to be our shepherds, to help us through, to offer guidance....that sort of authority. Sadly, I am aware that there are those in church leadership who don't see their role as compassionate servants, and instead abuse their authority and use it to enhance their own status, or as if they sit in judgment on others from some elevated position. I hope you don't have to endure those kind of things in your church. If that is your experience with your pastor, you may need to consider other individuals you can turn to for **godly** advice and support.

Nonetheless, the scripture is clear that we are to share all good things with those God has placed over us. That is part of what we see happening in today's readings. The disciples went out as Jesus had sent them, and then came back to let Him know how things had been going. The same thing happened time and again in Acts, as Peter, Paul, others were sent out on the various mission journeys, and then would come back to Jerusalem or Antioch to let the home base know how things were going, and what had happened. In the case of Peter and Paul, one of the issues brought to the home base was how to handle the non-Jewish converts. Since those converts had never kept the various laws in the Hebrew Bible prior to coming to Christ, the question arose of what needed to be required, and what things were uniquely part of the covenant with the Jews. Neither Peter nor Paul felt those decisions should be made on their own; they brought the question to the leadership for guidance.

It is important that you find a way to do the same kind of thing. It really is important to keep in touch with your pastor, or a small group leader, or some other person in your church who can assume the role of helping to watch out for you. You don't have to belabor every little detail with them, or run every decision by them. But you need to let them know how you are doing. And let them know honestly. Don't give them that stupid little answer that so often crosses our lips, "I'm fine." If they don't know you are struggling, how do you expect them to know you need their assistance? Share your prayer requests with them. Ask them for any biblical insights they could offer. Let them know how a sermon or a study impacted you when you needed it. Seek their counsel in tough decisions.

*We are **not** called to follow Christ all by ourselves!!* We are called to follow Christ in the community of believers. We are also not given leaders by God so that we can ignore them and not bother them with our struggles. God has placed them there for our welfare. I know, as a pastor, sometimes those struggles can feel burdensome to us as we spend hours listening and offering assistance....but it is a privileged burden to help carry the load of one of Christ's children. Take advantage of what God has provided for YOU. Help them do a good job: tell them what you need, ask them to pray, thank them for the times of support and encouragement....but don't let yourself fall into the trap of isolation. This may be a time God may want to teach them something through your experience, and to teach you something through theirs....don't cut off the opportunity.

And please, pray for your leaders, especially your pastor. Having served as a pastor in several churches myself, I cannot tell you how much it means to know that there are people in my church who are praying for me. I would also encourage you to do what the apostles did when they returned to Jesus, share with your advisors the good things God is doing in your life, not merely the struggles. Allow them to peek into the window of your soul, to see the fruit of their labor. It will do both of you good!

Day 153   Hebrews 10:35-39

As a pastor who has known a variety of people over the years, I have the sad experience of being aware of too many people who started out with the Lord, and for one reason or another, gave up. And the most amazing thing about it is that it isn't always who you think it might be. Sometimes it is people who are great leaders in the church, who are involved in many activities and clearly committed, whose example people have admired, but then something happens with them and they end up disappearing over time. This, to me, is the very point Paul is making in 1 Corinthians....don't ever think that it couldn't happen to you. In fact, I would argue that the stronger your commitment to Christ, and the more visible your ministry and your leadership God is using in the lives of others, the more intensely Satan is going to try to knock you out of action, using whatever means are necessary to do so.

One of the least preached about, but most scriptural characteristics God seeks to instill in His people is the ability to endure. And the only way people develop the ability to endure is by having to endure something. In the times of stress like that, you learn what things you can lean on to get you through. You learn about yourself, about your temptations, your needs, your values, and your weakness. You learn the best ways for YOU to draw strength from God to help you endure. All too often, we Christians forget to take the long view, allowing temporal things to pull us down while giving up too easily. Endurance is a choice. Read some of the stories by those people who were prisoners of war....there are several from Germany, Vietnam, and even hostages by terrorists. They can share insights to help you in your spiritual warfare. Talk to some saints you know who have gone through tough times and ask them to share their wisdom with you to help you through. Don't ever think you are safe. When we start thinking we are safe, that it can't happen to us, we are actually making ourselves the most vulnerable as pride takes root and we let our guard down. Choose to go after the long haul, the good race to the finish, to endure in the faith no matter what. And then seek out the help that you need from God and from fellow believers so that you will be one of those who endure to the end and are saved.

Day 154   Luke 7:36-50

In every divorce, there are plenty of opportunities to learn how to forgive or how to hold grudges. And sometimes the things which you might need to forgive are things that are very hurtful, things that are hard. Today, let's take a bit of time to discuss what forgiveness is not. Jesus didn't just let people off the hook. There were several times people heard Jesus tell them they were forgiven, but He didn't take away the consequences of their sins. In some cases, they were outcast. In others, they have the emotional and maybe physical scars of their past. Jesus set them free from the bondage of sin by granting them forgiveness, but He did not say that all of their struggles would end just because He forgave them. And surely some of those sins were heinous to Him. Yet He forgave....not because they deserved it, but because that is His nature, to forgive those who wronged Him, even if they don't deserve it. That is an important lesson for us to learn, if we are going to be

"Christians"…."little christs". We forgive because that is God's nature living out through us….we forgive because of what difference it makes in us and who we are. In other words, practicing forgiveness is about <u>us</u>, It doesn't matter what *they* did, or whether *they* deserve it, or whether *they* ask for forgiveness. What matters is who *you* are, and to whom *you* belong, and whom *you* choose to obey, and, possibly most important of all, whom you decide you want to be like: Jesus or somebody more hurtful and unforgiving.

Secondly, notice also that Jesus didn't pretend what they did wasn't significant. It was. He called sin, "sin." And He taught that sin always entangles and destroys. Maybe you are in your divorce situation right now because of somebody's sin….maybe your ex's sin, maybe your own. There is no need to pretend like it doesn't matter….that is a dead end road that resolves nothing. There is no need to pretend that you haven't been hurt or hurt others, or that you think what happened is okay and right. But with forgiveness, the choice is that you are going to do what is necessary for you to be right with God yourself, and that you are choosing not to let your future be determined by the sins of somebody else. You choose to forgive because your share of the sins have been forgiven, and because you want to be free from the control that your sin and the sins of others have had over you, so that you may walk freely into the future Christ has for you. And as you go into that future, you can go as others did in Jesus' day, with the words ringing in your ears and heart: go, and sin no more.

MY PRAYER FOR YOU THIS WEEK

This week, my prayer for you is for your strength and endurance. When you want to escape, may God grant you strength to fight to victory. When you want to quit, may God give you the strength to see it through. When the world crashes down and you feel overwhelmed, may God's strength enable you to dig your way out, one boulder at a time. In the name of Jesus, who is our rock and our strength, Amen.

Day 155   Nehemiah 7:1-4; 8:1-12

My attorney asked me if I wanted to attend the divorce proceedings at the court, and if I wanted her to accompany me there. I wasn't sure what she meant. Turns out in my state, at least, I could go by myself, I could go with my attorney, or my attorney could appear on my behalf instead of me. I asked her why I would want to do so, given that I had already felt great wear and tear on my emotions as it was. Her reply was that for some people, that proceeding becomes the ceremony of closure to the process of divorce, and the end of the marriage. I chose not to, but realized I, too, needed to make sure there was closure in some tough areas. I wonder if Jacob needed that closure when he, as Israel, returned to Bethel, or the exiles as they anticipated their return from exile. There were events I needed to go through as a divorced single that had previously been the domain of a couple….things like theater performances, worship attendance, celebrating birthdays and holidays, even driving on familiar highways. Some of these things happened naturally, or even serendipitously. Some happen by accident that I would have avoided had I but known. Some others had to be created to occur. There may be places you need to reclaim as your own. There may be some things about yourself that have always been there, but have long been buried in your relationship, and the time may now have come for you to reclaim those.

Closure is important. Some people need certain ceremonies. I have known of some who brought closure by crying until they could cry no more. Others I know have burned letters, pictures or some other symbolic act. Whatever yours may be, there needs to come a day and an act in which you can intentionally lay to rest the things that trouble you, bring some kind of closure and allow you to move on. It isn't something you can rush. Unfortunately, it *is* something you can avoid for a long time by stuffing your feelings and cautiously keeping away from things that would remind you. But, if you will prayerfully allow God to help you face those memories, and face the people and places that bring back those memories… painful though they be….you will be able to construct your own kind of closure that will prepare you for the next chapter of your life in a healthy way, ready for what God might bring. And maybe, like those Jews of old, you will be able to experience that the time of your exile is over. It's time to go back to the homeland of who God created you to be.

Day 156   John 12:1-11

For the people who opposed Jesus, having Lazarus walking around was a problem. As long as he was in the tomb dead, they could easily point out that Jesus didn't manage to keep His friend from dying, that he hadn't even hurried His schedule to go see him when he was sick. It suggested that Jesus wasn't as loving as everybody thought, nor as powerful. It suggested that there were indeed limits to His powers, and that undermined His claim to be the Son of God. But then Jesus called out for Lazarus to come out of the tomb....and when he did, that was a problem. Everywhere they went, when somebody would question what Jesus could and could not do, there was probably always somebody around who remembered that there was a Lazarus walking around who wasn't supposed to be. No wonder they wanted to kill him. Although, if you think about that, it really is pretty stupid isn't it? After all, he had already died once, and that didn't take the first time....what made them think Jesus wouldn't just mess it up again for them? Still, they just wished he was gone.

I'm sure you know something of what it must have felt like for them....someone walking around making life difficult. Or that time you go walking down the street, and pass that familiar face, a face you thought you would never have to see again. But the truth is, life goes on. There are times and events that will logically result in you and your ex being in the same place at the same time. It is just how life is. And no matter how uncomfortable that may feel, it is not the end of the world. That person may no longer be your wife, or your husband, but he or she remains the father or mother of your children. She or he remains a person with whom you have shared significant portions of your life, and who is woven throughout the memories of your life and the fabric of who you are....whether you like it or not. You might think life would be easier if that person wasn't around, and you never had to deal with them again. Whether or not that is true is irrelevant.... because it isn't reality. Reality is, he or she is there, and you will have those moments, and life goes on. So, like those Jewish leaders of old who were troubled with the presence of Lazarus, you have a choice to make. You can either pretend it isn't so, and live a life of denial and stress. Or, you can face the reality of what has happened in life square on, and find the meaning that exists in it. If they had done so, they would have realized that Jesus really was the Messiah, the Son of God, and ultimately found eternal life and salvation through Him, as Paul later did when faced with the same choice. Only God knows what you will find as you face your reality head on, looking to God to provide the meaning. You will have opportunity to make this choice many times in your future. Choose wisely.

Day 157 *Philippians 3:13-16*

In the grieving of divorce, there is often a rehashing over and again all the years, all the arguments, all the times you made decisions, and now you wonder what would have happened had you decided differently. Depending on your temperament, you can identify all those things that convince you it was all your fault, or you can come up with the conclusion that none of it was your fault. Both are probably wrong. But there comes a time when you have to change directions, a time when you have to turn around and look forward instead of looking back.

Paul knew this experience, as well. He knew what he had been.... he knew his past, he knew his credentials, he knew everything he had once pursued, but now it was no longer relevant because he had come to a different point in his life, a different direction. His way of handling this shift took place after his conversion, when he knew he had to lay aside the mistakes and misunderstandings he had based his life on previously, to step into the new life Christ was calling him to live. The same is true of you and I after a divorce. There may have been good times, there may have been bad times, there may have been good choices, there may have been poor choices, but there comes the time when we need to let go of what is behind and press forward to what is ahead in Christ. Certainly there is no value in rehashing old events about which you can do nothing. Certainly there is little value in beating yourself up for choices you wish you had never made. If your situation is one that is moving toward reconciliation, then you must look at how things were done that led you to this point of crisis so that in reconciliation, you can each find a different way of doing things. But if your direction has instead led to divorce, then you may have to just let go. Don't nurse the old grudges. Don't continually mourn the mistakes. Pick up your knapsack, so to speak, load it up with the things of your life that are worth keeping as you journey forward, and then walk away from the things that no longer are part of your life. This is not something done in the kind of anger and rage exemplified by the spouse who destroys clothes and pictures as if they can rid themselves of the hurt by destruction. Instead, it is a healthy acknowledging of life's reality, and with quiet acceptance of what has been, laying to rest the past so as to focus your energy and attention to the future. When you feel you are ready to do some turning toward the future, I suggest you make some kind of tangible act that represents that turning for you. Perhaps you could take a stroll, and as you walk, pray through the various memories that need to be left behind, and then, when you get to a fork in the road, or a corner, make a turn confessing to God that you have turned a corner in your life, and asking Him to guide you in the new direction you are taking. Maybe you have a better idea, and that's good. Whatever you do, however you accomplish it, imprint upon yourself this time of forgetting what is behind as you turn to press on toward the future God has.

Day 158   1 Samuel 25:1-28

How embarrassed Abigail must have felt, to have to run out and apologize for her husband's stupidity. But she did it. She swallowed her pride, went out and found David, and apologized for Nabal while offering the supplies David had requested in the first place. Embarrassment feels lousy, but it isn't the end of the world. Sometimes embarrassment and humiliation are a huge part of divorce. It can be embarrassing if others thought you had a perfect marriage and, now that it has fallen apart, you go everywhere without your spouse. This can be especially the case if your spouse is leaving you for another lover with whom he/she committed adultery. Particularly if others knew about it, and you were the last to find out. Not only do you have the feelings tied in with the divorce process, you also have to deal with betrayal, and maybe even people wondering what is wrong with you that your spouse would cheat on you. Maybe you have asked yourself the same question. I want to forego some "political correctness" in a way that might help with the embarrassment, if this is your situation. (If it is NOT your situation, then pause a moment right now and thank God you don't have to endure that.) Your spouse left you for the adulterous partner with whom they have been breaking the seventh of the ten commandments of God: "You shall not commit adultery." (Exodus 20:14, NASB) Now, thinking of that wording, there surely should be some embarrassment and shame, but if you are not the one committing that sin, it is not YOU who needs to have that.

Whether or not you are the one who should feel embarrassed or humiliated, "should" doesn't have much clout in the world of feelings.... you feel what you feel. The issue of being humiliated is actually a big topic of discussion in the Hebrew Bible. When you have been dishonored, your head hangs, your self confidence fades, your energy level drops....it is just a lousy experience to go through. But there comes the time you have to deal with the embarrassment face to face, and then move on. Maybe you need to confront a person, maybe you need to go back out into the group of folks you have been avoiding, maybe you just need to make your peace with yourself in prayer. There is a story about David in 2 Samuel, chapter 10, in which a foreign king had intentionally shamed some of David's messengers by cutting off their beards and clothes. David knew how hard their humiliation was for them, just as God knows how hard your embarrassment or humiliation is for you. David assigned the men some time to be away by themselves, to heal up a bit and then, once their beards grew back and their strength returned, they were able to walk into the city once again with their heads held high. That day will come for you, too. Ask God to bring you the restoration and strength you are lacking.

Day 159   Mark 10:13-16

We have previously discussed that, if there are children in your marriage, you need to look out for their welfare. And realize, it may not be just your own children if you have them, because marriage and divorce takes place in the context of a family, an extended family. There may be nieces or nephews who are hurting, knowing they may never see a favorite aunt or uncle again. For that matter, it is not that uncommon, unfortunately, for children to see their grandparents divorcing. And the child may be confused, or they may think they understand, when what they really understand is a twisted version of reality. When Jesus saw the children around Him, the scripture says He took them in His arms and blessed them. He knew children don't always have the easiest time in this world. Kids are often very mean to one another. Adults often get too busy to notice the kids around them. Parents can sometimes get so caught up with their responsibilities....or so absorbed in the struggles and decisions of divorce, that they may not see how much their kids are struggling, too.

Today, I want to challenge you to be like Jesus. Take a child in your arms and bless him. Give that child a moment of joy, knowing she is loved, knowing he is important, knowing that somebody has noticed her. Do your best to not put your children in the middle of your divorce garbage, don't try to convince the child you are right or to be on your side. Just bless him or her. He so needs a blessing in this hard time, and only you can give him the blessing of his mother or father, her aunt or uncle, his grandmother or grandfather. Let Jesus be your inspiration and example. Intentionally be a blessing to the children in your life.... even when you don't feel like you can, and you will find that you will be blessed right back! And remember, all of us make mistakes, that is why we need forgiveness and grace: do your best, and then trust God to make up for what you cannot.

Day 160   Hebrews 12:13-17

Just after my divorce began, a friend I hadn't seen in many years turned up on my doorstep to give me some words of encouragement. He had been through a divorce a decade earlier, and he offered what he felt were the most important words of advice he had to share. He merely encouraged me not to allow myself to become bitter. His divorce had been a particularly nasty one, and there had been a good deal of vindictiveness and greed involved that had taken him to the proverbial cleaners....at least, that's how it appeared to me from the outside. The lesson he had learned, and had to struggle to conquer himself, was how to not be bitter. The passage in Hebrews today speaks of bitterness as a root, a root that can grow, spring up, and defile many people beside just the one who is himself bitter. It is a temptation we all face when we have been hurt. You may even want to go back and reread Ruth 1, where the woman, Naomi (whose name means pleasant) had suffered many reversals in life: famine, displacement, widowhood, and the death of her only children are the ones that the story highlights. When she wandered back to her hometown and everyone greeted her by name, she told them not to call her Naomi (pleasant), but instead to call her Mara, which means bitter. She felt abandoned, betrayed by God, and now that her life had become bitter, she began to feel bitter as well. Hard times....such as divorce....set up that temptation.

Unforgiveness becomes the mortar by which the bricks of bitterness are held together. Bitterness is the root that defiles the pure work of God. Defilement leads to decay and destruction. My friend told me simply to not let myself become bitter. His implication is that it is a choice. His experience was that it is a poor choice with lousy consequences, and the path of bitterness takes a long time to retrace once you have gone down its way. Bitterness is like a rottenness in your soul that gnaws and nags, it slowly eats away your insides and festers in your heart. The root that is bitterness is a rotten root, and when it springs up, it shows itself in short temper, sour disposition, judgmentalism and depression. Bitter people are often lonely people, because nobody wants to be around them, except other people who are also nurturing their bitterness. Together, they drag one another down and feed the bitterness by grumbling, complaining, comparing war stories....just like the grumbling Israelites did in the wilderness. And the isolation from more positive people just creates more bitterness. The spiral is not a good one to get into.

We have planted a new garden at our house this year. As we cleared the garden, and then strove to keep the garden clear, it was clear pretty quickly that it is much easier to pull the weeds out before the roots have a chance to spread themselves and grow deep. Once they have dug themselves in, you have to dig forever, and can no longer just pull them, but have to get out the shovel or other tools to make sure you get all the roots out. The same is true with bitterness. The longer you let it grow, the tougher the root will become, and the harder to get it out of your soul. Take an assessment of your heart today. Look out for those weeds of bitterness, and start cleaning out their vile influence by offering them up to God.

Day 161   Philippians 4:4-8 (You might enjoy The Message Bible for this verse.)

Do you know that little round based on verse four? I suppose I have sung it countless times in my life. Does this verse ever bother you? Do you ever have those times when you just say to yourself, "but I just don't feel very joyful." Maybe you even feel more like crying or are in despair most of the time, so this verse is the last thing you would use to describe how you felt. Then, maybe you go another step, and start to feel guilty, because Christians are supposed to be happy people, aren't they? After all, it does say to rejoice ALWAYS. Then you can begin to believe that you aren't a very good Christian, especially if you know all the other verses that talk about joy and rejoicing in hardship. Well intentioned people may try to help you rejoice by telling you things like, "You know, it could be much worse, I know a friend who....," or, "You really ought to be glad you are out of that marriage, the way he/she was treating you." I'm sure you've heard others, and would even agree with me that there is some truth in what is said, but it still doesn't help change how you are feeling.

Let me make some suggestions and observations. First, despite the ideas some suggest, being a Christian does not mean that God will shut down half of the normal emotions humans experience....at least not until the day He wipes every tear from your eyes in glory. Notice that the implication of that concept, of course, is that there are tears which need to be wiped away! No, Christians have the same range of emotions as everybody else, like it or not.

Secondly, the Bible does not promise you will never have any hard times if you are a Christian. In fact, you could easily make the argument that it promises just the opposite, because we are following the example of our Savior who suffered for us, and who told us that we would have tribulation in the world. Thirdly, rejoicing and joy are not necessarily the same thing as emotional happiness, and are not based on our feelings and experiences. Remember in Luke 19 when the disciples had been out doing ministry and came back on "cloud nine," ecstatic and thrilled over what God was doing through them? In that passage, Jesus warns them not to rejoice in those things, but to rejoice that their names are written in heaven. In other words, not to let their experiences and emotional state be the foundation of their joy, and I think He said that because He knew just how fickle this world and our emotions can be. Instead, He pointed them to a different source for joy.

Joy is not an artificial smile placed upon our faces that comes out in half hearted "Praise the Lord"'s in hard times. Christian joy is a deep assurance that abides in the midst of tears and hurt, as well as happiness and excitement. Notice that prior to Philippians 4:8, Paul is addressing people who seem to be weighed down and worried, because this verse is a prescription to counteract those experiences, and to help them handle those struggles in a godly manner. His advice is that they turn all their worries into prayer, choose to rejoice in the Lord, and change their thought patterns. Tomorrow we shall talk more about what it means to rejoice in the Lord, but today, take a quick inventory of how you are doing with the other parts of these instructions. Are you keeping all your worries, or are you taking them to God in prayer? What do you let your mind dwell on, the hard things, the discouraging things, and the scary things about your life right now, or things that match the list in verse eight? Take a few minutes to discuss these matters with your loving Father.

MY PRAYER FOR YOU THIS WEEK

This week, I pray that God will give you a sound mind, free from fear, free from confusion, full of the Spirit of God and the wisdom that comes from Him alone. May your anxieties be laid to rest and your mind able to focus with clarity on the tasks God has given for you today, and each day, one day at a time. Amen.

Day 162   1 Samuel 25:14-33

At another point, we discussed the story of Abigail and Nabal in relation to her utter embarrassment at his inappropriate and foolish behavior. She seemed to respond almost automatically. Like she had done it before. Lots of times before. She knew he was a foolish man…. it would appear she loved him anyway. And part of how she showed her love was to intervene when he made serious mistakes by covering for him to shield him from consequences. If you come out of an abusive relationship, it may actually be that God has looked upon your need and you are in the midst of being rescued….even though it may not feel like it. Living in abusive relationships is addictive. It may not be the dream you always wanted, but it is at least something, and you come to believe that something is better than nothing, and better than the unknown future on your own. Sometimes a divorce will force an abusive person to face the issues they need to face so they can change. Sometimes it only causes them to pretend to change. Frequently, the abused spouse believes that the abuse was all her or his fault....when, in fact, much of the blame rests on the choices and issues of the abuser.

On the other hand, the abused person can come to believe that it was all the abuser's fault and they are absolutely innocent. I would suggest that there is no behavior by a spouse that justifies their being abused....there is no excuse for that horrendous behavior. But there is also no perfect person, and the abused spouse will also have their own issues. Sometimes the issue is rescuing, sometimes it is provoking, sometimes it is self blame, sometimes it is living in denial....there are many, although it is very difficult for abused persons to identify the issues objectively, as they have so long been told everything is their fault. If you have been abused, it is a good thing that you were able to love a person who treated you poorly, and that you were willing to stand by them and try just as Abigail tried. But Abigail's intervention did not keep God from holding Nabal accountable, and it won't keep God from holding your abusive spouse accountable....somehow...someday.

If you have been in an abusive relationship....whether physically being beaten, sexually abused, or emotionally and mentally abused, I want to strongly encourage you to spend some significant time and energy in self-examination. Why? Because if you do not face and work through the issues that are your own, the odds are extremely high that you will end up in exactly the same kind of relationship again. And honestly, do you really want another trip to the hospital? Do you really want to have to call your alcoholic spouse's boss with another lying excuse about being sick? Do you really want to have to pretend at church that your spouse is the most wonderful thing on earth, knowing that if you don't you will be terrorized when you get home? Or, the other thing that can happen is that you can simply replace one dysfunction with another.

You may need to get some counseling, an option that may make all the difference in your future. You may need to get involved in a codependency support ministry, or read some good materials on those kind of topics. But if you are going to have a real break from that kind of life and a true fresh start, it won't happen automatically....you have to intentionally face the issues and work on growing, so that God can help you into a new and better life. I don't know how great Abigail's marriage to David was, as David's marriages sure seem odd by today's standards. But it is clear that, unlike Nabal, David at least appreciated her for the wise woman she was....and for her, that was probably a breath of fresh air. Fresh air can come your way, too. Do what it takes to prepare for it now, and to make sure you don't end up making the same mistakes with the same kind of person in the future.

Day 163   Psalm 103:11-14

How far have you traveled in this world? As of this writing, the furthest east I have ever been would be when I visited the country of Jordan a few years ago. The furthest west would be either the Olympic National Park or maybe when I went out on a vessel whale watching in the Pacific. I used to drive from my home in Kansas to my college in Pennsylvania. It took 24 hours to drive straight through with gas and food stops along the way. I have driven to see my sister up in Washington State several times, and that road trip is about three days. When I flew to Jordan, it was something like 12 hours on the plane.... maybe more, I don't remember...it was a long time ago on an overnight flight, and I slept a lot. Often, on my cross country journeys, I am struck by the vastness of creation. I realize I am driving for hours and hours, but even driving all day is just a fraction of the circumference of the globe. And as I see all the cracks in the highway that they have tried to repair time and again as the earth has broken it, I realize the road might be six, ten, maybe even twelve inches thick. It is such a minute fraction of the earth's crust! Just a tiny smidgen of the earth's diameter. And then I think, as far as the east is from the west. That's a long way. A very, long way.

If you travel around our globe, you can head north for a long way. But when you reach the North Pole, no matter which way you go, you will now be going south. Obviously the same is true if you head south. In effect, south and north meet at the poles. But if you head east, you can keep going east around our globe indefinitely....you will never suddenly be going west. And the same is true if you head west. When God chose to describe how far He removes your sins from you when He forgives you, He chose east and west, not north and south. What are the sins that have scarred your life? Are there some heavy burdens of regret and guilt you have carried around for too long? You cannot get rid of them by yourself, regardless of how much counseling you get, or how much you try to be a better person, or how much you change everything about yourself. Because the debt of sin is one you owe to

God, and changing your present and future cannot change your past. But God has provided the way to wash you within, to make you clean and remove those hideous stains of sin. This comes through the sacrifice of Christ at Calvary on your behalf, and after having accepted that sacrifice as your own, simply coming to God in confession of your sin, asking for His cleansing forgiveness. At that moment, the sin is removed from you and placed as far as the east is from the west....infinitely far from you. Take some time right now to offer to God anything that needs cleansing and forgiveness. And then think about how far east you have been in your life, and how far west. Then multiply that distance by millions of millions....those sins are gone that far. Praise God, He is a mighty Savior, wouldn't you say?

Day 164   Matthew 19:26

Do you really believe this verse? Maybe you believe it in a theoretical way. But what about in your specific situation? Do you believe that nothing is outside the possibilities of God for the circumstances of *your* life? Are there walls that seem impossible to break through? Or obstacles too big to overcome? Maybe there is a brokenness, or some broken relationships that are beyond healing. Or there could be a flood of things that are more than overwhelming which are nearly drowning you. None of those kinds of things are outside the possibilities of God. God is able to do things that you would consider beyond hope, beyond repair, beyond victory, beyond imagination....but they are only beyond YOUR hope, YOUR ability to repair, YOUR power to gain victory, YOUR limited imagination. Nothing is beyond God's possibilities.

Now, of course, just because something is possible, doesn't mean it is automatically going to be what becomes reality. For example, it is entirely possible for God to simply destroy the world before you finish reading this sentence. But that doesn't mean He is going to do so.... apparently He didn't or you wouldn't be reading THIS sentence! It is possible for a parent to feed his or her child candy for breakfast, lunch and dinner every day....and the child might believe that would be their dream come true. But that doesn't mean the parent is going to do it.... because the parent knows that some possible things are not the best practical things. And God knows even better than that parent what possible things are the best practical things for your life. It's just that He is not limited by what WE think is possible.

So the possibilities of God are greater than the challenges of your life. But the choice of which possibility God wants to use, and the timing of when God wants to use that possibility, are God's decisions, not ours. Sometimes I think I know exactly what God ought to do. But God, knowing more than I do, chooses not to use that possibility, instead using another one I couldn't have imagined. And that, of course, turns out to be a better option anyway. Don't let your limited understanding and imagination determine your level of trust and hope....because God is bigger than that. What God does might radically stretch you, teach you, change you, empower you, expand your understanding of God.... BESIDES meeting the challenge you face. Just keep reminding yourself, "nothing is impossible with God!"

Day 165   Romans 8:26-27

Sometimes our prayers can become rote and boring. I always wonder how God feels listening to us pray, especially when I try to imagine us talking to our good friends the same way we talk to God. Like people who mention God's name every third word....you know: "O God, we just come to you, God, and want to ask you, Lord, to help us our God and..." well, you get the idea. What if you, Fred, said to your friend, Fred, that you wanted his help, Fred, if only he would pay attention, Fred? Bizarre, huh? Or the prayers that are a lot of words that we almost never hear ourselves saying in our other connections, like, "Dear God, we thank thee for this which we are about to receive from your bounty." Not a bad prayer, but how often do you think about something called bounty and who all do you call "thee"? Then there are times when we quickly list to God our concerns or needs as we scurry from one pressing task to the next. But to really take the time to have a heart to heart.... well, we just don't bother.

When life is changing and uncertain, or when it is hard and frightening, can be a good time to deepen your prayer life. So many things in your life may be completely restructuring these days, as you evaluate what you are keeping, what you are removing, what you are changing, and what you are adding. What if you applied those questions to the evaluation of your prayer life? In this time of possible restructure, would you like it to be different than it is? Are there some things about it that you want to make sure you never lose? Maybe it is that you have a special time and place with God, or some special terms of endearment you share. Are there things you want to remove....habits that have lost their meaning for you, or distractions that hinder your time with God? What about changing things, are there some things you have about your prayer life that you want developed more deeply, such as learning to support your prayers with scripture, or learning from the recorded prayers of past prayer warriors? Are there some things you wish to add into your prayer life? Perhaps a more dedicated time of praise and thanksgiving is in order. Perhaps including a time to sing some hymns or praise choruses to God as you pray. Maybe it is in the area of intercession you wish greater depth as you develop your prayer life. In any case, during the times when prayer becomes more urgent to us, we are given an opportunity to shape our prayer into something more meaningful, something in which the Spirit Himself joins us in power and guidance to make our time with God more precious with each passing day. In this time of a changing life, don't neglect the critical area of building a better prayer life as you put together the new directions your life will take.

Day 166   Hebrews 11:13-16

Have you ever been ashamed of God? You know, like in a situation where social friends are making fun of Christians, or commenting on how backwards anyone must be to hold the values Christians hold, and rather than speak up, you remain silent. I think most of us have had at least one experience in which we were tested about how we would respond in such a situation and fell short of what our ideal response would have been. Today, though, I want you to notice something just the opposite. Today's passage does not address whether or not you have been ashamed to speak up for God; instead, it refers to God's attitude toward us. God is not ashamed to be called OUR God.

Perhaps there have been times in your life when you feel unworthy, unloved, undesirable, unwanted.... you know, almost like you are an "unperson." You may feel that way because your ex has treated you that way. You may feel that way because others have treated you that way. You may feel that way because that is how you have treated others who have been divorced. Or you may feel that way because you have convinced yourself that the failure of the marriage was all your fault. But God does not base His opinion of you on those things. Any and all of the above things are not sufficient reason to cause God to be ashamed of you. In fact, the opposite is true.

God bases His opinion of you on a more eternal foundation. God's foundation includes the fact that you are His own handcrafted creation. A foundation that includes the fact that He deemed you a person for whom it was worth dying on a cross. His foundation also includes the fact that you have decided you wanted to live with God forever in heaven (if you have done so).

He is proud to have you as part of the family. He is pleased that you have chosen heaven as your eternal home. He is not ashamed of you. You are not some black sheep of the family who has to slip in the back way. One time, with Job, God told Satan how upright Job was. Another time, with Jesus, He announced that Jesus was His beloved Son, and He was pleased with Him. And there will come a time when He will make the same kind of announcement about you. Because He loves you. Because He has redeemed you. Because He has saved you. Because He has called you His own. Because He knows you have yearned for heaven. He is not ashamed to be your God. We need not be ashamed that we are His children or that He is our God. Shame belongs to the kingdom of darkness. Hold your head high and give praise to the Almighty God, your God, the God, who is not ashamed of His relationship with YOU!

Day 167   Psalm 1:2-3

I have something I have always wished I could see, kind of a strange thing. I have always heard about tree roots, in terms of their depth and breadth, that there often is more tree underground than above. So I've always thought it would be kind of neat if there was a museum somewhere that had managed to pull out an entire tree with its root system intact. I am especially struck with that concept when I mow the lawn or work in the dirt, and find a big root much further away from the tree than I anticipated. Or when I walk down a sidewalk and see a place where it is bowed up due to the roots that have grown underneath. I have a chore ahead that I'm not really excited about. You see, the house we own needs lots of work, and different kinds of work. One of the chores awaiting my attention is the clearing out of some pretty tall weeds (that were just cleared out a few weeks ago!) and getting rid of the occasional wild trees that have sprung up from seeds here and there among the weeds. I don't get very excited about it, because I know I can't just cut them, or easily pull them, but will have to deal with their root system. We have mimosas, redbuds, elms and I don't even know what. But somehow their seeds have landed in my yard and taken root. I will have to pull them, or dig them, or somehow poison them to keep them from coming back....none of which is very much fun. Some of the roots seem to go very deep, while others seem to spread out very wide. A couple of times I have been hiking on trails near waterfalls and seen entire root systems wandering down the rocky hillside, exposed to the air, yet taking such a firm grasp on the rocks that they support huge trees up above. Roots are amazing things, drawing life and moisture out of a wide variety of conditions. And, as a result, we have apples and pears, acorns and walnuts, magnolia blossoms and mimosa blooms.

You can be like that, if you trust God, delight in His word, and are obedient to His commands. I know we have talked about this image before, but it is such a powerful allegory, is it not? How widely do your roots spread? How deep do they go? How good are they at drawing every bit of nourishment they can find? Where are the streams of water from which you draw? Every once in a while, since I live in Kansas where high winds are not at all uncommon, I see a tree that is blown over during a storm with a clump of roots at the base, because its root system was weak, no depth, no breadth, no strength. Trusting in God is not the foolish thing many people believe it to be, such as the unbeliever I saw on television last night, scoffing at the Christian faith. Instead of being foolish, developing a strong and practical trust in God is something that will get you through both the storms and the dry times of your life. Maybe you could find a way to enhance your root system today. A new habit of spiritual discipline, or a new personal challenge to memorize scripture, read through the Bible this year, whatever. Perhaps connecting with fellow Christians in a new way or with different Christians than you normally see. Or it could be in one of your life practices, such as trusting God with your finances by giving more than you are used to doing, or taking on a challenge from which you would normally shy away. Roots are sent out so a thirsty tree will be nourished, or so a person thirsty for God will find their hearts satisfied.

Day 168   Matthew 6:25-33

I don't know about you, but this is a passage that comes back to me time and again over the years. Sometimes I turn to it on purpose because I know I need to hear the message, other times I am directed there by various readings I do or sermons I hear. I end up back at this passage because it is a passage I need to be reminded of time and again in my life. I have observed many divorces, and in some cases, one person manages to finagle things in such a way that they come out of the process with financial ease while the other is left struggling. Usually that happens when one person is not honest with the court and hides money one way or another. Of course, it always occurs to me that they may hide the money from the court and their ex, but they cannot hide it from God, and they will be held accountable by Him for their dishonest actions. (If that is you, you may want to unload some guilt and remedy that situation now.) Most of the time, however, I observe that both parties are left with debts, struggles and fears. And worry. Worries about a lot of things. Things like how the bills are all going to get paid. Worries about how the divorce will affect the children. Worries about whether you will spend the rest of your life alone. Worries about how the ex's new partner will impact your children. Worries about faith— will the children give up on God? Will my church still accept me? Worries about simple things, like how the children will fare when they are at the other house. Worries about holidays—will Christmas ever be the same? Will I ever enjoy Thanksgiving again? Worries about the future, such as will I need to go back to school? Will there be enough for me to retire on? Worries about the possibility that your ex and his/her lawyer will find something else to come after you about that will end up costing a bundle. And what about the children? What if they turn against me? Will they ever know the truth, or only the slanted version they have been given?

This passage is worth reading quite regularly. And I would encourage you to find some different Bibles so you can read it in several translations, because I have found that the wording in one translation will hit me one way, then another translation's words raises insights I missed in the first. But regardless of which translation you read, there are always certain messages that come out. For me, some of those messages are: 1) nothing is ever achieved by worry; 2) take care of today, deal with tomorrow's cares when tomorrow comes; 3) don't get distracted from your focus on God as your first priority; and 4) God knows and will care for your every need Himself.

You know, I have known and loved this passage for over 30 years. You'd think by now I wouldn't have to be reminded of its message. But I do. Regularly. Maybe it's my personality type. Maybe it is a function of this era and culture. Maybe it is because of the pathway my life's journey has taken. But for whatever reason, I regularly have to be reminded that these truths apply to my life, and are there for me to claim and cherish. Especially on those days that I allow worries to mount up in my life. Or when I begin to think it is my responsibility to solve all the problems I face, when I need to be learning to lean more on God for the answers. Maybe this passage is a challenge for you today, or maybe it is already a core part of your life. Whatever your situation, I want to encourage you to find several translations of the Bible and read this passage over several times, letting the message of the phrases soak into your consciousness, and seeking to hear the hope in them afresh. Then ask yourself, "How can I apply what I am reading to my life today?" God knows what priorities work and what is useless. Do you?

MY PRAYER FOR YOU THIS WEEK

This week, I pray that God will do something special in your life, give you some little gift, some little joy, some surprise or unexpected moment to lift your spirit. And, as you experience that moment, my prayer is that you will be able to savor it, to allow it to saturate your spirit, to soak it up as a ray of sunshine in the midst of a stormy life, that you may know deep in your soul that God does, indeed, care for you. Amen.

Day 169   John 4:1-4, 16-18; Judges 15:1-2;
1 Samuel 25:43-44; and Ezra 10:1-5

There aren't very many references to divorce in the Bible, and even fewer biographical details of anybody who experienced one. In terms of women, Mary was almost divorced by Joseph when he found out she was pregnant, and it could be suggested that Ruth was sort of "divorced" from the unnamed kinsman who refused to redeem her, and then there is this lady at the well in Samaria. Two men we know by name whose experiences could be construed as divorced were both men whose wives were given to somebody else in marriage, effectively creating a divorce type of circumstance. These two were Samson and his Philistine wife, and David's promised marriage to the daughter of Saul. There are also references to the men there in Ezra, too. This woman at the well is the only New Testament person we observe who has been divorced, male or female. And I want to waste a few minutes as you are developing your own theology of divorce to make some observations about this woman and what we might learn by considering Jesus' interactions with her.

I am going to focus pretty narrowly on this lady, specifically dealing with how Jesus responds to the fact that she is divorced. The first thing to notice is that Jesus goes way out of His way to see her. Did you catch at the beginning of the passage that Jesus said He needed to go through Samaria? Well, in terms of options, He didn't have to go that way. In fact, most of the Jewish people from Galilee would have specifically NOT gone that way. But Jesus knew He had a divine appointment with this woman, and it was for that reason that He HAD to go through Samaria....something pretty commonly acknowledged among the commentators. The fact that He went so far out of His way violating the social customs of the time, is indicative of the high value that Jesus was willing to place on: 1) women; 2) Samaritans...i.e. renegade Jews at best, the despised outcasts at worst; 3) persons who have been divorced or otherwise failed in the relationships of life. Often the people He cared for were the ones others considered to be "outcasts." He no more discards her for being divorced than He does because she is a woman or because she was a Samaritan, all of which were grounds others would have used to judge her. Those attitudes existed not only back then, but also in many churches today. However, Jesus does not act in a way that affirms such calloused rejection of people God created and loves. Instead, He works in a way that demonstrates the absurdity of that attitude.

Not only does He go out of His way to meet her, He also makes clear to her that He knows of her situation as a divorced person and a person living in an illicit relationship. When she is done talking with Jesus there at the well, her response makes it very clear that she feels loved and accepted, not judged and rejected. Not that He condones couples living together, or groundless divorce, but He always values the person involved, sometimes in spite of the circumstances. She is so excited to discover that there is a place for her in the plan of God that she runs back to the village to tell all her friends about Jesus. I contrast this with divorced people whom good church folks often treat as if they are less for their having been divorced.

I wonder how that woman felt BEFORE she and Jesus talked. I suspect she felt pretty lonely. And, in today's terminology, she must have had pretty low self-esteem, after having apparently been rejected time and again by men she loved, and ostracized by the people of the village. But once she had the sense that the Messiah Himself did not reject her, she was no longer afraid of what others would think.

Divorce hurts. And it is not something that is easy to get over, if indeed one ever does completely get over the experience. Like many wounds, once healed, there are often scars that remain. But Jesus did not judge this woman by her wounds, by her scars, nor even by her view of herself. He saw her through the eyes of God. Through those eyes, she was just like the rest of us....individuals God has created whose lives have been marred through the suffering and sins of this world, yet whom God continues to love. If you learn nothing else from this lady, learn this: it really doesn't matter what anybody else thinks of us, what matters is what God thinks of us. Surely it grieves God's heart to see us make poor choices of our own, or suffer due to the poor choices of others. But rather than see us as marred and worth rejecting, He sees us as creatures in need of help and healing. And most of all, He sees us as individuals in need of love. When the Samaritan woman understood His response, she knew that no matter what anyone else thought Christ loved her. Though an entire village might reject you and expect you to go to the well in the hot sun by yourself rather than in the morning with others, be assured that Christ considers *you* worth going out of the way for, no matter what village rejects you, no matter how much *you* feel like you have failed in life. *That was enough for her, and it is enough for you and me as well. Christ loves you.*

Day 170   John 4:21-30

We revisit this story today, and will do so tomorrow, for some other issues worth considering. I want to focus today upon what happened in this lady's life once she met Christ in such a profound way. The scripture tells us that she suddenly was very excited, dropped her things and ran back into the village telling them about her experience with Jesus, inviting them to come meet Him themselves. As you struggle to discern what your future with God might be, examine the story of this woman from Samaria. I want to make what some might consider a radical suggestion from this text: this woman's witness in her town is evidence that God is not only willing, but desires to use people who have been divorced. (Notice, I didn't say He desires the divorce, but that His desire is to use people includes those who have been divorced.) She is used of God in a highly effective manner....she brings most of the village back to Jesus, which I find to be very interesting, considering that the "apostles" only came back with bread. It was this lady, not those apostles, that God used to reach an entire village with the message of the Messiah. Perhaps she was willing to be used by God and they weren't yet willing to see that God loved people such as these. Just as they weren't so sure she was worthy of being loved by God either. Does any of this sound familiar to your experience with some Christians? Does Christ consider a person who has been divorced worthy of His love and attention? The Samaritan woman certainly thought so. Can Christ use a divorced person to build the kingdom of God? Her story is evidence that He can and does! He used her to reach people the disciples could not or would not reach. I have mentioned before, a divorced person can have a different kind of connection with other divorced folks. Maybe it was the fact of her past experiences that opened the door for her to share so effectively with the people of her village, they could tell something was different after her encounter with Jesus.

I want to make a few observations for your consideration. Notice, Jesus didn't say that *the reason* it was okay for her to go tell about Him was because she was divorced before she met Him. That is a distinction church people often make that we will discuss more fully tomorrow. In fact, Jesus doesn't put any qualifiers on whether she can be used by God or not. He dismisses her concern about the difference between the Jewish faith and the Samaritan faith....centering His attention on the worship of God in spirit and truth through Himself as the Messiah. Not only that, but, to what must be the consternation of many church leaders today, He also has no problem ministering through her even though she is a woman. She takes her place alongside a number of women in scripture used by God in significant ways, from the matriarchs to Miriam to Mary to Priscilla and forward. However, for our purposes, it is perhaps most astounding that He does not even bother to raise with her the issue of whether her divorce affected her acceptability and usefulness for the Kingdom of God. She has connections with her village that the apostles do not have.

Isn't it funny that He doesn't make a point to send her into the village to witness? He does not disqualify her, nor does He specifically commission her, yet she is used of God in a mighty way. Perhaps we sometimes make too much of trying to know if God is calling or choosing us for various tasks. Maybe the call of God is as simple as being so awestruck by what God has done in your life that you automatically want to share it with people you know who are in need of God's touch. She didn't need Jesus to tell her which people to go visit with, she knew there was a whole village back home who knew nothing of Jesus, and felt obligated....no, privileged to be the one to pass along the message. She didn't wait for Jesus to do some special ceremony to send her. She didn't wait for the apostles to come back and hold a council about her fitness for this ministry. She simply responded to the need she knew was there. And God honored her efforts. Not only by touching the hearts of villagers through her, but by preserving her story in scripture to this day as an example of a person redeemed by God. God used her. God can use you. You don't have to wait for somebody else to give some kind of stamp of approval. Do what she did, look for the needs around you, and minister to them.

Day 171   John 4:1-42

And so, today, we come back to this lady at the well one more time. Among the various ways Christians have viewed divorced folks down through the years, one that comes up now and again is the view that tries to draw a distinction between someone who was divorced prior to coming to Christ, and those who divorced after their Christian commitment. Interestingly enough....or, maybe, sadly enough....those who draw that distinction tend to be more forgiving for those who were unbelievers than they are for the struggles of their fellow Christians! And so, with the story of the Samaritan woman, those with that view would point out that her divorces took place prior to her coming to Christ. Only with that can they explain her actions, since their divorce theology is built on the notion that divorce can be "forgiven" only if it occurs prior to becoming a Christian. (I already referred to my view on this earlier.) As if to say that if your divorce occurs after you come to Christ, then that somehow disqualifies you from being "forgiven" or used of God. Of course, all of us would believe that Christians, especially, need to seek the highest standard and ethics in their lives, we are to pursue the ideal, and a loving, committed marriage for life is unquestionably that ideal. But the reality of the Christian walk in this world is that we all struggle in one way or another. You and I both know Christians whose tempers are not pleasing to God, or whose language is filled with gossip and slander, or any of the other multitude of ways in which we fall short of God's ideal life. The concept of complete forgiveness for divorce only if prior to one's encounter with Christ contains an underlying assumption that does not ring true in the experience of any Christians I know. It is as if somehow being a Christian means there will never be difficulties or failures in your life. But you know that was not true even before you divorced, let alone afterward. Frankly, it is kind of sad to think that someone actually believes that God would be more forgiving to rebellious sinners who come to Him than He would to His own children who struggle as they try to live for Him!

I believe that God mourns over the failure of any marriage, as it is indicative of the fallen state in which we live. But I also believe He mourns over all worldly suffering, and that He takes us as we are to help us grow and to use us for His purposes. When I look at the life of this woman at the well, there is nothing to indicate that Jesus had the attitude that it was okay to use her to reach others only because her divorce occurred before she met Him. He did not put the qualifications on her that are all too often placed on divorced folks today. Now, don't get me wrong. I am not saying that we should act as if being divorced is not a big deal, any more than we should not be concerned over someone's violent temper. We are to be striving to live the way Christ would live in our shoes....in fact, allowing Christ to live through us in our experiences. If we have honestly come to God about our experiences and our situations, as well as our failings and frustrations, we simply throw ourselves upon the mercy and forgiveness of God. Jesus makes no restrictions on His willingness to use this woman's life in His mission to the world based on the timing of her divorce. It is simply not an issue to Him in this regard. Certainly, He points out His disapproval of her current "live in" situation, but she is able to easily distinguish between His disapproval of that lifestyle from disapproval of her....<u>something she does not experience with Jesus</u>. All too often that is a distinction neglected by many Christians in their actions. No, God is the kind of being who recognizes and defines right and wrong, holiness and sinfulness, good and evil. For the latter item in the pairs, He offers redemption. For the former, He prescribes the goal and provides for us the perfection we cannot achieve on our own. His calling for us all, no matter what the situation of our lives, no matter the background from which we come, His calling is always for us to be His witnesses, the people who tell the story of what difference He makes in our lives. Not only those who have great marriages and struggle with sin in other areas of their lives, but also those of us who have suffered the pain of difficult marriages and divorce. Let your life reflect the example set by this troubled, then transformed woman of God!

Day 172   Mark 14:66-72

Coulda, woulda, shoulda. Have you ever wished that you could go back and do things differently? More than once I have talked with divorced folks who have looked back over their marriage, and wished they could. Perhaps something said, perhaps time not spent investing in the marriage that might have made a difference. Sometimes what I hear as the person looks back is a statement about the lack of wisdom in marrying that spouse in the first place. Often it is phrased as, "What in the world was I thinking? What did I ever see in him/her?" Sometimes that 20/20 hindsight is such a curse, because we can rehash questions from the current perspective without realizing that we truly did not know at that time what we do now.

I see the same thing in the lives of people of the New Testament. We read the parables and the stories and we marvel that the people of Jesus' day, not even the disciples seemed to understand, what we see so clearly, that Jesus was the Messiah and, *of course* He had to die and be raised from the dead. But the truth is, we see that because we view the events through post-resurrection eyes. In the same way, we see things that we could have chosen more wisely in our past because we see them with eyes that have come to the other side of the choices and their consequences. *Of course*, if we had known, some of those choices would have been different. But real life is, we didn't know, and we made our choices then based upon what we knew then; some of those choices were good, some not so good, but all are the realities of our pasts.

Peter made choices, too. And much has been made of the threefold denial he made concerning his relationship with Jesus. In this account, Jesus looks at Peter after the denial, and then Peter goes out weeping bitterly. At that moment, besides all the other emotions he must have felt, he surely wished he could go back and change things. But he couldn't. And neither can you and I. The marvelous thing is the restoration of Peter in John 21, where Jesus three times asks Peter about his love, and then charges him with a ministry with the people of God. Whatever else happened in that exchange, Peter came to terms with his denial. He was able to accept that part of who he was and what he had done, and know that it all was something God would forgive, and even use. I would suggest that Peter was at peace about it all after that restoration encounter. It is interesting that <u>every Gospel</u> contains the denial by Peter, including some details that very possibly only Peter knew. It is as if Peter wanted people to know he had failed in this way. I can imagine him hearing about the people writing the Gospels, and saying to Mark, or to Luke, "Make sure you include my denial, people need to know that I did that."

What had been a shame and embarrassment to him, became a lesson from which he learned about the incredible grace and forgiveness of God, and it was a lesson he wanted everybody to know. He was willing to be the example. How many times have we Christians through the generations found hope in knowing that even a denial like Peter's can be forgiven, and a person as weak as we are found a place in the ministry of the kingdom?

As you look back and discover choices that you may be regretting or unable to understand now, I encourage you to remember Peter, and follow that example. Seek time alone with God to discuss those choices, and allow Him to restore your soul. Accept that none of us are perfect, we make choices that, in retrospect, we think were poor choices. Let those experiences teach you lessons that can impact your future choices, and let them be something you can share to help others as they struggle to make choices, or as they live with regrets of poor choices. God is in the renewal business. If He can do it for Peter, He can do it for you, and He can do it for those you know. God's grace is amazing!

Day 173   Deuteronomy 24:1-4

This passage is the Old Testament passage containing the Mosaic instructions about divorce. The only one. In Genesis, of course, we have the story of creation in which the original design is most clearly presented, and the story of how that design becomes flawed through the entrance of sin into our world. Some of the rabbis of Jesus' day understood this passage as a command of how to handle a situation where there has been cause for divorce. There is an odd phrase in here that creates the difficulty in interpretation, because nobody knows for sure exactly what the intended meaning is of the words which are the grounds given for divorce. A literal meaning is something like: "the nakedness of the matter." In fact, if you look at the passage, your own Bible will probably have a different wording of what the cause of the divorce was than this literal sense of the Hebrew words which is so unclear. The rabbis used to argue over their meaning. Some thought it meant adultery, <u>but</u> the punishment for adultery was stoning to death, not divorce! There are other theories out there, but I don't intend to pursue them, as you can find them in the commentaries if you have an interest. Instead, we are going to look a bit at what this passage is trying to teach, and what we may or may not do with that teaching.

If you read the whole section carefully, you will note that the primary point of the passage is that if a man divorced his wife, and she remarries and that marriage ends in divorce, the first husband is not allowed to take her back as his wife again. At the same time, there are some indications of the appropriate process of divorce included, this whole idea of a writ of divorce....it had to be more than just something spoken, she needed to have a written document, because of the precarious situation in which she would be placed. But the passage is not about what grounds are legitimate for divorce, nor is there a command to divorce over some issue. At the same time, however, it is also clear from the passage that divorce *is* taking place among the people. While some are quick to point out that this passage does not suggest that God approves of divorce or commands divorce or gives acceptable grounds for divorce, they are *slow* to point out that the passage also does not condemn divorce, or express God's disapproval of divorce, or forbid divorce. It actually feels more like the passage is simply commenting on what is already occurring in the society, and is setting a particular boundary and guideline for those occurrences.

It is not so much that divorce is God's idea here, as it is that God recognizes the reality of the world in which we are living, and seeks to temper the effects of the Fall by providing a limit by describing one area that is not to be allowed. I would suggest that if divorce was strictly forbidden by God, that this would have been the crucial moment for God to mention that. But it isn't mentioned, even though it is clear that divorce was occurring and needed some regulating. Not that anyone of us would say that God's perfect and ideal design is for marriages to end in divorce. Of course not. But what in this fallen world does operate exactly according to God's ideal design? God takes brokenness and imperfections and mistakes and blemishes and turns them around for good. Note especially how God used the awful injustice of an unwarranted death sentence to purchase salvation for you and I through the execution of Jesus. I have heard people say that folks who get a divorce are just taking the easy way out. In some cases, that may be true. However, most of the folks I know who have been divorced would not describe it as "an easy way out." In fact, they would call it one of the most difficult things they have ever experienced in their lives. I have said before, I believe that God's heart breaks with each marriage that ends in divorce, and He weeps because of the pain and suffering that go with it, as well as the fact that it indicates how far we have drifted from God's ideal there in the Garden. But God works within the system that exists for us, neither offering approval to the place we have gotten ourselves, nor denying the necessary realities brought about by human frailty and hearts hardened by sin's awful influence. As you seek to find your place in the Kingdom of God as a divorced person, hold on to the fact that God's heart is heavy just as yours by that difficult time. His grace, forgiveness and strength are offered to you just as much as to any of the other broken people in our world. And praise God that it is offered, because I don't know how I would make it without God's help, do you?

Day 174   Proverbs 11:14

Probably by now you are realizing that to make it through some of the tough times you have had, the support of friends and confidants has helped you keep going. Maybe you have discovered that some folks are really good advisors and friends, while others would be best kept at arm's length because of the way they handle confidences, or because you have experienced their bad advice. Somewhere along the way, it is important to let those who care for you know how much they mean to you, and how much their support or advice has helped you. And, odds are, your need for wisdom and encouragement aren't over. In fact, I would suggest that having a good circle of advisors and supportive friends is an important factor throughout life. There will be other times when you may want an outside perspective, or someone to lean upon. And, those relationships need to be reciprocal....those very friends and advisors may one day need you for the same reasons. Don't ever let yourself become so self absorbed that you become only a taker, and never a giver. Let the ways you have experienced meaningful support or advice help you learn how to be a more effective supporter and advisor for those who seek your aid. In my case, through my experiences of divorce and subsequent events, I have learned so much more about how to come to the aid of others struggling with divorce, ways that I didn't realize were important prior to my experience. I have come to realize what things mean more, and what things mean less (and, hopefully, this book contains things that help more!). Carefully look for those to whom you may be called to be a support and advisor, and then carefully offer your support and advice in ways you have learned are truly useful.

Before we leave this topic, let me raise another area for your consideration. The issue is a simple one, you know who your support network is, do you know who the support network is for your children? You see, you must remember that how all this impacts them is significantly different from how it impacts you. It may be that you may need to be more actively involved with their teachers, their youth minister, their friends....maybe even arranging opportunities for them to spend time with a pastor or counselor. They, too, are struggling. And, unfortunately, in many ways, you are too involved with the struggle to be the objective outsider they may need. Give them not only permission to seek support, but help make sure those opportunities are there for them. They may or may not realize your role in that accomplishment, but that doesn't matter, because it isn't about you, it's about them. The goal I hope we all have for our children is that they will grow up to be emotionally as healthy and well grounded as possible. It may take some intentional efforts on your part to help make that happen. A little support and wise counsel now may help avoid the need for greater support and counsel later.

MY PRAYER FOR YOU THIS WEEK

This week, I pray that God will draw you close. As Jesus said when He saw Jerusalem so long ago, His desire is to draw you close under His wings, to shelter you there. I pray that you experience afresh what it means to know that God's protection for your life will keep you from all genuine harm, even in the midst of the pains and sufferings of this earthly experience. Amen.

Day 175   Philippians 1:3-5

As I write this devotional, I am sitting in a hospital where my 91 year old dad awaits test results and doctor recommendations for a possible surgery today. At that age, of course, any significant surgery is risky. As I waited through the night, I found myself thinking about the things so many of us think about at times like this....all summed up in the notion that life is so fragile, and we never know how long we have anybody in our lives. I count myself truly blessed to have had the father I have had, and to have enjoyed his company so long already. It seems to me that these lessons are worth being reminded about once again....at least for me, and maybe for you, too. As you deal with the ongoing struggles of regaining equilibrium in a divorce situation, and wrestle with the myriad of decisions and hurts that come your way, it can become very easy to be so wrapped up in yourself and your struggle that you lose track of the fact that there are so many others in your life who are also special, and who need to be valued by you even in the midst of the struggle. There isn't a person in your life who you know for sure will still be living tomorrow. Don't let the treasuring of these special folks get crowded out by the overwhelming issues of your daily living. Perhaps now would be a good time to make time to create a list of some of those special names, and join Paul in giving thanks as you remember the people God has placed in your life.

Day 176   2 Peter 1:16-18

As Peter was writing the words of today's passage, I wonder how he felt? You can tell by the tone that he was absolutely overwhelmed by even the memory of that incredible event. Remember how that story is told in the Gospels? (See for example, Matthew 17.) Do you remember that Peter was so beside himself that he just had to say and do something, so he offered to build little tabernacles there on the mountain to commemorate the moment? I suspect Jesus chuckled when He declined the offer. If you stop and think about Peter's life, he had a lot of really cool things to remember. Like when he was out walking across the water....at least for a little while. Or the times Jesus helped him in his fishing efforts. And especially the time Jesus told him to catch a fish to get the coin to pay taxes with! Can you imagine what it must have felt like to be holding a basket with a little bread and a piece of fish that just seems to never run out as you handed it out from person to person? We will never know how much he treasured the time during the seaside barbeque when he and Jesus, just the two of them, shared that private moment after the resurrection. The day he preached and thousands were saved surely had to be a high point for him. And maybe right up there would have been his visit in Joppa where we Gentiles first learned that Christ was our savior, too. What a life he had!

But I suspect that you have had quite a life, yourself! Yesterday, we took a little time to remember some special *people* in our lives, I wonder if today wouldn't be a good day to remember some special *times* in our lives. If you were penning a letter such as this little letter of Peter's, what things would warm your heart? What times in your life stand out as moments when you knew God was at work in you and for you? Take a few moments to savor some of those precious memories. Remind yourself of some of the things God has done for you down through the years. Recall some of the life lessons He has taught you, and consider how you might apply them to your life today. Remember the Psalmist tells us to forget none of His benefits? Are there some you have kind of forgotten, and need to remember today? Write them down, share them with a friend, pray them back to God with thanksgiving. Maybe it's time to take that proverbial stroll down memory lane with the Lord at your side.

Day 177   Matthew 5:31-48; 19:3-9

These are a couple of the passages that many church people will use to decide your status as a divorced person. These are also passages that you can choose to pretend aren't there, or can study and pray about carefully to understand what they mean for your life from this point on. You see, each of us is accountable to God for how we handle the scriptures. There are some individuals I know who strongly disagree with my understanding of divorce and scripture. But, you could just as easily say I strongly disagree with theirs! You have to sort out and decide the meaning of these scriptures as best you can, and then decide how you need to apply them to your life, because ultimately, it is between you and God. However, don't too easily discount the hard things, just because it is convenient. Having said that, I will share some of the things I believe about these.

First, I believe there are two things very clear in the scriptures: 1) marriage is a very sacred thing involving not just a man and a woman, but also God; 2) the way things are experienced in this fallen world is a long way from how God intended things to be before sin reared its ugly head. In the first of these passages, we find this concept in the verse that says we are to, "be perfect, as your heavenly Father is perfect." (NASB) Excuse me? Perfect? Ooh, that is a big word. It seems to me that a lot of what Jesus was doing in the Sermon on the Mount was to challenge the common religious understanding of the day. Blessedness was not truly about material prosperity and easy living, but found in the midst of persecution and mourning. Keeping the commandments was not about following a set of rules with outward actions, but a matter of the heart, and at the heart level, nobody kept all the commandments. Nobody. Not even the people who THOUGHT they did. I know people like that today, don't you? As if to drive home the point, Jesus makes this comment about the requirement of perfection.

I believe part of the purpose of this divorce passage in Matthew 5 is that, along with the comments about anger and adultery, Jesus is trying to get His listeners to hear that they aren't perfect, even if they have been outwardly avoiding the actions the commandments forbid, inwardly they are breaking them in their hearts. There are entire discussions written about these two passages, and especially what Jesus intended when He said that Moses permitted divorce. Some say Jesus is trying to make them understand that it wasn't commanded as the Pharisees were saying, but only allowed. Or that Jesus is trying to help them understand how far they have come from the original idea. They suggest He is indicating the need to get back in touch with God's original intention. Others say He is explaining the only legitimate grounds for divorce....adultery....and is in agreement with the teaching that divorce is allowed in cases of adultery, as opposed to the suggested "any reason" concept that had reached the point of frivolity.

I kind of have a different take on this whole thing....and it is, again, what has had meaning for me. It seems to me Jesus continues to try to help these people move past the outward actions to the matters of the heart. When they ask if a man can divorce a woman for any reason, and Jesus challenges them, He includes in His response the statement that divorce was allowed because of "your hardness of heart." Not "their" hardness of heart, but "yours," which implies that Jesus wasn't merely talking about the people in Moses day, but is trying to make us all understand how far we have really drifted from God, even if we believe we have lived perfect lives. He doesn't make light of divorce, because He doesn't repeat their phrase "for any reason," which you could take several ways. But, He also doesn't say that it should cease to exist. Instead, it seems to me that He simply makes His statement from the perspective of someone with a clear view of the realities of fallen people inhabiting a broken world. The possibility also strikes me in these discussions about adultery and remarriage, that Jesus, like Malachi before Him, was speaking against the notion of someone divorcing his wife so he can marry another (in Malachi's day, one who was younger and "more attractive"). It may well have been that men were convincing themselves (as they often do today), that it is okay to divorce your wife and then take another younger one. Jesus indicates that such plans constitute adultery, even though you got your divorce before you married that other woman.

Well, those are some of my musings....just a very few. You will need to find your own, I am not going to explain all my belief system in this matter, because you need to work things out with God for yourself, just as I have had to do. In any case, the scripture does not treat divorce nearly as lightly as so much of our society and our entertainment industry do. Nor does Jesus indicate that divorce is the unforgiveable sin with no hope of forgiveness or a future, as sometimes overly legalistic Christians do. To be responsible Christians, we need to reflect well on these matters. My prayers are that you will be sensitive to God's words to you concerning these things.

Day 178   Deuteronomy 8:1-7

Sometimes in life, we learn things in ways that illustrate the old adage that "a word to the wise is sufficient." Other times we fail to catch those opportunities, and learn, as they say, by way of the "school of hard knocks." If you are like me, you have had plenty of each. And, if you are like me, sometimes you can feel like you are tired of learning at all, you just want to be left alone to go on about your life. However, it is just in the nature of life and human beings that all of life is a learning experience. Every day we pick up something new, try something different, experience something unknown....it is just part of life.

Some of the things we learn in life have a deep and lasting impact on us. Some of the lessons we learn by experience are especially that way. I know that there have been times I have been told things like to keep my hands away from things that are hot, lest I get burned. But the times I have grabbed a hot skillet, thinking it will only be a second to get it over to the sink, I learned a very strong lesson that they really meant it when they said not to touch anything hot! The impact was completely different.

Perhaps you, like me, have read many times the passages about the Israelites wandering through the wilderness. And perhaps, like me, you have read and heard many times the scripture that tells us man does not live by bread alone, but by every word that comes from the mouth of God. Today's passage, however, is the context of that verse, with an interesting tidbit. God wanted the people to follow His commands. He wanted them to know they should spend their entire lives with that priority the practice of their lives. So He didn't merely tell them. He intentionally decided that this was one lesson they would need to learn by experience if they were going to remember it. In verse 7 we find the crux: God chose to let them hunger so that they could be fed with manna and thus learn by experience that bread alone isn't enough….God's word is what we need to live our lives. They didn't forget that lesson. The Jewish ceremonies tied with Passover always include a reminder that it is God who provides the bread, and who led His people through the wilderness….reminders even now, thousands of years later!

If you had asked the people, they would have said that God had abandoned them, left them to die in the wilderness and they never should have followed Moses out there. But when the manna fell, they discovered they weren't abandoned, and that God did care about their needs, that God can be trusted to provide…even if it didn't seem like it at the time. I wonder how your experience relates to these things. Could it be that God has something He is trying to teach you that you can only learn by experience? Could it be that you are not so sure that God knows where He is leading you, or what He is doing in your life? Could it be that God wants to provide in a way you will never forget? Could it be that the resistance you are kicking up is actually hindering what God wants to teach you? The key to this whole passage is humility…. God wanted them to become humble, so He let them hunger and fed them Himself with manna. Humility teaches us that God is in control, not us; that God's commands can be trusted, even if we think we know a better way; and finally, humility teaches us that God never abandons us, no matter what we think or feel to the contrary. So, what are you learning these days?

Day 179   Nehemiah 1:1-4; 2:11-18

Away from home as a displaced person, Nehemiah knew that his homeland was in rubbles. The work of rebuilding Jerusalem was far from complete, and he knew he needed to do something about it. So he takes a risk, gets official approval, makes the journey back to Jerusalem, and then, one night, he wanders the circle of the city examining the damage and disrepair of the walls. From there, he begins a plan to rebuild, step by step. He meets opposition from those who want to keep him and his people down. But he perseveres, and the work gets done, with Nehemiah believing that the work he is doing is what God has called him to do. It is clear he had a great love for his home city. How heavy his heart must have been when he got the word about the devastation. And with tears overcoating his dedication, he observed the tremendous task facing him as he examined the condition of the walls. But then, the next day, he and his people began working to rebuild.

Do you relate in any way? When you look at your home, do you observe a brokenness, a devastation that has swept away what you once held dear? Perhaps just thinking about these things makes your heart heavy. Perhaps the memories bring tears to your eyes. Perhaps the possibility of rebuilding your home seems a daunting task. Patience, diligence and a plan helped Nehemiah accomplish his great work. It will take the same from you. Your world will not rebuild overnight.... there are loose ends that may take years to sort out. There may be times you want to quit, or that others pressure you somehow to give up. Only diligence and perseverance will get you through, one step at a time. A plan, though? Maybe you don't yet have a plan. Or maybe you just have hints of a plan. A plan begins with priorities. Nehemiah arranged things so that he and his workers would not be distracted from the work they were doing by other things that would pop up. At the same time, some of their work was done with a sword in one hand and a trowel in the other, because he knew that defense of the city could at any moment become the new priority. You will need to determine some priorities for yourself, and may need to hang on to some defensive measures to keep yourself and your children safe through it all. I would suggest that you make as one of your priorities the decision that you will rebuild only in ways that are honoring to God. That you will refuse shortcuts, that you will not compromise biblical standards nor settle for being less than who God has designed and called you to be. One of those standards is that you stand for truth, but you speak that truth in love. There may be moments when hate just overwhelms you....and that is not the time to speak. There may be times when your children need to know that you truly love them and will stand with them through this tough time. And just as any pioneer who started building a new village, so you will have the opportunity to build something new. Make sure that the new life and home you build are worthy of the name Christian. When you have that as your commitment and priority, you can persevere knowing that you are not building alone, but in the strength and guidance of the Lord.

Day 180   Matthew 18:23-35

But why should I forgive that person for what they have done? Oh, that question can so easily arise in a divorce. I know of divorce situations where one parent keeps children away on Father's or Mother's Day. I know of divorce situations where one partner had hidden money....sometimes a great deal of money....to keep from having to split it with the divorcing partner. I know of divorces where a partner let the ex pay alimony for years after the partner's remarriage, only changing things when the ex accidentally discovered the marriage. I have known of people putting clothes and possessions in the street, destroying or selling all the ex's possessions. I have known of partners defying court orders time and again. I have known of partners even doing malicious things such as having utilities cut off, or forcing an eviction, or flaunting an affair....the list is almost endless. These people surely do not deserve to be forgiven! How could God ask me to forgive them? After all they have done?

The difficult fact to face is found in today's parable, and you may not believe it, or want to accept it, but it is the truth. You are not forgiving anybody because they deserve it. You are forgiving because you are forgiven. The hard part to really grasp is, you are forgiven by Christ in spite of the fact that YOU don't deserve it, either. And to make it really plain, this parable teaches us that no matter how much somebody has done evilly against us....it is nothing compared to how odious our sins are before God. The worst anybody has ever done to you....and some of those things can be pretty awful....the worst thing is the equivalent of ten dollars compared to the hundred millions of dollars God has forgiven you. To refuse to forgive somebody....even your ex....is the highest form of insolence. How dare you not forgive! How dare you think that YOU are more important than God, that YOU would have the right to not forgive when God has forgiven you! Oh, we all tend to discount our own sins as not being nearly as bad as the sins of somebody else....but that is a lie from Satan. Even the smallest sin is an awful stench in God's sight....and God chooses to forgive. Forgiveness, perhaps more than any other characteristic of life, gives us the opportunity to be like Christ. And if you are going to move on well and healthy in your life, forgiveness is the road you must walk.

Day 181   1 John 3:1-2

I absolutely love the tone of this verse. It is incredible. Let me play with the words with you for a few minutes, to see if I can help you be as awestruck as I am when I read this verse. I think of it in these ways: *Consider how much God loves us....He not only calls us His children, He adopts us into His family as His children. Look at the kind of love God has for us, the kind of love that calls us His children, and then goes on and makes us His very own kids. Do you see how God exercises the love He has for us? He calls us to be His, and then takes that love and through it, makes us His.* What is sad is, I don't think these even do justice to the wonder of God's active love. But it is so precious. God wants us to be in absolutely intimate relationship with Him, absolutely bonded with Him as kin. Not only as kin, but in the tenderest and most dependent of relationships....as His beloved children. The kind of relationship that includes expectations and responsibilities, obligations if you will, on the parent....of our Father in heaven!

I guess what amazes me is that He didn't have to do that. He could have just saved us like He did when He rescued Israel from danger so many times in its history, and called it good enough. He could have simply forgiven us, and left it at that. Or He could have just considered us good friends, and had us come live with Him as His guests. Maybe even as special guests. But He doesn't. He wants us to be more than that, He wants us to be His children! He wants us to be family! He wants us not to be merely His guests, but to actually belong with Him in heaven.

I know that sometimes, some of us can get kind of down on ourselves, think we're not much, like some kind of misfits. But He doesn't care about any of the things we get down on ourselves about.... He still considers us worth adopting into His family as His children. Sometimes, some of us think just the opposite, that we are the greatest thing on earth. And we can be something pretty great: **children of God!** But we never received that privilege on the basis of who we are, only on the basis of what He has done! It is a marvelous thing to be called, not only called, but actually become, children of God. How about spending some time with your Daddy today, letting Him know how much you like being part of the family?

Day 182   Psalm 34:8

At some gatherings I have attended in recent years, there is a little saying they banter around. The person leading the gathering will get up and say, "God is good...." The people are then supposed to respond, "All the time." And then the leader says, "All the time...." And the people respond, "God is good." That seems to me to be the current variation of what we used to do in the 70's, when small groups would rather spontaneously burst into the Bill Gaither song, "God is So Good." The emphasis is twofold in these things: 1) the goodness of God; 2) the constancy of His goodness. But have you ever really taken time to stop and ask yourself what is meant by the goodness of God?

Some people believe that doing good means to avoid doing anything that would ever bring harm. While that contains truth, that makes goodness into nothing more than the absence of harm or evil, leaving it with no essence of its own. *Being* good impels one to *do* something, to do things that are beneficial, things that are kind, things that are helpful and that are more than just the bare minimum. It is extending one's efforts beyond oneself for the sake of others. Someone who is good is someone who can be counted on to be consistently trustworthy in every relational interaction. Someone who is good is someone you would never have cause to fear could harm you....unless, of course, your harm was the consequence of your own poor choices. Because someone who is truly good will also be truly righteous, truly just, never defending evil behavior and irresponsible actions. Hence, God can be a good God, and still allow people to experience the consequence of eternal hell. In fact, He wouldn't be truly good if He didn't allow that, if He simply ignored evil actions and pretended like they didn't matter. We would never allow a court justice to perpetually release convicted murderers as if nothing had happened, because we know that is not right, just, or good. God is ultimate good, because not only will He not ignore evil and leave it unpunished, He chose, for the benefit of humans He loves, to take the punishment Himself in our place upon the cross, so that the truly repentant can know forgiveness and experience the goodness of God forever. He chose to do those things not only because He loves us, but because He is also good. Always. In every choice. By every action. With all His being. God is good.

Have you experienced God's goodness for yourself? Can you recount things in your relationship with God that have demonstrated for you personally that God is indeed good to you? Are you able to trust that the things which seem to you not to be so good just now, God will turn into good before everything is said and done. Maybe not today. Maybe not tomorrow. Maybe not even during your earthly sojourn. But when all things are seen from the perspective of eternity, you will find that God is indeed good, pure good, and that everything you have experienced from His hand has been, in fact, ultimately and absolutely good. Revel today in the reality that the God you worship, the God you love, the God who created you and loves you and saved you is good today, tomorrow, and always.

INTRODUCTION TO SPECIAL
OCCASION/HOLIDAY DEVOTIONALS

Luke 9:59-60

There are, perhaps, no times impacted by divorce more than those days that can be so special in our lives, but which can also be so painful and memory laden. I am speaking about the holidays and vacation times that have so many traditions and memories built around them. And now, with the divorce, new dimensions and layers are added that complicate these special times, cloud the emotions, and bring in a new sense that somehow, your privacy has now been invaded. For example, in my state, if you have minor children, you can't just decide on the spur of the moment you want to spend the weekend at the resort town across the state line, you have to first give your ex 24 hours notice that you are taking the children out of state. One always wonders what would happen if they decide to object.... will you find yourself back in court? And, of course, there is also a bizarre negotiation that occurs when you tell the kids, "Hey, let's take the weekend and go out to that theme park we all enjoy so much," and hear the reply, "Nah, we really don't want to go. We just went last weekend with the other parent." Ohhh, okay, so now that place and memory that used to be so special has now become off limits, or, at the least, tentative and negotiable?

There can be a real discomfort as you find your privacy now scattered to the winds. The kids talk about how much fun they had at their birthday celebration over at the other house, and you wonder what is going to be said about your celebration with them. Or, you may not even be able to PLAN your celebration very easily. They may come and ask what you have planned for Christmas Eve, because, at the other house, they are trying to work out plans to go somewhere and need to know when they can leave. With our children, one thing that was weird, but seemed to help the complications, was that they made two separate wish lists of gifts for Christmas or birthdays, so that we didn't have to be concerned that we or the grandparents would accidentally duplicate a gift with the other branch, and thus the child have to choose whose to return. But sometimes even that was difficult, as a gift I had desired to arrange had already been spoken for unbeknownst to me by somebody on the other side. Sometimes you just want to scream: "it isn't any of his/her business....this is MY home, and I ought to be able to plan a simple celebration without having to go through all this hassle!!!" Then you realize that divorce, far from being a quick and easy court process is actually a very complicating and destructive event. The special events in the kids' lives were especially hard, as they graduate high school or college and you have to negotiate time to celebrate with them, and have to accept that you may not get to be involved in what is the most important time in YOUR heart.

I wish I had some easy answers for you. There have been plenty of times when I wished things were simpler or easier, and plenty of times when I felt something could or should have been done differently or better, but I just had to live with the situation. I think the best thoughts I can offer might be these: 1) it isn't easy....but life rarely is, so just do the best you can and let it go at that; 2) there will be many times you will miss being with your kids that may be very difficult to miss....but don't focus on those, focus on the times you CAN be with them; 3) don't worry too much about the privacy thing, frustrating though it may be. If you are doing your best and living the way you believe God wants you to live, what difference does it make that you are being so carefully observed or invaded? Might end up being a pretty good witness! I tend to think that people whose lives are so absorbed in the details of their exs are pretty sad people who have no life of their own. I just decide that such entanglement is that person's issue; I'm going to live my own life, do the best I can do, and focus upon enjoying IT! Finally, 4) try your hardest to keep your love focused on the kids, and avoid as much as possible creating situations that are more awkward than they need to be. Realize they negotiate the difficult waters of separated parents, they will experience and create enough complicated times without you adding to the mess.

God bless you. It is just hard. But it isn't forever. Love can always be shown and shared, and, even if the ways you used to do so are no longer available, new ways can be created. I would suggest you read these special day devotionals a few days prior to the event, but you may decide that for you, they would be best read on the day itself. Hopefully they will contain something to help you navigate the frustrations, disappointments and joys of the special events in our lives during the early years of your divorce.

Your Birthday

Read Psalm 90:10-12

It is your birthday, again! It's an amazing thing, isn't it, that this was your birthday before you got married, it was your birthday during your married life, and it remains your birthday! Disruptive as divorce may seem, there are things that refuse to change just because of a divorce. One of the nice things I learned during this time of life was how to enjoy some things just for myself. There won't be a special present from your spouse, or the traditions that may have developed around your birthday celebration with that person, but that doesn't mean you won't be able to celebrate! In fact, you can celebrate your own way, go to a restaurant that YOU like, or prepare the meal that is YOUR favorite, or invite some of YOUR friends over....or, if you have kids, take them somewhere fun to build a memory together....assuming, of course, your ex is cooperative on that (and sadly, often many are not). It may be that you have other family members you haven't gotten to celebrate with in years, and may want to reconnect with them for this birthday. Or, perhaps you have already met somebody new, and will have a quiet celebration with that person.

However you choose to celebrate it, you still have a birthday, and it is an important day, so don't ignore it. Instead, find a meaningful way to make a new celebration. And, I would even go so far as to suggest a celebration that might not have been accepted in your previous marriage....maybe a little way to indulge yourself with a weekend getaway or trip to a local spa. Maybe, instead, celebrate by doing something special for somebody else at the homeless or battered shelter, or a hungry person on the other side of the world.

For some of us, this birthday also signifies some other things. Things like a biological clock ticking while you are back out in the single world. Or feeling too old to ever find anyone again. Or perhaps it makes you realize that you are not at the point in life you had hoped you would be by this birthday, since so much has now changed in your life. But, for better or worse, your birthday remains. I want you to know that the One who oversaw your birth years ago, is available for your celebration. I encourage you to look at this birthday celebration as the start of a new chapter in the celebrations of your birthday: the chapter of childhood parties is gone, the chapter of young single life parties is over, and now, the chapter of your married birthdays has closed....who knows what the next chapter will hold. So go, celebrate, enjoy the start of this new chapter. And make sure you invite God to attend your party. Oh, by the way, HAPPY BIRTHDAY!

Ex's birthday

Read Matthew 14:1-12

I had an odd thing happen the other day. In going about my daily business, something was said that made me realize that a couple days previous had been my ex's birthday. It had slipped by completely unnoticed. Because my life has moved on, and I have no ongoing connection with my ex, as my children are old enough that their relationship with her is outside of their connection with me. I know some people continue to be in contact with their ex for things like this, and that seems to work for them. Others are like me, who have gone other ways and simply have no contact with their ex, and that seems to work for us. In other words, at least in my opinion, there isn't a way you HAVE to handle this, some RIGHT way you have to do things. Instead, you just have to figure out ways to do things as they work best for you. I do know that for many who are fresh out of divorce, the ex's birthday can be pretty difficult, especially when there was adultery involved and you have some kind of awareness that the two involved are off celebrating and having a good time, having left you behind in a world of hurt. But let it go....that is your ex's life, you can focus on yours. And don't be so sure that someone who is moving forward in a relationship that started out as adultery is going to be as truly happy as you might think....you may want to remind yourself of Galatians 6:9-10.

Now, for those of you with young children, there are other issues involved. You can certainly leave the birthday of your ex to be what it is, and not be involved in any way. But I would encourage you to consider what I think is a bit higher pathway, although it is also a difficult one to take. I would encourage you, at the least, make sure your children realize it is their mom or dad's birthday. And I would also encourage you to go one more step, if the children are young, find out if they have been able to arrange a present. If not, then how about, for the sake of your kids, helping them make something, or taking them shopping, or give them some cash so they can feel good about their participation in their parent's birthday. It also lets them know that you believe those days are important, and that you are trying to teach them that value for their own lives. But don't kid yourself about what is going to happen. Odds are very high your ex will NOT call to say thanks for having helped the kids with their gifts. Nor can you assume that your ex will have the common decency to reciprocate when YOUR birthday rolls around. But you aren't doing it so that there will be reciprocation....you do it because of the kind of person YOU want to be, and you do it because of what you want to teach your children about what kind of people you hope they grow up to be. Your ex is actually irrelevant in terms of your participation....it is about you, it is about teaching your kids and helping them be quality people. And, if it really bothers you, then maybe you can take the cash you would have had to spend on them for a present in the past, and buy yourself dinner out, or buy a special "just because" gift for your kids. Maybe, someday, they will understand. And, even if they don't, you have done what you know is a noble thing....and that can feel pretty good! And that can help a lot, because sometimes it feels more like watching the party when Herod's daughter was dancing, and special loves of your own feel betrayed as was John the Baptist. But that's okay, it isn't your celebration to be part of, anyway. Let them have their party, you spend the day in whatever way works best for you....maybe having your own party, celebrating that you can do whatever you want with the day now.

Wedding Anniversary

Read John 2:1-11

The first time this date rolls around can be a very emotion filled day, perhaps blindsiding you with an intensity you didn't expect. Memories flood. The day that for, perhaps, years, has always been an important day of celebration suddenly can become a day of mourning. You may want to find a way to mark this first anniversary with something you do on your own, something only you can create to match your emotional makeup. If I remember correctly, that was the day I chose to go back to the church where I had been married to sit by myself for a time of reflection and prayer. That may not be the kind of day that would be helpful for you. *You* may feel like celebrating….especially if your experience is that you now feel freed from a very difficult and/or dangerous marriage. For some people, it is helpful to be alone dealing with the emotions of the day in your own private way. For others, spending the day with close friends or family may be an important support or time of encouragement. I found that the personal time I spent, reflecting on the wedding, the marriage, the divorce, and trying to understand what it all could mean for me, was perhaps my most helpful moment of closure. It didn't take much….just half an hour or so….but it helped me put a finality to what was happening, since my anniversary date came during the middle of the process of divorce.

There are lots of passages in the scripture that use weddings to illustrate God's love and other lessons. From now on, whenever you read those passages, they will impact you differently than they did when you read them prior to your divorce. Today's passage contains the imagery of the joy of a wedding celebration, with Jesus right in the midst of it. He was in the midst of YOUR wedding, too. You had hopes and dreams that day, imaginations of the days and years ahead. But now, you realize that many of those hopes and dreams lay shattered on the ground, and instead of joy, they bring sorrow to your heart. Jesus was present, whether you realized it or not, both as the dreams were fulfilled, and as they began to decay and shatter. You may have called upon Him in those times, you may have ignored Him, but He was there all the same. And on this day when you try to absorb the immensity of all that has transpired, take a few moments to cherish the dreams that came true which might otherwise get lost in the shuffle. And maybe take some time to grieve those things that fell apart. Find things for which to give God thanks. Seek His healing and peace for what has been, and His direction for what will be. In your mind's eye, image Jesus present in person at your wedding, as well as through the joys and sorrows of your marriage. But also visualize Christ standing there with you just now. Allow Him to wrap His loving arms around you, let his embraces give you the strength, healing and hope to go on from this day, and through His power and grace become a better person as you move into a new future.

Anniversary of Filing or of Divorce Date

Read Ephesians 4:22-24

Well, you have made a significant milestone. If you are reading this devotion on one of the dates above, then you have made it through a cycle of holidays, anniversaries, birthdays, memories piled upon memories. The first year, it seems, much of what happens is that you experience the grief and the loss, perhaps also some of the sense of newness and opportunity. After you have made that first cycle, though some things will still be hard, there can come a sense of moving on as the process of rebuilding and redefining takes place.

Today, I want to suggest that it might be good to examine the path you have walked, and identify the hand of the One who has led you through that path. Can you see how far you have come? Surely you can still sense all the hurt, all the things that you have lost or that have been thrown out of place, but can you also recognize the ways in which some things are starting to come back together? For example, is your emotional state more stable now than a year ago? I remember identifying that progress with the notion that the depression I felt was of shorter duration, or more sporadic than when I first began. That is, at first, I tended to feel that despairing struggle on an hourly, or maybe even continuous basis. But as time passed, the struggle would only interrupt the day, or the week and a more stable sense was what dominated most of the time. *That is* progress. You will have made progress as well, and it is important to recognize that progress and focus on it rather than focusing only on the things that still might weigh you down. Can you also see the ways in which things have not turned out to be as bad as you perhaps thought they might have been? Maybe you didn't think you could live without that spouse, maybe you thought you would lose everything, maybe you thought nobody would care about you. All sorts of fears and myths pop up in those early days, but now, with the perspective of time, you discover that some things are not as bad as you had imagined they would be.

And so, as you experience this anniversary that you had never wanted to have, take a few minutes to grieve the losses. But also take time to celebrate the progress, even if that progress feels tediously slow. Remember, progress IS progress...the speed at which progress is made is not nearly as significant as the fact of progress. This process is just a hard one to experience.

Most importantly, consider and identify areas in which God has cared for you, provided for you, encouraged you, helped you. Think about some of the individuals whose support has helped you get where you are. And give thanks, because with God's help you have weathered some pretty tough days, probably the worst of the days, and that truth can encourage you that God will help you weather whatever is ahead as well. God bless you today, my friend. May your heart experience a bit of healing, hope and peace on this significant day.

Date Divorce Becomes Final

Read Joel 2:15-17

Well, this is it. Today is the day you enter the world of being a divorced person. It is the day that the marriage is officially over. For many divorcing folks, the marriage was actually over long before, but on the day the gavel falls, it is over in no uncertain terms. Done.

You may have very mixed emotions. I want you to know that God walks with you every step of the day, today. He is at your side as you walk to court (if you do), and He is at your side when you leave that same court divorced. He walks with you into the home with no spouse at your side. And He walks with you in the confusion, sorrow and struggle you may experience today. Some people experience this day as the day to be glad they are out of that rotten marriage! Others will sense it as a dreadful experience, when something very precious doesn't merely die, but is literally strangled to death. I can't imagine how those three felt when, there in the midst of the furnace, they found they weren't walking through the flames alone, but as surely as God walked beside them there, so He walks beside you today.

When that gavel falls, for almost all of us, there is a gratefulness or relief that at least the awful process of getting a divorce is over and done with, and now you can begin to move on and put your life back together without all the uncertainty that is such a part of divorce.

I have no profound words of advice for your day. Sorry. What I have are words of compassion. You are not alone. There are those of us who have been where you are, and we know how hard it is, and how confusing all the emotions can be on this day. Do what things are necessary for you, but I do encourage you to do those things out of faith, not out of fear. In other words, going out and getting drunk is probably not the best way to handle it, because your actions lead away from God, not toward Him. But do what you feel would be most helpful for you.

Some people go to the court, some do not. Some find a friend and go to dinner or a movie. Others stay at home alone, silently shedding tears in private. Find a way that is meaningful for you on this day to let go, to sense the completion of the moment, and maybe just to rest at the end of this stressful and arduous process. Remember your children in the midst of it all. Remember your God....find time to pray, maybe spend a little extra time in the scriptures or with your pastor.

There is, however, one thing I want to say to you. No matter how bad your marriage was, there is nobody in heaven rejoicing over this day of divorce. Instead, this becomes just one more evidence of the fallen and broken world in which we live, and God's ideal was for so much more. We will see that ideal one day in heaven. I believe there is a tear, so to speak, on God's cheek for every time a gavel strikes shattering a marriage vow taken long before. But know this, that sorrow (and yours) does not mean that God gives up on you, on your future, or on His ability to work in and through your life. No, God does not give up.

And don't you. There are things ahead in your life that will make this day seem like just a distant memory. God will walk with you there, as well.

Weekend Holidays—Memorial Day, Labor Day, MLK Day, President's Day

Read Exodus 31:12-17

I don't know whether any of these holidays are special in your family or not. Most of them aren't for me, but sometimes we did do some cemetery visits and services on Memorial Day, and in my first marriage, her side of the family often liked to go away for the weekend for Memorial and/or Labor Day. Apart from that, they are just long weekends to me....and that depends on where I am working! I have a friend, though, who likes to go to the car races and has for years, so for him it really is a family thing. But me, an occasional picnic will cover it most of the time.

What about you, though? If there are important traditions in your family, then once again, you need to figure out how to adapt them to your new situation. However, for many of us, I suspect that the biggest thing we need for these kinds of times is rest. My wife points out how often I use holidays (like many guys do) to accomplish projects, rather than to relax and enjoy the break. But I am learning, and I hope you are, too. Sometimes you just need to have time to rest, relax and refresh. It is significant, it seems to me, that when God made the designations about time, seasons and holidays He built into the format time each week for rest.

In this highly stressful process called divorce, when was the last time you really took time to just relax, to rest, to just enjoy some time away from everything? We need that. God knew that. And we need to know it. I want to encourage you to use these weekends....especially during the first year....as times to honestly just kick back and relax, and allow yourself to be refreshed a bit body and soul. God intended you to have a break once in a while. Take advantage of the ones our government also decided to establish!

Valentine's Day

Read 1 Corinthians 13:4-13

Are you a sap for Valentine's Day? Do you love the roses, the sentimental cards, the romantic candlelight dinners and the starry eyed lovers in chick flick movies? If that is you, then this first Valentine's Day may be difficult for you, because you feel like love has let you down. Maybe the memories that well up bring more pain than nostalgia. Maybe you work in a place where you are surrounded by people receiving flowers or making reservations at restaurants to celebrate their love. Yet no one awaits you at home, and you feel like there is no one upon whom to shower your affection. Today's scripture reminds us that love does endure. It hopes all things, believes all things, and never fails....so why does it feel like it has so miserably failed for you this Valentine's Day? The answer, of course, is painfully obvious: real love, God's love, is far beyond the feeble attempts of humans to emulate it in their relationships. Sometimes a marriage reflects well the love of God that lasts through time. Sometimes we fall far short as dreams and plans give way to disappointment and brokenness. As you deal with all the emotions you may be feeling this day, I want to challenge you to reflect on a couple of biblical passages in your own search for real love.

First, is the famous 1 Corinthians 13's description of love as defined and demonstrated by God. Read it over again, carefully and slowly, noting which things describe the love of you and your ex during your marriage relationship, and which things simply do not mesh with your experiences. In doing that, you can learn in a fresh way what love really is, and in what ways your marriage, or your own love, did not reflect accurately God's description of what true love is like. It may help you to understand the areas in which you and your marriage had gone astray.

Then, I want to encourage you to read Ephesians 5:22-32, a passage often used at weddings. But what I want to point out to you is Paul's statement that he is actually speaking about Christ and the church, not merely the human reflection of that relationship found in marriage. So I want to suggest, as you find yourself in a new situation on Valentine's Day, that you not let your holiday be bound only to your human relationships. Perhaps you could celebrate Valentine's Day by reflecting on the love relationship in your life that surpasses all others....the way in which God loves you, has given Himself for you and seeks to make you the best you that you can be. It is an incredible love that Christ has for His church, and for you as a member of it. Then, as part of your Valentine celebration, find a way to show love to somebody in your life, just as a reminder that though your marriage may be ending, love never ends. Let it remind you that the source of love who is within you, God Himself, is still able to work through *you* to show love to a world so desperately in need of *genuine love.*

Easter

Read John 20:1-18

I bet you didn't know that I am the world's greatest Easter egger, did you? My kids know it. Whether or not they believe it is an entirely different matter. Every Easter, when my children were young, we would take time to have Easter egg hunts with plastic or candy eggs. If weather was nice, it was outside, if not, it was inside. The rules we set up required that the eggs had to be visible....at least in part....from at least one angle without having to move anything to see them. Easy as that sounds, the truth is sometimes it became very challenging to find all the eggs. One of my favorite life memories. And you know what else? Easter is one of my very favorite holidays. I love why we celebrate it, I love Holy Week services and sunrise services and ham dinners and coloring Easter eggs and you can just keep on going. The resurrection, more than anything else, is the defining truth of the Christian faith that distinguishes it from every other religion in the world.

And so, Easter also, therefore, became one of the difficult holidays after my divorce. To celebrate it without my children in the years they were at my ex's home....that was so very hard. But the focus was never about the bunny or the eggs or the candy....it was always about God. The kids Easter baskets were filled with goodies, but there was also always a gift related to the faith...a cd, a Bible, something to remember why we were celebrating. And that is the first bit of advice I have for your celebration of this holy day....keep the focus where it belongs:

on the Lord Jesus Christ, crucified, buried and resurrected for you and for me.

In addition, I would encourage you that this holiday, more than any other, takes on new potential in light of your divorce. The holiday is about resurrection, new life, hope when there seems to be no hope, victory over death, Satan and darkness, and God's ability to work something wonderful out of something awful. God can bring resurrection into your life post divorce as well. There can be new life, there can be hope in even the blackest times, there can be victory and power and God will do it in your life just as surely as He did at the tomb, if you will but trust and be obedient to the best of your ability. As you celebrate Easter with whatever traditions you have developed, this year, I encourage you to offer the holiday as a symbolic prayer to God for His new life to enter into the darkness that entombs your heart in the processes of divorce.

Mother's Day and/or Father's Day

Read Ruth 4:11-12 and Ephesians 3:14-15

So, are you a mother or a father? Then one or the other of these days is about you....at least in part. If you are not a parent, then this day still is important to celebrate, as you remember your own father and mother, and then I have a few words for you below as well. But for those of you who are parents, then these days are especially poignant in the time of divorce. I will address just a few things, with a few simple thoughts, as you celebrate these holidays.

First, if you are the parent whose "day" is being celebrated, I want to suggest that you choose to make this day not about you. That is always a good idea, although one rarely followed in our culture...a good lesson toward the development of humility. However, that isn't why I am suggesting it. Instead, it is because you have a mother or father, who need to know your appreciation, so focus on them. And, additionally, you have a child or children who are struggling over the upheavals of their lives, and in this new environment may not know how to navigate the waters of this holiday in a way that will appease all involved. They need you to smooth the waters for them. One of my precious memories was from this time after the divorce, when my son was over for Father's Day, and probably didn't have money to be able to do much in terms of a gift. I suggested to him that what would mean the most to me was simply for us to have some fun together, so we headed out to a nearby amusement park and spent the day riding rides and watching shows. It has become one of my favorite memories, and though I can't speak for him, I do think it provided him an easy way to figure out how to celebrate that day with me without creating unnecessary stress. We had a lot of fun.

Secondly, if it is NOT your "day," though you may be grieving the situation, and struggle with the absence of your children on this day, I want to encourage you to hold to the high ideals. As you will find elsewhere in these writings, remember that the individual to whom you once were married, remains the father or mother of your children. If nothing else good ever happened in your marriage, you do have the blessing of the children, and it is your responsibility to instruct them in the ways of the Lord, which includes the command that they honor their father AND their mother....with no mention as to whether father and mother are divorced. Help them to honor the other parent well, because it demonstrates that you, too, seek to be obedient to the commands of God.

Thirdly, again, if you have children, relish their love on this day. Realize that they love you, no matter what has happened. They may be confused, they may be struggling, but you are still important to the little ones God has placed in your care. Take this day to realize how important you are in their lives, the role that only YOU can play. The changes due to the divorce may be making it more difficult for you to be an effective father or mother, but difficult doesn't mean impossible. Do the best you can. Love your kids. Let them love you.

And last, if you are mourning on this day the fact that your marriage ended in divorce and you never got to have the children you dreamed of, I want to encourage you as well. Realize that God may have chosen to spare you the hardship and heartache that comes through divorce when one has children, because you see their little hearts breaking and their eyes welling with tears. What once had been a team effort becomes instead a complicated businesslike arrangement....a far cry from the loving homes God intends for children to grow up in. One day, God may give you another union into which children may be born, and that opportunity may turn out to be something wonderful. God does know best.

Independence Day—Fourth of July

Read 2 Corinthians 3:17

As if there hasn't been enough fireworks already, right? Isn't it amazing how every holiday changes simply because of the dynamics of divorce? One of my favorite memories was watching night sky fireworks with my children when they were small, listening to them "ooh" and "ahh," and their disappointment when the presentation ended. And we have gotten to be around some larger cities that seemed to specialize in fireworks. My step children like fireworks, also, but they always liked to shoot them off themselves, and since their dad lived in an area where fireworks were banned for personal use, they would almost always try to come to our home for the Fourth, so they could shoot firecrackers to their hearts' content. And, with me having a touch of pyromania anyway, that is just fine with me! We have lots of fun.

A few years ago, my uncle was selling his old home place, where we used to do our fireworks when I was a kid. We decided that since it was the last time he'd own the property on Independence Day, some of us cousins got together with the folks and whatever kids were around, and reenacted those displays of yesteryear. I made up some batches of homemade ice cream (like back when), everybody pitched in some fireworks and food, and we had a grand time, just like the good old days….even down to the pinwheels that still wouldn't take off right on the pole, just like they didn't years and years ago! We laughed ourselves silly! I think all the folks there of the next generation thought we were nuts! And who am I to argue? What is interesting is that the celebration was more likely to happen and easier to plan for in my second marriage than if I had still been in my first marriage….for lots of reasons. So, in this case as least, what felt like exile and devastation at the time, turned out to be freedom and joy!

Why do I share these things? Well, partly to help you realize that changes due to the divorce does not eliminate precious memories, nor limit the possibility of making new ones. In fact, there might even be ways in which it is EASIER to make new special memories than it might have been were you still in your relationship.

The truth is, in all things, the key is to stay in tune with the Spirit of God. We celebrate the freedom we have here in America on the Fourth of July, but the truth is, real freedom is only found by walking with the Spirit of God. That Spirit makes all things new, grants us victory, empowers us, sets us free, gifts us and just generally allows us to enjoy life no matter the circumstances, because our hope and our freedom and our joy are found in the Lord, not in the earth. So, this Independence Day, feel FREE to do something new, something old, something fresh, something just plain old fun for fun's sake! And if you happen to have an extra buzz bomb, set one off for me....they are great!

Halloween

Read John 7:1-10

Some Christians don't believe in bothering with Halloween, and if that is you, that's okay, you can skip over this if you want to do so. For others of us, though, Halloween has lots of fun memories of time with our kids. Carving pumpkins, finding that perfect costume, door to door with kids and candy, fall festivals at church, bonfires, parades, bobbing for apples, whatever. I remember when my kids were little, we had a certain circuit of friends we took them to where we knew they would be safe, and those friends often had special treats they had prepared knowing that our kids were coming. It was always such fun to see how the kids enjoyed dressing up, and see the fun they had running around with friends in their costumes. If you have children, now that you are divorced you may only get to spend Halloween with them every other year. You come to realize, as they are growing up quickly, that you won't have much longer to enjoy the childhood fun of Halloween with them.

You may want to find alternate times with them....after all, you don't usually carve the pumpkins on Halloween anyway. You may want to find alternate traditions....have you taken them out to a pumpkin patch ahead of time to select the pumpkin? Or maybe you could make an adventure of going from store to store looking for the largest one you can find. Maybe, if you haven't ever done so, this could be a good year to make sure the kids know that Halloween means "All Hallow's Eve", the evening before All Saints Day. That could give you an opportunity to discuss with them some of the great Christians down through the centuries, changing your focus from the evening to the meaning of the following day. Or maybe, during the time you don't have your kids with you, you could choose to do something to make Halloween special for other children, like hosting a neighborhood Halloween party, or volunteering for the fall party at your church, or just really enjoying decorating for trick or treaters who might come by your home. Or maybe you will simply move to a different chapter of your life and let Halloween become a part of your past....and that's okay, too, because that is the natural cycle of many things in life.

Just make sure your children don't get shortchanged in whatever the holiday has come to mean to them....after all, the best Halloweens are the ones that truly are about children. It seems that Jesus and his family regularly participated in the festivals and celebrations in Jerusalem, those annual celebrations were important for his family, and they are important for yours. Whatever your celebrations have been for Halloween, find a way to make the family part of the celebration valuable, because, after all, that is what really matters anyway, isn't it?

Thanksgiving

Read Ephesians 5:19-20

This verse from Ephesians is one that I have always appreciated. Always giving thanks, it says. That means, even in the midst of and the aftermath of divorce. Give thanks. For me, Thanksgiving was an especially difficult day with the divorce, because so much of family tradition that meant a lot to me was marred. At the same time, it also became a precious day, because I was able to spend it with my family of origin more regularly than was the case in my first marriage.

I remember that first Thanksgiving after the divorce was really hard. I spent that first Thanksgiving without my children, as they were at my ex's house that first year. I decided that I didn't want to be around family at a Thanksgiving table, as the empty slots would probably bother me a great deal, so I decided to volunteer at a soup kitchen for the Thanksgiving Day meal. I was glad I did, it gave me a different meaning than I had experienced before, and allowed me to avoid the empty chairs that first year, even though it turned out the soup kitchen ended up with much more help than they needed.

This Thanksgiving, whether you have children or not, and whether they are with you or not, one thing I would suggest is that you force yourself to focus upon the intent of the day: the giving of thanks. You may not feel terribly thankful, you may be reeling with the consequences of the divorce, but that does not mean there are not things for which you can give thanks to God. Maybe this has never been part of your Thanksgiving Day traditions. Maybe all you usually do is offer a quick prayer at the dinner table. It is time to reclaim what the day really means...the recognition of who is God and who is the one created by instituting a fresh and appropriate giving of thanks. For life. For food. For family. For health. For the beauty of nature. For whatever you can add to the list....dedicate some REAL time to give God thanks....if not with family members, at least carve out some time of your own. I understand that sometimes not all family members are on board with the meaning of Thanksgiving, so you may need to do that as your own time....or you may be the one who gently helps transform the holiday for them.

And, as usual, I would suggest keeping some traditions, and maybe starting some new ones. Even if you are by yourself. Are there certain foods that you especially associate with Thanksgiving which help give the holiday meaning for you? I have a list of those. Some are from my family from long ago that I brought even into the first marriage, some are things I learned during that marriage, and some are things that I have chosen since the divorce as options I can now choose for myself if I want. And now there is a new richness developing as my new wife brings in fresh traditions and meanings of her own.

What would you like YOUR Thanksgiving meal to be? What would you like your Thanksgiving traditions to be? For me, this is a significant holiday, and as you enter into it for the first time since your divorce, I urge you to find a way to capitalize on the significance, hard though it may be emotionally. Stake a claim and make your Thanksgiving a holiday for a lifetime. I believe you will be glad you did.

Christmas

Read your favorite Christmas passage, and maybe sing a Christmas carol.

This year, as we were decorating the Christmas tree, I got out some bubble lights to put on the tree. My step daughter asked me why they were called bubble lights. I was surprised she hadn't seen them before. My wife told me that this was the first time I had gotten them out and put them on the tree. This is our seventh Christmas as a married couple, and it has been twelve years since my divorce. I don't remember if I had any on my Christmas tree the years I was single or not, but it really struck me that I had never gotten them out for our tree since we have been married. Now, the reason is not just that I am an emotional sap. Some of the cause is the fact that my wife's kids have a lot of decorations of their own, and their own traditions, and since my kids are grown, I wanted to honor their traditions as more important for this time than my own have been. Still, the time finally came when I could put out the lights, without a twinge of melancholy that attends difficult memories.

Christmas is, for most of us Christians, one of the most special of holidays. For us divorced Christians, it can also be one of the most difficult. How is Christmas for you, this year? The first Christmas after a divorce is especially hard. Whereas you may have had traditions for both Christmas eve and Christmas day, in many divorced situations where children are involved, this year you may be able to spend time with them only for one or the other of the time slots....not both. The house can feel pretty empty when you return from dropping off the kids, or while you are waiting to get to see them. And if you don't have children, I suspect that you will especially feel the emptiness in the home, since the one you have shared Christmas with in the past won't be at your side this Christmas. In my case, the majority of the ornaments and Christmas decorations I have are loaded with memories from the time they were purchased or the people they represent.

And yet, I have also supplemented those decorations with others that I have bought since my divorce that are things I enjoy myself, not to mention ones that my new wife and I have selected together. Along the way in my life, there has accumulated a variety of new traditions, new memories, that overlay the old memories. Things like a certain joke gift that appears year after year, or Christmas Eve fondue—a tradition brought by my new wife. And finally, now, the bubble lights are on the tree. You see, the new traditions have blended with the ones that I kept from the past to form the new, fresh Christmas traditions filled with new meanings. Some of them are simple changes, like trekking out in the cold to find the perfect Christmas tree to cut and bring home, instead of unboxing the old artificial tree. Some are more complicated, involving adapting schedules to coordinate with all the children, as well as the selection of important traditions from both of our families as we create our own celebration of Christmas. But it seems to me that, it all boils back down to the fact that the bubble lights are back on the tree. Christmas, though changed, still has a place in the restructured post divorce life, as well as contributions to tradition that have come through my remarriage.

Christmas claims its place in my life because the story of Christmas has never changed just because my marital status did. And my connection with that story and that Savior transcends all the decorations, all the celebrations, and all the memories. Though I regularly missed the days when Christmas was so easily a joyous holiday, as it frequently turned into a holiday with schedules that were difficult or impossible to juggle and negotiate. And yet, at the core of Christmas, there remains an underlying theme of God's love and faithfulness. Perhaps it is best summed up in one word that is specially highlighted at this special time of the year: Immanuel. God is with us. Though my experience of the holiday is now different, and sometimes includes empty spaces and times without the usual presence of those we have loved, still the One who has loved us always remains, because the core promise of Christmas is a promise that takes on new depth of meaning as your life changes….and that promise is: GOD IS WITH US….GOD IS WITH YOU! Let that simple and profound truth redeem Christmas for you as you begin building your own new kinds of celebration.

YOUR RELATIONSHIP WITH CHRIST

This section is offered to help you clarify and maybe gain better understanding of your own spiritual standing with God. Only you know your own heart, and your own relationship with God. Actually, the scripture says that even our hearts can deceive us (see Jeremiah 17:9), so it is important to check our internal senses against the clear teachings of scripture. The first thing I want to encourage you to examine is to recall whether or not you have ever committed your life to Christ. That time is described in many ways, but it is a time when you acknowledge your sin and shortcomings to God, ask his forgiveness and receive adoption into the family of God. Have you experienced that moment in your life? If you don't know for sure, then odds are, you haven't or at least haven't understood when you did and need to clarify for yourself your standing with God.

The scriptures teach that we can KNOW we are securely in God's hand, not merely hope, wish or dream it were so. It is called many things, such as being saved, or born again, but whatever terms you want to use, it is important to know that you belong to and have been accepted by God as His own. One of my favorite passages is 1 John 5:11-13....I strongly encourage you to take time to read it now (there is a table of contents in the front of your Bible....make sure you find 1 John, and not merely John....they are not the same book). For me, this passage makes things pretty clear, as it boils it down to one simple question: do you have the Son of God, or do you not? He is more than willing to partner with you through life, to make you His own dear child, to cleanse you from sin's poison within your soul.

Another helpful scripture is 2 Corinthians 5:21, which you will want to read, but I am going to paraphrase in this way: "For our sake, God somehow made Jesus Christ 'become sin' so that we could become God's righteousness through Christ." A basic outline of what God intends for us can be described as if God offers you and me an exchange, a swap:

1) It is not our place to establish the spiritual rules of the universe; we simply learn how God established them from the teachings of scripture. These rules are real, just as real as gravity that always pulls us toward the earth....we didn't set that one up, either.

2) Sin deserves to be punished ("for the wages of sin is death"—Romans 6:23, NASB). For this discussion, sin can be defined as doing something that is less than God's perfection, or neglecting to do those things God has commanded. In either case, it is simply acting in ways that are not all God designed or desires us to be. Face it, we are a long way from perfect!

3) Though Jesus did not sin, He suffered punishment by death... which is the penalty for sin, not the penalty for a righteous person like Jesus. So Jesus paid a debt He did not owe and accepted a punishment He did not deserve....He has a credit balance, so to speak.

4) However, you and I have sinned. I have yet to meet the perfect person who has never done anything wrong, or always done everything good they could and should. Sometimes we think our sins are smaller than those of others, or not enough to count. When it comes to salvation and entrance to heaven, God doesn't measure our sinfulness by degrees, only in terms of perfect or imperfect (see James 2:10).

5) You and I deserve the punishment of death, because that is the consequence of sin (not merely physical death alone, but death defined as eternal separation from the source of life, separation from God—which is the central concept of hell).

6) Since Jesus didn't sin, He didn't deserve death, He deserved life. It was we who sinned, and we deserve the death. So the deal Jesus offers is this: we can have the life He deserves, if we will trust Him to apply His death as the substitute penalty owed for our sins.

7) We, however, have to actively accept that offer. A wealthy man can write you a billion dollar check, but it will not make you wealthy until the day you accept it as valid and cash it or deposit it to your own account. Jesus has written you something worth far more than a billion dollars….have you accepted the offer, have you deposited His gift into your life's account? Not sure? Don't know how? Read on.

What we have been discussing is the initial start of the Christian life. It is accomplished, amazingly enough, by simply believing the offer and accepting Jesus' death on the cross as payment for your sin. How? By telling God so! The idea is we trust that God will accept Jesus' sacrifice as an appropriate payment on our behalf, rather than trying to find some other way to pay the penalty myself. Many try other ways such as being good, overcompensating to "make up for" their poor actions, or self help programs. Strange as it may seem, that is the solution God chose to make available, and since He makes the rules, we should probably use His solution and not try to make up our own, right? Some object, and claim that all the other religions can't be wrong, that surely God doesn't have only way to reach Him. But let me ask you, if there were other ways we could make it by our own efforts, do you *really* think He would *unnecessarily* allow His Son to suffer and die? I wouldn't do that with my son, would you?

Accepting the offer of Christ is accomplished by committing your destiny, your forgiveness and your life to Him, trusting He will make His solution work for you. All you have to do is tell God that is what you want, that you want your life to be more pleasing to Him, you want to quit those things that defile you and you want to accept the offer of forgiveness purchased for us through the cross of Christ. But being a Christian isn't merely asking Jesus to come into our hearts and forgive us; it is ALSO committing ourselves to Christ as the ruler and guide of our lives, committing to follow Him and His teachings to the best of our ability. Jesus isn't about handing out tickets to heaven, He is about calling disciples to follow and learn from Him. He is about adopting us into His family, making us His beloved children.

So, what keeps YOU from taking advantage of God's offer for your life? If you haven't already, I invite you to get right with God at this very moment. Below are additional scriptures you can look up to help you better understand these concepts. There is also a short prayer you can use as a guide in your connection with God if you like. But know this: God wants YOU to be part of His family, and to experience the forgiveness He has provided in Jesus Christ. He won't force you to do so, but He invites you to come to Him. *It's okay if you don't understand it all....the truth is, none of us fully understand all that God has done. But just come to God with what you DO understand, and let that be the beginning you need in this time. God is the One who understands.*

If you do know Christ personally, then I encourage you to examine the depth and commitment of that relationship. Are you following? Will you follow, no matter what, even through this most difficult of experiences? I guarantee you this: if you truly have given your life to Christ, then God's promise and my experience is that you will not have to walk through the tragedy of divorce by yourself....God Himself will walk with you. And that assurance, at least for me, makes all the difference in the world.

I probably shouldn't leave this topic without pointing out one more thing. Sometimes, people I have dealt with feel unsure about these things. They think that maybe they didn't pray right, or they weren't sure if God answered because they didn't feel what they thought they ought to feel, or they had other ideas and attitudes that create doubt. I want to encourage you to notice that in all the scriptures we are examining, God never says, "maybe." When it comes to God doing His part, He always says that He *will*, He *shall*, it *is*. The scriptures never say of God's promises that He might, it could be, or maybe He will. God can be trusted to follow through on what He has promised. Even if you don't feel like it. Even if you aren't so sure you did everything perfectly. Remember, God knows your heart and your intention, and it is there that He looks. So don't let yourself fret over whether you said exactly the right words to God, or had your eyes closed when you prayed, or whatever. Just have a heart to heart with a God who loves you more than anything, and who will ALWAYS keep His promises for you.

ADDITIONAL SCRIPTURES ON SALVATION

Luke 5:32
Luke 19:10
John 3:16-17
John 1:12
John 1:1-4, 14
Acts 4:12
Acts 16:31
Romans 3:10-12, 23
Romans 5:8
Romans 6:23
Romans 8:26-39
Romans 10:9-10
2 Corinthians 1:20
2 Corinthians 5:14-21
Galatians 2:16-20
Ephesians 1:7-8
Ephesians 2:8-10
2 Thessalonians 1:4-12
2 Timothy 2:11-13
Hebrews 4:12-16
1 Peter 1:1-5
1 John 5:11-13
Revelation 3:20

SAMPLE PRAYER

God,

I am looking at my relationship with you, and find that it is not what I want it to be, and that I have not been all you have wanted me to be. I do believe in your love for me, and your willingness to help me and to save me. I am sorry for all the times I have disappointed you, done things that were wrong when I knew I should have done otherwise. Forgive me for those sins. I want to become your child, and I believe that Jesus' paid the penalty for my sins when He died upon that cross. I come to you to ask you to make me your own, and give me life eternal in your presence. I give my life to you, and will do my best, with your help, to follow you all the days of my life. I love you, God, and appreciate what you have done for me, and look forward to getting to know you better in the years ahead.

In Jesus name, Amen

SCRIPTURAL REFERENCES RELATED TO DIVORCE

The following verses are intended to be a pretty comprehensive list of the scripture references related, either directly or through implication, to divorce. Some are guidelines about the process, some are stories of individuals whose life experience may have included divorce or a similar event, and the Romans passage is one where the marriage commitment is used as an illustration for another point. They are offered without comment here for your own perusal. Comments regarding various of the verses can be found elsewhere in this devotional as well as in volume two. I have chosen not to include verses about marriage itself (except the Romans passage), as the relevant marriage verses are referred to in some of the passages already, and can be found from them.

Deuteronomy 24:1-4
Judges 15:1-8
Ruth 4:1-12
1 Samuel 18:17-29, 25:44, 2 Samuel 3:12-16
Ezra 9:10-12, 10:1-44
Nehemiah 13:23-31
Malachi 2:13-16
Matthew 1:18-25, 5:31-32, 19:1-12
Mark 10:2-12
John 4:1-42
Romans 7:1-6
1 Corinthians 7:1-17
1 Timothy 3:1-13, 5:9-16
Titus 1:5-6

TOPICAL INDEX

(BY DEVOTIONAL DAY)

Index Of Scripture References

(By Devotional Day)

2 Kings
6:8-17 Days 90, 119
6:24-25 Day 73
7:1-15 Day 73

Ezra
3:8-13 Day 95
10:1-5 Day 169

Nehemiah
1:1-4 Day 179
2:11-18 Day 179
7:1-4 Day 155
8:1-12 Day 155

Job
1:13-22 Day 99
2:1-10 Day 37
2:11-13 Day 151
13:13-16 Day 38
19:23-27 Days 39, 40
23:8-10 Day 36

Psalms
1:2-3 Day 167
15:1-5 Day 30
18:1-6 Day 148
18:27-43 Day 148
27:1-2 Day 88
30:4-12 Day 11
34:8 Day 182
37:1-9 Day 85
41:4-13 Day 108
46:1-11 Day 16
57:1-11 Day 120
71:1-3 Day 2
73:1-17 Day 59
90:10-12 Holidays: Your
    Birthday

Psalms cont.
103:11-14 Day 163
127:3-5 Day 86
136:1-9 Day 51
141:1-4 Day 80
147:1-6 Day 104

Proverbs
3:5-6 Day 21
11:14 Day 174
15:13 Day 102
17:22 Day 102
18:10 Day 2

Ecclesiastes
12:13-14 Day 48

Isaiah
1:1-3 Days 14, 86
26:7-10 Day 77
30:15-17 Day 92
41:10 Days 3, 79
42:1-6 Day 94
43:1-5 Day 10
46:8-13 Day 35
49:13-16 Day 135
58:13-16 Day 141

Jeremiah
17:7-8 Days 121, 122, 123
31:21-23 Day 81
32:17 Day 134
42:1-43:7 Day 29

Daniel
3:18-30 Day 144

Hosea
7:8-12 Day 27

AUTHOR'S BIOGRAPHICAL NOTE
AND CONTACT INFORMATION

Richard Crooks is an ordained American Baptist minister who has been in ministry since 1983, and has served a number of churches and as campus minister in college ministry. He holds Master's degrees from Central Baptist Theological Seminary and Hebrew Union College.

After his wife filed for divorce in 1998, opportunities opened for special ministries with individuals struggling with divorce in their lives, which has led him to identify the need for tools like this to help God's children who might be in the midst of divorce. Through a variety of experiences, he is keenly aware of the devastating impact divorce can have in the lives of families, including not only the couple, but children, parents and grandparents as well. His own struggles and contacts in ministry bring personal impact to these pages. Richard does not claim to have all the answers, nor to have handled all of the issues perfectly himself, but believes it is important to have support, resources and tools from those who have shared the struggle to help divorcing individuals navigate the treacherous waters of divorce.

The father of two, he remarried in 2004, and is step father of four children. He and his wife, Nola, have been instrumental in helping others struggling with the impact of divorce, both through ministry opportunities as well as with friends and family. Soon to be published is <u>Vol. 2: Spring and Summer—Seasons of Renewal and Warmth</u>, which focuses on the process of moving on after the divorce is settled, with ideas, tips and warnings for the next phase of the journey. Watch for publication announcement on his website at *www.findinggoddevotionals. com*, as well as the blog and facebook page. If you desire, you can contact him through email to *seasonsofdivorce@gmail.com* or through the *findinggodintheseasonsofdivorce* facebook page. His writing can be found on *www.findinggodintheseasonsofdivorce.blogspot.com*.

CPSIA information can be obtained at www.ICGtesting.com
Printed in the USA
LVOW120427021012

301058LV00002B/2/P